CW00689229

A Wandering Voice
A Diary of Birdsong

A Wandering Voice
A Diary of Birdsong

Michael Waterhouse

with a foreword by
the Right Honourable Norman Lamont MP

and illustrations by
Philip Snow

Bellew Publishing • London

This edition first published in Great Britain 1996

Bellew Publishing Company Limited
8 Balham Hill, London SW12 9EA

ISBN 1 85725 118 0

Typeset by Antony Gray
Printed and bound in Great Britain by
Hartnolls Ltd, Bodmin, Cornwall

To the memory of my mother
Caroline Waterhouse
and my parents-in-law
Robin and Jean Hastings

ACKNOWLEDGEMENTS

I would like to thank my wife, Lucinda, for introducing me to Edward Grey by way of a copy of *Capital of Happiness*; my uncle, Sunny Marlborough, for allowing me to live at the Lince Lodge in the early eighties; and my friends William Astor, David Bulmer, Roderick Balfour, Wenty Beaumont, Jamie Chichester, Nick de Rothschild, Richard Wellesley, Derek Frost and Jeremy Norman, who all in their own way have contributed much to my love of birds and the countryside. Also Anthony Bailey, who has patiently hunted down and acquired on my behalf books by Grey, Hudson, Warde Fowler and Seton Gordon, in addition to Stephen Tennant's collection of bird books from Wilsford.

In particular I would like to thank Carole Gregory who toiled over the word processor for the best part of eighteen months in her own time, and Edward Hay who assisted with the editing as the diary was compiled.

In a bibliography on page 239 I have listed the books I have used or quoted from but which I have not fully credited within the body of the text. I thank the British Trust for Ornithology for permission to reproduce extracts from *The New Atlas of Breeding Birds in Britain and Ireland* 1988–1991 (D. W. Gibbons, J. B. Reid and R. A. Chapman, 1993), published by T. and A. D. Poyser.

I would like to acknowledge the great kindness of the heirs to the estate of Sir Edward Grey in allowing me to quote so extensively from his writings.

I would also like to thank Peter Jackson of Heart of the Lakes Ltd and Colin MacQueen of Peak Cottages Ltd for sponsoring this book. It has been jointly decided that the author's royalties will be donated to the Derbyshire Nightingale Macmillan Cancer Care Appeal.

Finally I am most grateful to Norman Lamont for writing the foreword to *A Wandering Voice*. It is particularly appropriate he should do so, for like Grey, not only did he occupy one of the three great offices of state, but he is also an accomplished and enthusiastic ornithologist.

FOREWORD

I have always found it very difficult to identify birds by their song. For a keen ornithologist that is deeply frustrating. I have tried everything, including studying closely the phonetic representations in books. Such representations are dead, lifeless and useless. I have tried listening to tapes in my car and CDs at home. But I still find it difficult to master the art of identifying birds by their song.

Of course, I can tell a few common species, like the robin, the wren, the willow warbler and the chaffinch, and common moorland birds, like the curlew or the lapwing – who couldn't? But what I find difficult is to identify by their song birds that I cannot see and perhaps have never seen. Warblers and 'little brown jobs' are particularly difficult to identify anyway. So song can be the vital clue.

How I envy the person who can walk into a wood on a glorious early May morning when there is an outpouring of song and reel off fifteen species at once without a single bird being visible. If there is one gift that I would like to be given it is that of remembering bird songs.

Bird songs cannot be described on a piece of paper any more than can a piece of music. But just as E. M. Forster in *Howard's End* describes the effect of Beethoven's Fifth Symphony on the listener, so too written descriptions of bird songs can convey something of the quality of the song. Sir Edward Grey's writings in a mysterious, magical way do leave in the reader's mind a haunting impression of a bird's song. I have never forgotten the first time I read his passage in *The Charm of Birds* comparing the song of a blackcap and a nightingale and then judging the blackcap's the more beautiful.

We all have our own favourites in birds and bird songs. Neither Michael Waterhouse nor Sir Edward Grey rate the appearance of the blackbird highly, but I never cease to be astonished by the beauty of the bird: that extraordinary bright orange beak against the jet black of the body. Its song, of course, is universally among the most highly praised, but for me it is second to none. I remember during one General Election in my constituency feeling very tired and downhearted. I was walking up some drive on Kingston Hill overgrown with lilacs. There had been a shower and suddenly a blackbird started to sing among the dripping leaves. Instantly it became for me the natural bird of the suburbs and of my constituency. It lifted my spirit. It was the first time I had really ever noticed how beautiful the song was. Every time I hear it now I think of that day.

In my opinion Sir Edward Grey has genius as a writer. If he had never been Foreign Secretary, *The Charm of Birds* would still be an English classic, alongside *The Compleat Angler* and *The Natural History of Selborne*. Take his description of a dipper:

> When the woods are hushed and white with snow, and the burn is pinched with frost so that only a narrow dark channel of running water shows between the ice and snow at the side of it, there on some stone in the burn the dipper will stand and sing. It is water rippling over a stony bed that he frequents; the soft luxuriance of the chalk stream has no attraction for him. His song seems part of the sound of the rippling water from which he is never away.

Can anyone say that is not as fine a piece of writing about birds as can be found anywhere?

In this book Sir Edward Grey is described as an amateur naturalist. That is far from just. Today we have the advantages of modern science and equipment and of more knowledge in identifying, analysing and studying the behaviour of birds. But Sir Edward Grey was a real countryman with a deep insight and profound understanding of the habitats of birds.

Take this description of a wood warbler:

> The wood warbler is well named. It is a bird of full-grown woods. It does not frequent gardens and shrubberies, as the chiffchaff and willow warbler do; it lives in big trees, especially beech or oak; so indifferent is it to bushes that it seems almost to prefer woods, where the ground is bare, as is so often the case under beech trees.

That shows a truly detailed knowledge of wood warblers. You would not get that in today's compact, modern guides, describing every species in fifty lines.

Many politicians have found refuge from the hurly-burly of the world in contemplation of birds. Sir Edward Grey and Neville Chamberlain both studied the wildfowl in St James's Park. I did, as I am sure Kenneth Clarke has done. Sometimes the charm of birds can take one's mind quite off immediate problems. When negotiating the Maastricht Treaty in Luxembourg, I came out of a difficult meeting for some fresh air and immediately saw my first ever black redstart. I was only able to return to the meeting with the greatest difficulty. But the meeting went much better from then on.

Michael Waterhouse reminds us how when in 1906 the Akaba Crisis erupted, Sir Edward Grey did not want to return to London because that Sunday, the second Sunday in May, was 'Beech Sunday', the day he always set aside, looked forward to, 'counted upon', to visit a dearly loved beech wood at the fleeting moment when the trees were in tender green leaf and their beauty 'indiscribable'.

Michael Waterhouse enables us to compare the countryside of Grey with today's. Michael follows the tracks of Sir Edward from Hampshire to Northumberland. But he goes via Parwich Lees in his beloved Derbyshire, and Wales, Spain and Scotland. I particularly enjoyed his diary in Jura. His vivid description of the dunlin ('incessant feeders that constantly prod the sand and are agile in flight, darting this way and that') and of oystercatchers ('piping angrily' below the 'towering Paps of Jura, today capped in cloud') brought back to me the two visits I have made there.

Grey described how certain birds had declined under what he called 'modern agriculture'. Today Michael Waterhouse gives another grim list of vanishing birds: the sedge warbler, and the cirl bunting, perhaps in the future even the song thrush and the skylark. Of course, there are gains the other way, such as the collared dove and the fulmar, but it always seems to be the attractive species that decline and the less attractive ones that increase.

Today species are decreasing ever more rapidly and in some cases, terrifyingly, we do not know why. When we know it will be too late.

We need to do more to save our birdlife. Michael Waterhouse says he hopes the destruction of the Flow Country in Sutherland has now been halted. When I was a junior minister at the Treasury, at Nigel Lawson's prompting I was pleased to remove tax relief from the forestry that had done so much harm to that area. Nigel's notices were fiscal and quite right too. But I had the added pleasure of explaining to Treasury officials how dense forestation interfered with the flight path of the red-throated diver and resulted in the loss of breeding habitat for the greenshank, the golden plover and the dunlin.

Michael's book is full of insights. I did not know the cuckoo had developed egg mimicry, or that people thought the bearded tit was now related to the thrush family. I loved his description of the spotted fly catcher having 'spaniel eyes'.

Michael writes with great knowledge, not just of birds and the countryside but also of the place of birds in literature. To bring them all together in one volume is a delightful and significant achievement.

THE RIGHT HONOURABLE NORMAN LAMONT MP

EDWARD GREY
by John Singer Sargent, dated 1913

INTRODUCTION

> One who reviews pleasant experiences and puts them on record increases the value of them to himself; he gathers up his own feelings and reflections and is thereby better able to understand and to measure the fullness of what he has enjoyed.
>
> EDWARD GREY, *The Charm of Birds*

My love of birds was rekindled in my early thirties when I rented the Lince Lodge in Blenheim Park. Situated on Bladon Water at the southern end of the Park, it became a sacred refuge at weekends from the pressures of life in London. I began by making limited observations on the local birdlife at Blenheim and later, in August 1986 when we moved to Derbyshire and bought our home, Parwich Lees, I kept a more formal notebook which I have maintained to this day.

My inspiration for keeping a diary stems from reading the writings of Viscount Grey of Fallodon, author, naturalist and statesman. His book *The Charm of Birds*, first published in 1927, was reprinted each year until the outbreak of the Second World War. Like Jan Karpinski, who stated in his introduction to *Capital of Happiness* that the main purpose of producing his book was to make Grey's writings on birds more accessible, I quote passages from *The Charm of Birds* to draw attention to both a remarkable work and a remarkable man. I share the same deep affection for Hampshire and Northumberland that Edward Grey once had. I have tried to retrace his footsteps, discovering the birds that he loved and wrote so colourfully about and then endeavouring to describe them and what is happening to them now. Modern farming techniques have had a devastating effect on bird habitat and population.

Finally, I make no apology for my participation in country sports. In his book *The Birdman*, Henry Douglas-Home wrote, 'It is my experience that sportsmen of all kinds are usually the best naturalists and conservationists. They admire nature and try to live in harmony with its mysteries.' I hope this diary demonstrates both the strong ties which exist between conservation and sport and that one can participate in the latter while at the same time keeping faith with a love and respect for nature. There is a strong and misguided movement to ban hunting with hounds – part of the tapestry of our countryside for many hundreds of years. Because so much of the debate against is based on ignorance or political expediency, I believe that it is vital for the view of the countryman to be heard.

TO THE CUCKOO

O blithe new-comer! I have heard,
I hear thee and rejoice.
O Cuckoo! shall I call thee Bird,
Or but a Wandering Voice?

While I am lying on the grass
Thy twofold shout I hear;
From hill to hill it seems to pass
At once far off, and near.

Though babbling only to the vale,
Of sunshine and of flowers,
Thou bringest unto me a tale
Of visionary hours.

Thrice welcome, darling of the Spring!
Even yet thou art to me
No bird, but an invisible thing,
A voice, a mystery;

The same whom in my schoolboy days
I listened to; that cry
Which made me look a thousand ways
In bush, and tree, and sky.

To seek thee did I often rove
Through woods and on the green;
And thou wert still a hope, a love;
Still longed for, never seen!

And I can listen to thee yet;
Can lie upon the plain
And listen, till I do beget
That golden time again.

O blessed bird! the earth we pace
Again appears to be
An unsubstantial, faery place,
That is fit home for thee!

WILLIAM WORDSWORTH
(1802)

MAY

Wednesday, 3 May

If there is one place that has contributed more than any other to my love of birds over the years it is Needs Ore. I've been visiting this heavenly spot for over fifteen years, ever since Jeremy Norman and Derek Frost took on one of the coastguard cottages in the late seventies. The Needs Ore cottages were used by customs and excise officers until the introduction of the wireless in the early part of the century. Now owned by the Beaulieu Estate, they are located at the mouth of the Beaulieu estuary in the New Forest. The cottages face a small creek which at low tide plays host to a multitude of hungry waders and wildfowl. From 1 March onwards the marsh on the seaward side becomes a noisy gullery. Across the Solent flicker the lights of Newtown Bay and further west, Yarmouth. Behind the cottages lies the nature reserve of Blackwater and its surrounding meadows which were today being enjoyed by hundreds of brent geese, and a good contingent of wigeon.

Jeremy is my closest Cambridge friend. We met while cramming for our university entrance at Davies, Laing & Dick in Holland Park. We both passed in on geography but were soon frightened off by the fact that at Cambridge it was treated as a science rather than an art-subject. We fled to the Faculty of Archaeology and Anthropology and lived happily ever afterwards! He is one of the most creative entrepreneurs of our generation. After Cambridge he acquired a publishing business and more recently has been very successful operating in both the leisure and property sectors. He has had a lifelong interest in natural history and when not travelling abroad with Derek, his spare time is spent at Needs Ore.

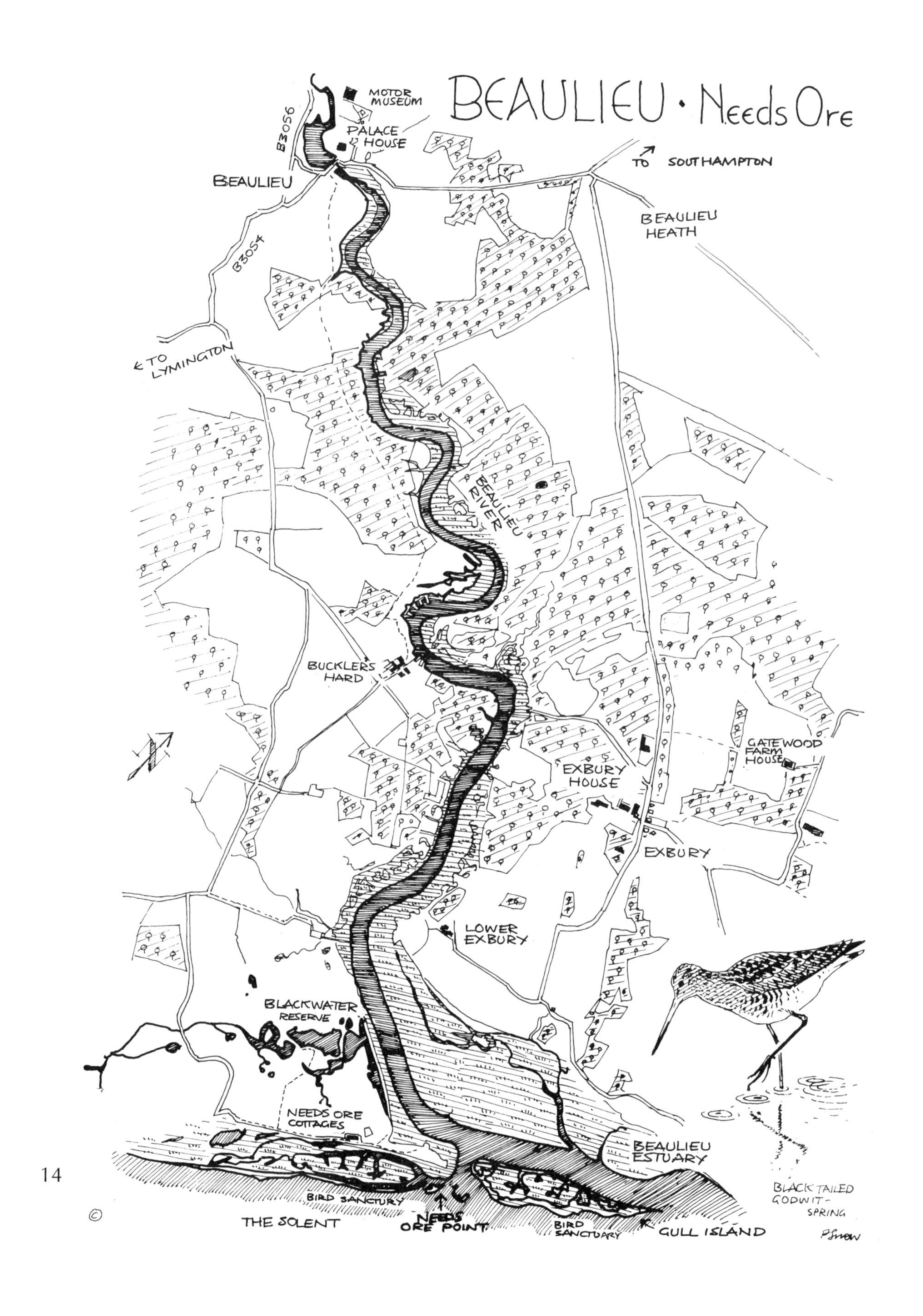
BEAULIEU · Needs Ore
MOTOR MUSEUM
PALACE HOUSE
B3056
BEAULIEU
TO SOUTHAMPTON
BEAULIEU HEATH
B3054
← TO LYMINGTON
BEAULIEU RIVER
BUCKLERS HARD
GATEWOOD FARM HOUSE
EXBURY HOUSE
EXBURY
LOWER EXBURY
BLACKWATER RESERVE
NEEDS ORE COTTAGES
BEAULIEU ESTUARY
BIRD SANCTURY
THE SOLENT
NEEDS ORE POINT
BIRD SANCTUARY
GULL ISLAND
BLACK TAILED GODWIT - SPRING
P Snow

A glorious sunny morning. I walked to Blackwater before breakfast. The estuary surroundings were full of every sort of joy sound and joy flight imaginable. Taking full advantage of the bank-holiday Mediterranean weather, countless birds were at the peak of their courtship ritual.

On this still morning the distant call of the cuckoo came from all points of the compass. One particular bird seemed to have decided on a change of tune. The entry in *The Country Diary of an Edwardian Lady* for midsummer's day starts: 'The cuckoo is beginning to change his tune, a little later he will be saying "cuc-cuckoo" instead of "cuckoo".' The well-known rhyme goes:

> The cuckoo comes in April
> Sings his song in May
> Changes his tune in the middle of June
> In July he flies away.

My bird broke into a chorus of cuc-cuc-cuckoo on two separate occasions, well over a month earlier than it is supposed to. The adult cuckoo does leave Britain early in the summer (July) but the young birds stay with their foster parents as late as September. They then migrate on their own, finding their way unaided to their African winter quarters.

Living in the Derbyshire Dales I always seem to be one of the last people to hear the spring cuckoo. I only enjoy one or two instances of local song a year. This may well be because of a lack of woodland on the limestone hills.

The cuckoo is the only one of our birds that rears its young by fostering them on other birds. It adopts a large territory and, having ejected one of the host's eggs, will deposit an egg in anything up to a dozen nests. In this way it can produce many more offspring than if it had to feed them all itself.

I watched a cuckoo fly close by over one of the Blackwater reedbeds. This was unusual in itself; as Wordsworth reminds us, they are more often heard than seen. It was no doubt prospecting for nests to target among those belonging to the hapless reed warblers which have recently arrived in numbers from Africa. The rushes were alive with their churring song. With its long tail and sickle-shaped wings the cuckoo in flight looks like a bird of prey, and this was why he was aggressively mobbed by a good old black-headed gull.

The cuckoo is one of Nature's miracles. It has even developed egg mimicry. Cuckoos which prey on reed warblers and meadow pipits will lay eggs closely resembling those of the victimised birds in pattern.

No sound in nature is more eagerly awaited in Britain than the song of the cuckoo in April. Last night Jeremy and I walked up to the seafront road at dusk on a balmy still evening to listen for a nightingale. The lights of Yarmouth twinkled merrily across the Solent. But on this particular occasion the maestro would not come on stage. We were not to be disappointed. Way out across the Forest a cuckoo was gently calling long after the light had finally gone.

Thursday, 4 May

We drove over to Beaulieu at dusk to meet Jamie Chichester, having made a plan to go in search of nightingales and nightjars. Jamie is one of my oldest friends. A real countryman with a wealth of knowledge on trees, shrubs, birds and wild flowers. He is a modern day Colonel Hawker with a passion for country sports.

To hear the call of a nightjar on a warm summer's evening is an unforgettable experience and there was one waiting for us just outside

the nursery perimeter. Jamie's nursery lies on the edge of the New Forest and is surrounded by a young conifer plantation infilled with a mass of purple rhododendrons. The time to go and listen is at dusk when the woods begin to echo with their eerie churring calls. The monotonous soft reeling song is not high pitched like that of a grasshopper warbler but more of a mechanical sound like the revolutions of a distant machine. For a moment we thought there were two males calling. In fact it was merely a distinct change of pitch caused by the movement of a single bird's head as it perched along the length of a branch.

Grey finds something mysterious about the song:

> It is a most soothing sound, maintained for long periods without a break. No one acquainted with it and hearing it for the first time would guess that the noise was made by a bird at all. It is of that class of stationary, soothing, continuous sounds, such as the hum of a threshing machine, or the noise of waves on the shore heard at a distance, which dispose us to sit still and listen indefinitely.

The nightjar has a good deal in common with the woodcock. They are both night-time feeders and with their superb camouflage they spend the day roosting on the woodland floor. At dusk they are great entertainers in terms of song and movement. The nightjar's flight is silent but acrobatic, as it wheels, twists, turns, floats and glides in pursuit of the moth. Its hawk-like features of a long tail and pointed wings produce the manoeuvrability necessary to take such insects on the wing. It is the only bird that competes in the same airspace as the bat. An interesting characteristic displayed during their dusk sorties is a loud wing clapping similar to that of the much larger short-eared owl. The male has distinctive white spots on its wings which make for a ready form of identification, in much the same way as the grey plover sports heavy black spots under its armpits.

We did not see a nightjar in flight this evening but we did enjoy a number of roding woodcock. They emit a curious combination of grunts and high-pitched bat-like calls as they complete their territorial flypast.

The nightjar arrives on our southern open heathlands from Africa in the middle of May – ours was an early bird. Its numbers are sadly decreasing which is almost certainly connected with the gradual encroachment on to our heaths of housing. Nightjars need bare ground for their nest site. They nest among the dead debris that follows forest harvesting and will not nest on growing vegetation. In the last twenty years or so the increased felling of conifer plantations has had a positive effect on nightjar populations.

Particularly graphic is the old-fashioned nickname for the nightjar – the 'goatsucker'. A combination of its large gape and the fact that it often feeds in the vicinity of grazing flocks where insects tend to congregate must have led shepherds of old to assume the nightjar preyed vampire-like on their animals.

Entranced by the performance of this single bird we drove off towards Needs Ore to see if we could make it a double with a nightingale. It was a lovely still clear night with the sweet smell of the fresh May blossom in the air. We stopped at one or two likely places on the edge of the Forest but heard nothing. We finally descended on the pretty little village of

Buckler's Hard where Jamie heard a single bird a week or so ago. Lights were on in the houses, the bar in the Master Builder's Hotel was doing brisk business and the green and red navigation lights of the incoming yachts glided up the river. The nightingale was also present – deep in the riverside scrub – but he was not very obliging. Just once or twice we were given the merest taste of that powerful song. He was there, and we had heard him, and that was all that mattered.

I only once before heard a nightingale sing in England and that was five years ago to the day at Needs Ore. I was driving Jeremy Norman down to his Hampshire cottage at the beginning of the May Day weekend in 1990. As the coastguard cottages came into sight, I was relating how some months ago a local bird watcher had told me that during the month of May nightingales could be heard singing in the driveway hedge fronting the creek. It was 1.00 a.m. in the morning and a dark night. The sea was calm as a light yet cold north wind was blowing off the mainland and out to the island. Across the Solent the lights of the old medieval port of Shalfleet flickered reassuringly. Our car window was open and we savoured the fresh salty smell of the sea.

Hardly had I finished telling him of my conversation with the birdman than we heard a song of such power that it was audible above the noise of the engine. We stopped the car and listened. No more than three yards away a nightingale was singing his heart out from the depths of a hedgerow full of gnarled and weather-beaten trees and bramble scrub. He sang and sang and was not remotely upset either by our presence or the glare of the headlights. Maybe he was just too tired to care after his long flight from the continent. In the far distance another retorted with his 'chock and wheezes'. A nightingale singing in the stillness of a dark summer's night has immense pulling power and is surely one of the wonders of nature.

The nightingale has real charisma. He has his part in Greek mythology. He has inspired poets down countless generations and his rumoured presence will excite the attention of normally uninterested everyday folk. Why? It certainly isn't because of his looks. He is an altogether unremarkable creature with a warbler-like brown back and white belly, but with a redeeming rich rufus tail that he flicks in indignation if spied upon in the undergrowth. He is shy and retiring and more often heard than seen. He is a skulker who lurks in dense thickets of scrub and a well-camouflaged ground feeder who perches and nests low down, barely off the ground.

There are, I feel, three reasons why the nightingale is such a welcome visitor to England. Firstly the quality of his song, secondly the fact that he sings at night and lastly his sadly increasing rarity.

The nightingale may not be the best technical performer – the blackcap and blackbird can probably lay claim to this award – however, for power and variety of song he has no equal. In *The Charm of Birds*, Edward Grey describes the nightingale's song as follows:

> Let us suppose a lover of birdsong to be walking slowly, with ears alert, about an oakwood in the latter half of May. The big trees stand sufficiently apart to encourage plenty of undergrowth – thickets of thorn and bramble, hazel and perhaps some bushes of whin. He hears, one after another, various songs familiar to him – thrush,

blackbird, garden warbler, blackcap, willow warbler, whitethroat and others; he selects the song of each with pleased attention: suddenly he is struck – it is almost a physical impact – by notes of an energy, force and dominance with which none of the others can compare. The song is not a linked phrase, like that of the blackbird: it is repetition of one set of notes; then a pause, and then a different set of notes: in this the plan of the song resembles that of the thrush. We cannot tell which notes will follow a pause. 'Jug, jug, jug' is an expression used to describe the most usual and typical notes. But the supreme achievement of the nightingale is a loud, clear, sustained note that fills the air. The best notes of other birds, blackcap or blackbird, come distinctly from the point where the bird utters them, and seem to reach and terminate at the listener's ear; but the supreme notes of the nightingale envelop and surround us so that we lose the perception of the point whence they proceed: it is as if we were included and embraced in pervading sound.

Although I have only heard a nightingale sing in England on a couple of occasions, I have been lucky enough to enjoy some memorable performances at Sotogrande in southernmost Spain. The birds are eagerly awaited around 1st April each year. Some will use the lush thick shrubs below the cork oaks as a refuelling point on their way north while others stay to stake out a nesting territory. We visited Sotogrande in 1991 – it was a particularly early Easter and the weather was cold and cloudy. On our last day the sun broke through and the nightingales appeared out of thin air. The garden became a chorus of song. It took me some time to locate a singing bird. This nightingale shook visibly as he performed, his throat swollen and body vibrating as he recoiled violently on the more powerful notes. There are long wheezes as he builds up to a 'choc-choc' crescendo – on and on he goes with at times machine-gun-like velocity. He spills forth an incredible variety of rich notes, some fast, some slow, some deep, some high. There is no way that this song can be described as melancholy, which some commentators down the years have suggested. It is a song of exuberance and happiness, as described by Wordsworth:

O Nightingale! thou surely art
A creature of 'fiery heart'
These notes of thine – they pierce and pierce;
Tumultuous harmony and fierce!
Thou sings't as if the god of wine;
Had helped thee to a Valentine;
A song in mockery and despite;
Of shares, and dews and silent night;
And steady bliss and all the loves;
New sleeping in these peaceful groves.

Also John Keats in the first verse of 'Ode to a Nightingale' writes:

'Tis not through envy of thy happy lot,
But being too happy in thy happiness,
That thou, light-winged Dryad of the trees,
In some melodious plot

Of beechen green, and shadows numberless,
Singest of summer in full-throated ease.

If anybody does portray the nightingale as a doleful creature it must be because the bird sings at night. Being alone at night can be a frightening experience – the darkness, the solitude, it is often a time for melancholy brooding. In 'Ode to a Nightingale', Keats tells how he often thought of suicide and of there being no better moment than when listening to the nightingale's song on a balmy summer night. Here we have an association of unhappiness with the nightingale and with some of the most lovely poetry in the world:

Darkling I listen; and for many a time,
I have been half in love with easeful Death,
Call'd him soft names in many a mused rhyme,
To take into the air my quiet breath;
Now more than ever seems it rich to die,
To cease upon the midnight with no pain,
While thou art pouring forth thy soul abroad
In such an ecstacy!
Still would'st thou sing, and I have ears in vain –
To thy high requiem become a sod.

The original culprit for associating the nightingale with sadness is surely Greek mythology. Procne, daughter of the King of Athens, was changed by the gods into a nightingale and so great was her sorrow that she sang, pressing her breast against a thorn.

In the spring of 1990, I read this lovely passage from the poem 'Fishing' by Dorothy Wellesley at my father-in-law, Robin Hastings', memorial service in Winchester Cathedral:

Lovely the mercury, the flutter of the sea,
And the squares of the quicksilver nets,
And the drops of the sea divine,
As the fishes took the road to death,
Little waifs, little souls,
Lovely in their living and dying ever,
For luminous their fins as feathers in the sun,
Sunny their scales as the sheen of the jay,
– When silly tomboy, in sunshine he screams –
For inwardly lit are they;
Inwardly lit of their own light it seems,
Knowing a clarity ungiven to the day,
As on the branching reefs undersea they alight and
sway,
To the swell like swarming starlings in a windy tree.
Yet intimate with shadows that in air cannot be,
Dark are they, brooding, knowing, yet gay,
Shaft of sunlight theirs, deeps the lark never knows,
No, nor even the nightingale crucified on the spine of
the Rose!

The nightingale is famed as a night-time songster. In fact he performs just as competently in the daytime, but during the long days at the end of May and early June his song in England is likely to be drowned by the rich voices of the blackbird and blackcap. Nobody really understands why they sing at night; however, two other night-time songsters, the sedge and grasshopper warbler, have much in common with the nightingale. They all thrive in dense cover in addition to being summer visitors which migrate at night from the African continent. The male birds tend to arrive about ten days before the females to set up their territories which they defend with song. They sing heartily in the daytime, then it is thought they continue in the silence of the night to attract females passing overhead.

Unfortunately, we are hearing the joy notes of the nightingale less and less in England. Edward Grey hinted at their decline around his Itchen cottage as early as the turn of the century.

> Time had been when, for some years, a pair had bred in the old chalk pit close to me, but that time was no more. One year the male had been in full song day after day and night after night; then one night in mid-May, there was a silence that was never broken there by a nightingale again.

I suspect the pressure of modern farming is an important reason for the decline in their numbers. Nightingales are found in small deciduous woods and copses – particularly those with rotational coppicing – in addition to overgrown hedgerows and commons with dense thickets of thorn scrub. The densest populations of birds occur in woods with a five- to eight-year coppicing cycle. If the cycle is longer than this the canopy becomes too dense and light cannot penetrate down to the undergrowth. Eric Simms in *British Warblers* writes:

> The process of coppicing small woods gave cyclical advantage to nightingales and garden warblers. Unfortunately thirty per cent of woods of less than a hectare in size were cleared between 1947 and 1972. Clearance had been encouraged by government grants and the Common Agricultural Policy has made farming more worthwhile then forestry. There have also been changes in the style of land ownership with financial institutions taking over from private landowners; in 1977 such bodies purchased more than ten per cent of all land sold in England and Wales. In many instances ancient woods have been sold and replaced by even-aged conifers or by farmland.

The nightingale above all frequents deciduous woods – particularly oaks under-planted with hazel – where a low cover of brambles and nettles is likely to develop and provide their favoured cover. A national decline in coppicing together with a general loss of deciduous woodland to modern farming and forestry practices have therefore taken their sad toll on nightingale numbers. Distribution, however, remains much the same running south of a line from the Wash to the Severn.

Friday, 5 May

Spent the night at Needs Ore.

We took Jeremy's new boat out on to the Solent for an hour or so after tea. You could still feel the heat of the sun at 6.00p.m. We passed Gull Island at the mouth of the river which gave us the opportunity to view the terns that have recently arrived. Three species of tern nest here in the summer. There are approximately fifty pairs each of sandwich and common terns. The sandwich terns are the largest and earliest to arrive. They are best identified by their overall whiteness, and their yellow-tipped black bill. Both species have nested on the shingle among the black-headed gulls, as they benefit from their neighbours' aggression towards intruders. Unless you get very close it is impossible to tell the common and Arctic tern apart. As we took the boat up a creek towards the Exbury shore we did get close enough to a common tern to see the black tip to the orange-red bill. The common tern tends to be a much more southerly bird than the Arctic tern and it is also seen inland to a greater degree. Any bird nesting south of a line from the Farne Islands to Anglesey is almost certainly a common tern.

After the black-tailed godwit, the bird I most associate with Needs Ore is the little tern. About ten pairs nest here every year and they are closely guarded by the local Nature Conservancy warden. Because they like to nest on stretches of fine beach or shingle ridges, they are always subject to human disturbance in the summer. As a result of protective measures across the country, they have increased to over 2,000 pairs. I walked up the creek in front of the cottages and a pair were chattering loudly on a small mudbank. The little tern is a charming tiny coastal tern that likes feeding in lagoons and creeks inside the seawall. The creek in front of Needs Ore cottages is the perfect place to watch them fishing. What I imagine was the male bird took off from the mudbank and hovered like a humming bird before diving down some twenty-five feet with a splash and taking a fish. This he proceeded to present to his mate amidst much high-pitched chattering. It is easy to understand why this dainty little bird has attracted the nickname 'sea-swallow'. It has a distinctive yellow bill with a black tip and unique yellow legs as far as the tern family goes. It arrives in Britain in April and leaves by September, going south to spend the winter in the rich fishing grounds along the West African coast.

Sunday, 7 May

We arrived at Rievaulx in North Yorkshire to stay with my brother-in-law and sister, Rick and Libby Beckett, yesterday evening. The abbey looked quite beautiful in the low evening sun.

My brother-in-law has one of the prettiest homes imaginable at Rievaulx. The estate consists of the village and a mile or so of the Rye River valley which is bordered on its steep sides by dense luxuriant woodland of oak and ash. There is no finer place to walk on a May morning and listen to birdsong. I went for a short walk before breakfast – the weather was fine but just beginning to show signs of breaking up. The ash and the hawthorn were not yet out but the wild cherry blossom made up for them. The woodland floor was a carpet of bluebells, forget-me-nots and wild garlic. The woods were alive with singing birds – chaffinches, blackbirds, song thrushes, blackcaps, chiffchaffs, willow warblers, wrens and nuthatches – even a solitary pied flycatcher. I watched a garden warbler sing for the first time this year. It might be a nondescript bird yet it really puts its back into its song. Its whole body was quivering as it performed from the top of a hawthorn bush.

I was alerted to a pair of dippers on the river by their metallic 'clink' call note. One of the birds was sitting under the bank and was invisible, apart from its snow-white chest. It then flew on to a stone in the middle of the river where it bobbed up and down and proceeded to give itself a wash and brush-up, pruning itself and shaking vigorously. I've only once seen a dipper feeding and it is a truly remarkable sight. I was staying at Arkengarthdale in Swaledale over the late May bank holiday in 1987. We were sitting on the pretty stone bridge over the Arkle beck below Scarr House. The dipper slipped off a stone into the water and actually walked along the stream bed under water. Experiments have shown that when the dipper walks upstream with its head down looking for food, the force of the fast current against its slanting back keeps it on the bottom. Again, I have only once consciously heard its liquid warbling song and that was pointed out to me by my friend Edward Hay whilst walking down the Middleton Dale at home in Derbyshire. Invariably you see them flying 'kingfisher like' downstream with a whirring of wings, emitting a sharp alarm call.

After I returned from my walk I sat in front of the house and marvelled at the view before me. A huge lush valley with thick wooded sides. Nature is so busy here. In the words of Dorothy Wellesley, a pheasant 'chucked and whirred' within yards of me; then there was the distant drumming of a great spotted woodpecker. And up and down the River Rye flew a constant traffic of colourful goosanders uttering their indignant growling calls.

The Benedictine monks certainly knew how to choose a home.

Tuesday, 9 May

Parwich Lees is an unusual house for the Derbyshire Peak District. Historically the area was relatively inaccessible and aside from a few big estates and the local lead mining it was not particularly prosperous. Consequently 'good-sized' country houses are few and far between. Parwich Lees is bigger than the average farmhouse, with lighter and

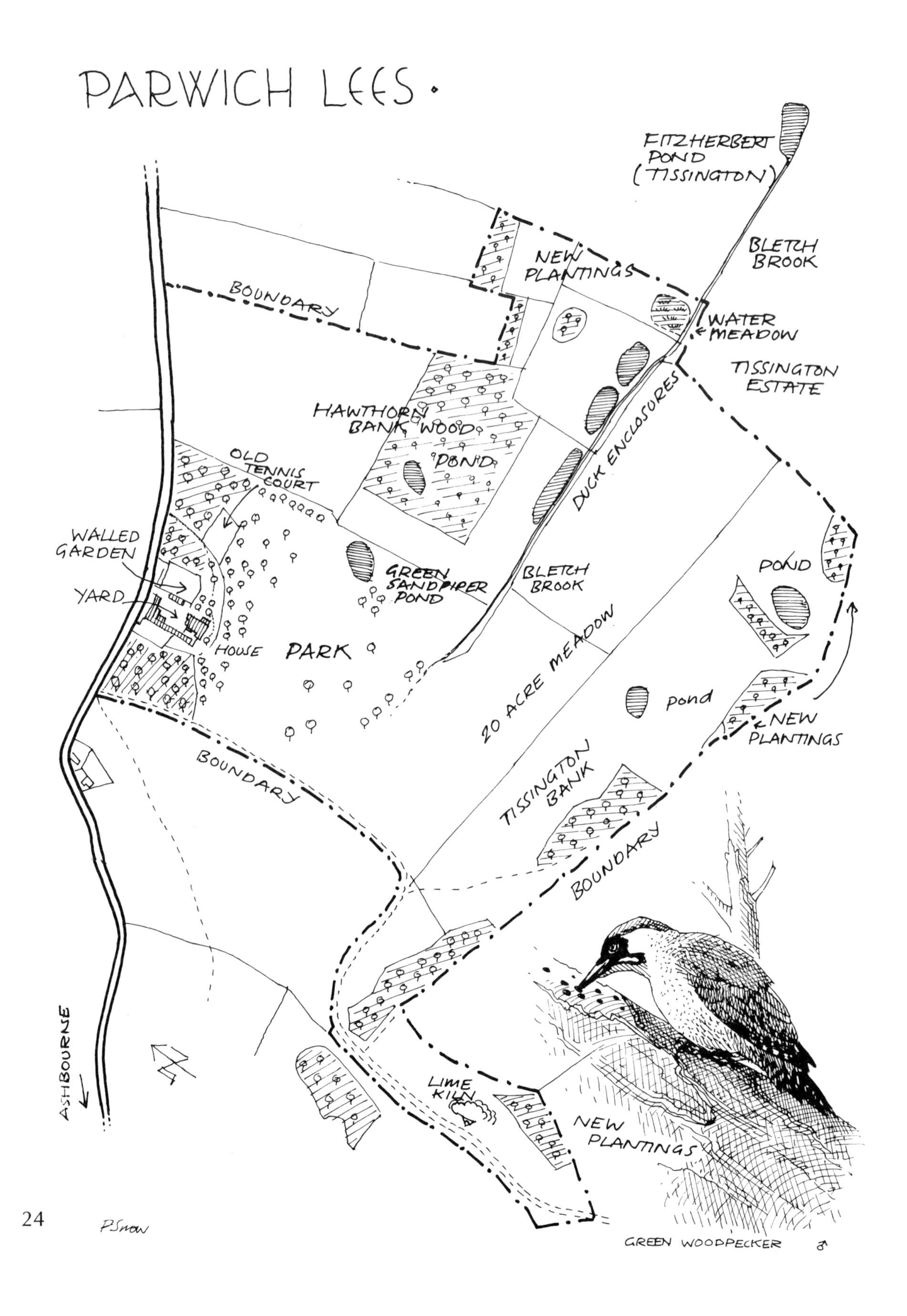
PARWICH LEES
FITZHERBERT POND (TISSINGTON)
BLETCH BROOK
NEW PLANTINGS
BOUNDARY
WATER MEADOW
TISSINGTON ESTATE
HAWTHORN BANK WOOD
POND
DUCK ENCLOSURES
OLD TENNIS COURT
WALLED GARDEN
YARD
GREEN SANDPIPER POND
BLETCH BROOK
POND
HOUSE
PARK
20 ACRE MEADOW
pond
NEW PLANTINGS
BOUNDARY
TISSINGTON BANK
BOUNDARY
ASHBOURNE
LIME KILN
NEW PLANTINGS
P. Snow
GREEN WOODPECKER ♂

more spacious rooms, yet not as substantial or architecturally imposing as some of our local 'halls'.

The house and yard have been enlarged at various stages, giving rise to a confusion of both limestone and redbrick farm buildings at the back. The front of the house, built with local limestone, presents the most pleasing aspect. Around 1800 a small Georgian façade was built on to the original farmhouse, adding four large rooms and a handsome staircase. At the turn of this century the two downstairs windows were replaced by large 'bays', outside which the lawn gently drops into the valley by way of a ha-ha.

The house is now approached by the backyard. We dispensed with the front drive when we bought the house and replaced the gravel and rather funereal yew trees with lawns. The yard has a number of attractive features. It is dominated on the west side by an imposing coachhouse and on the east by the walled garden. The latter was not marked on the 1844 tithe map and was probably built in 1857, the date on a charming little belltower by the back door which was used to ring in the farm workers. At the foot of the wall on the east side of the yard stands the old stone sheepdip, proof that not so long ago it was a working farmyard.

Parwich Lees was once a large farm for this part of Derbyshire, comprising two hundred and fifty acres. Over the years it has both been independently owned and part of the Alsop Estate. It was sadly split up and sold in the 1970s. In 1987 we were lucky enough to buy back ninety acres in front of the house. On this I have planted a number of small copses of mixed woodland totalling around ten acres.

What makes Parwich Lees so special is its situation. It faces south, sitting on the lip of the Alsop dale, with lovely views both down the valley and across to a steep bank which backs on to the Tissington Trail (the old Ashbourne to Buxton railway line). At the bottom of the valley is a twenty-acre meadow with the tiny Bletch Brook emerging from the ground half way down the north side. It is this stream that provides the main source of water for my duckponds.

I counted twenty-three ducklings feeding on the chick starter crumbs. I think they represent the two broods that were reared under the relative security of the plastic dustbins. Another brood has hatched under one of my bantams. I found yet another nest with seven eggs at the other end of the enclosure and successfully sat them under a broody.

A sedge warbler has arrived in the ditch hedge behind the enclosure. This one was in exactly the same place as last year, except that it arrived a week or so later. Its song is very distinctive. It is much more varied and rapid than that of the reed warbler. It chatters and whistles and chirrups, whereas the reed warbler 'churr churrs' and 'jag jags' in a rather monotonous fashion. Seen through the binoculars, the sedge warbler was conspicuously streaked with a long creamy eyestripe whereas the reed warbler is a uniformly brown bird. The location of this particular bird demonstrates that the sedge warbler frequents a wider habitat than the reed warbler, which sticks entirely to reed beds. An old country name for the sedge warbler is the 'mock nightingale' as this lively little bird will sing night and day when it first arrives back in Britain.

Grey saw this warbler as the extrovert among our summer visitors:

It is impossible to write of the sedge warbler without using epithets or expressions that apply to mankind rather than to a bird. When such expressions are used here or elsewhere they are intended, not as literal descriptions of the bird's nature and character, but to give the impression that the bird's appearance and ways produce upon a human observer. The sedge warbler is like a comic spirit among birds. The eyestripe gives a jaunty look; its demeanour and movements are very lively. The natural song is apparently akin to that of the reed warbler, but it is harsh in tone and the bird interpolates various imitations of notes of other species. Warde Fowler, in a book already quoted, describes how he saw and heard a sedge warbler imitate, as if in mockery, the fussy chuckle of a blackbird scared by a false alarm and flying off in unreasonable perturbation. The bird will often flit out almost under the angler's foot from some thick growth on the edge of the stream, as if its nest were surely there, when as likely as not the nest is in the hedge outside the water meadow. Sometimes it seems to frequent the reeds, as if it made common cause with the reed warblers; and yet we come upon it in bushes on higher ground in dry places not adjoining water. It is as if the bird wishes to show us that it can be indifferent to the neighbourhood of water, which we have thought indispensable to it. It is lively and noisy all day, but also sings at night. If one sleeps out of doors, various birds, especially the dunnock, may be heard to utter the occasional snatch of song; but with the exception of the nightingale and grasshopper warbler the only one of our songbirds that I have heard sing frequently and even continuously at night is the sedge warbler. The song lacks melody, but the bird is a pleasant and animating presence.

Sedge warbler numbers have been declining in Britain probably through a combination of drought in their winter quarters and habitat loss by way of wetland drainage and intensification of agricultural methods. The Sahel drought in West Africa has caused a decline in numbers since 1968 as returning birds use this zone for feeding prior to spring migration. Following the most severe failure of the rains in 1983, fewer than five per cent of adult sedge warblers were estimated to have survived and returned to their breeding grounds in England. Today, there are an estimated two hundred and fifty thousand sedge warbler territories in Britain.

Wednesday, 10 May

A lovely hot day with all the indications that we are moving from spring to early summer. The chestnut and sycamore trees are now out – the oaks and limes are well on their way and the beech is a fresh green. Our copper beech is now fully out, forming a russet umbrella over our stone birdtable which at this time of year doubles as a 'waterhole'. The fields are covered in buttercups and the old tennis court is congested with forget-me-nots. The garden is alive with the twittering of colourful goldfinches.

I found a moorhen's nest in an 'island' tuft of grass within feet of my central feeding point in the duck enclosure. It contained seven delicious buff-coloured eggs, speckled with red and brown.

I heard two birds for the first time this year which signifies the beginning of summer. I spent the morning at my business partner's house that sits on the edge of the moors to the Baslow side of Sheffield. While working in the garden I was entertained by a whitethroat. Grey evidently found the whitethroat as entertaining as the sedge warbler:

> Its song is fussy, as if the bird were always in a hurry or slightly provoked. Sometimes the tones and manner suggest scolding. The bird is fond of roadside hedges which have thick undergrowth and so thrusts itself upon our notice; but it also frequents clumps of woodland, especially where there are patches of bramble. In spite of what is said above about the bird and its song, the prevailing impression it gives is that of excitement and happiness and its animation and vitality are a pleasant feature in the places that it chooses to inhabit.

The cockbird is very well dressed with a grey head and snow-white throat which it puffs out while singing. It is a very fidgety bird that has a jerky bouncy song flight. This is often performed over hedgerows and it can often be seen helicoptering out of cover and then diving straight back in. The old country name for the whitethroat is 'nettlecreeper', which reflects the bird's favourite nesting place.

It was the failure of seventy-five per cent of the whitethroat population to reappear in the spring of 1969 that drew attention to the effect of the Sahelian drought on migratory birds. The bird suffers dramatic swings in its population depending on the climatic changes in its wintering grounds south of the Sahara desert. There are an estimated six hundred and fifty thousand pairs of whitethroat in Britain today but the species has never really recovered from a series of setbacks over the past twenty-five years.

In the afternoon I walked down to throw the ducks some barley and heard the forceful song of a garden warbler in the hawthorn bank. Its song is difficult to distinguish from that of the blackcap but it tends to go on for longer and is much more rapid and even. For sheer quality, Grey preferred the blackcap.

> The garden warbler's song is very good: in one respect it surpasses that of the blackcap; it is more sustained; but the bird never seems absolutely to clear the throat and let out the sound so pure and free as the blackcap does. To my ear the opening notes of the blackcap's song and those of the garden warbler are so alike that I hear them with a doubt of which bird I am listening to; but the garden warbler goes on and on for a longer time and yet never seems to liberate its voice upon the air so completely as a blackcap does. In other words, a garden warbler's song seems always on the point of an achievement, to which only the blackcap attains.

Warde Fowler in *A Year with the Birds* comes to much the same conclusion as Edward Grey:

> But they differ in two points: the strain of the blackcap is shorter, forming in fact one lengthened phrase 'in sweetness long drawn out', while the garden warbler will go on almost continuously for many minutes together; and secondly the blackcap's music is played upon a mellower instrument. The most gifted blackcaps – for birds of the same species differ considerably in their power of song – excel all other birds in the soft quality of their tone, just as a really good boy's voice, though less brilliant and resonant, excels all women's voices in softness and sweetness.

The garden warbler is a rather nondescript bird which makes up for its bland looks with a beautiful song. It is stockier than a blackcap and arrives a fortnight or so later. In my experience the two birds frequent different habitats and can be compared to the chiffchaff and the willow warbler. The blackcap and chiffchaff seem to prefer larger, more mature deciduous trees whereas the garden warbler is often found in the company of the willow warbler in the hawthorn bushes.

In the evening I picked up the two larsen traps and took them down to my friend Robert Shields in the village. We placed one of the traps in Robert's garden. A mistle thrush immediately dived down on the decoy magpie in the cage demonstrating the bird's natural aggression. I knew there must have been a nest in the vicinity and sure enough within minutes we found one prominently displayed in the fork of an apple tree. Grey also had little problem in locating their nests.

> Some nests are so exposed that it is surprising they ever escape. The mistle thrush builds early, when there is little cover and deciduous trees are still bare. The nest is large and is often placed more aloft than those of the song thrush: it is therefore very conspicuous. Indeed it has been said that 'you do not find a mistle thrush's nest; it finds you'. The mistle thrush, however, is a bird of some size and high courage: combat is often to be seen between a pair of mistle thrushes and a jackdaw; and it is probable that sometimes the mistle thrushes are able to protect the eggs or young.

Friday, 12 May

Spent Thursday night at Needs Ore having driven down from our Leeds office. Went out for a short walk before breakfast. A pair of squeaking little terns hovered acrobatically in the nippy east wind that was blowing the tide up the creek. A pair of gadwall flew over the saltmarsh, the drake distinctive with his white wing patches. Two black-tailed godwits sat on the mudflats at the mouth of the creek. Both birds were in their lovely russet breeding plumage. The local warden says they do not breed in the Blackwater meadows so they are probably on their way north. They were accompanied by a grey plover, a ringed plover and three dunlin, the latter also in their fine summer clothes. There are still a good number of brent geese here; I cannot think why as it seems very late. As I returned to the cottages, the first swifts I've seen this year dashed overhead.

One solitary wader stood out on the edge of the creek. It was larger than a redshank with long elegant green legs and a slightly upturned bill. The greenshank appears very pale with noticeably white underparts. When it took off in a fast erratic flight, it uttered a lovely penetrating three-note call – 'too-hoo-hoo'. In flight it has a conspicuous white rump and the white feathers extend well up its back in a

distinctive V shape like that of the curlew. I should really add the greenshank to the little tern and the black-tailed godwit as the birds I most enjoy seeing at Needs Ore. Indeed, the greenshank can be seen at most times of the year here although infrequently and in small numbers (usually singly and rarely more than three). Upwards of fifteen thousand pairs of greenshank now nest in northern Scotland – north of the Great Glen and in the Hebrides – but they are not a common sight in Britain; a few overwinter with us in the south (maybe the Scottish nesters?) but most sightings will be passage migrants moving through to their winter quarters south of the Sahara. The greenshank has slowly increased in numbers as a nesting bird in Britain. The bird was badly persecuted by egg collectors in the nineteenth century, the eggs being much sought-after as the nest is particularly difficult to find. They like to nest on open expanses of wild, flat moorland containing small ponds and lochans. The recent extensive planting of the Flow Country could check their present expansion. The tax benefits granted on planting forestry in the sixties and seventies led to large tracts of northern Scotland being planted. Thanks to the vigilance of the RSPB, combined with pressure applied on government departments, the destruction of the Flow Country has now been effectively halted.

I have been lucky enough to watch greenshanks on their nesting territory when staying at Ledmore near Ullapool in June. The bird circles high above its territory uttering its flutey too-hoo call from a quivering stop-go flight. It will dive down on to a tussock and perch there for some time displaying its distinctive white V-shaped rump. Finally it takes off again, climbs steeply to a great height and repeats the performance. The greenshank was Seton Gordon's favourite songster:

> Edward Grey once told me that he had heard most birds' songs, but that he had never heard the greenshank sing. The song of the wandering greenshank is one of the most beautiful – perhaps the most beautiful – of all the songs I know, and the singer sometimes remains in the air for half an hour uttering, without pause, his flute-like song.

With his frequent fishing trips to the Highlands, how strange that Grey never heard its song. Perhaps the greenshank represents another recent conservation success story.

SPOTTED REDSHANK & RUFF

There are two other exciting waders which one can sometimes see at Needs Ore at this time of year while they are *en route* to their northerly nesting grounds. The ruff and spotted redshank were not in evidence this time, but when staying on 6 May 1989 I was lucky enough to catch sight of both. There was a much rarer single reeve in the Blackwater meadows identifiable by the long slender neck, smallish head and beak together with a characteristic plumage that reminds me of a hen pheasant. Britain is on the western edge of their breeding range and fewer than ten pairs breed here each year, mainly on wet meadows in East Anglia. The spotted redshank is more common at Needs Ore and is nearly always seen on migration. Last July I saw a single bird at Blackwater that was returning early and had probably failed to nest. The beautiful black summer plumage of the spotted redshank can only be matched by the grey plover and it is very unusual to see the latter in this state in Britain. The spotted redshank is larger than the redshank. It has longer legs and no distinctive white wing bar.

Arrived at Blenheim at 10.00 a.m. after a drive of an hour and a half from the New Forest. I have such happy memories of past times at Blenheim. I spent a good deal of my youth staying with my grandparents. For a child, the house was a gigantic Aladdin's Cave with endless opportunities for games and exploring. The acres of gardens, lakes and parkland were a young birdnester's paradise. It was here I learnt both to shoot and to love and respect nature. There were thirty wonderful Christmases, surrounded by a large family, and then there were three immensely happy years at the Lince in the early 1980s. The Lince was built in the late eighteenth century as a folly when Capability Brown was brought in to mastermind the lake and parklands. It stands at the junction of the Rivers Glyme and Evenlode and has a lovely view down on to Bladon Water. In much the same way as 'the Cottage' on the Itchen was a special refuge for Grey, so the Lince was for me. It provided the perfect weekend retreat from the stresses of working for a West End advertising agency.

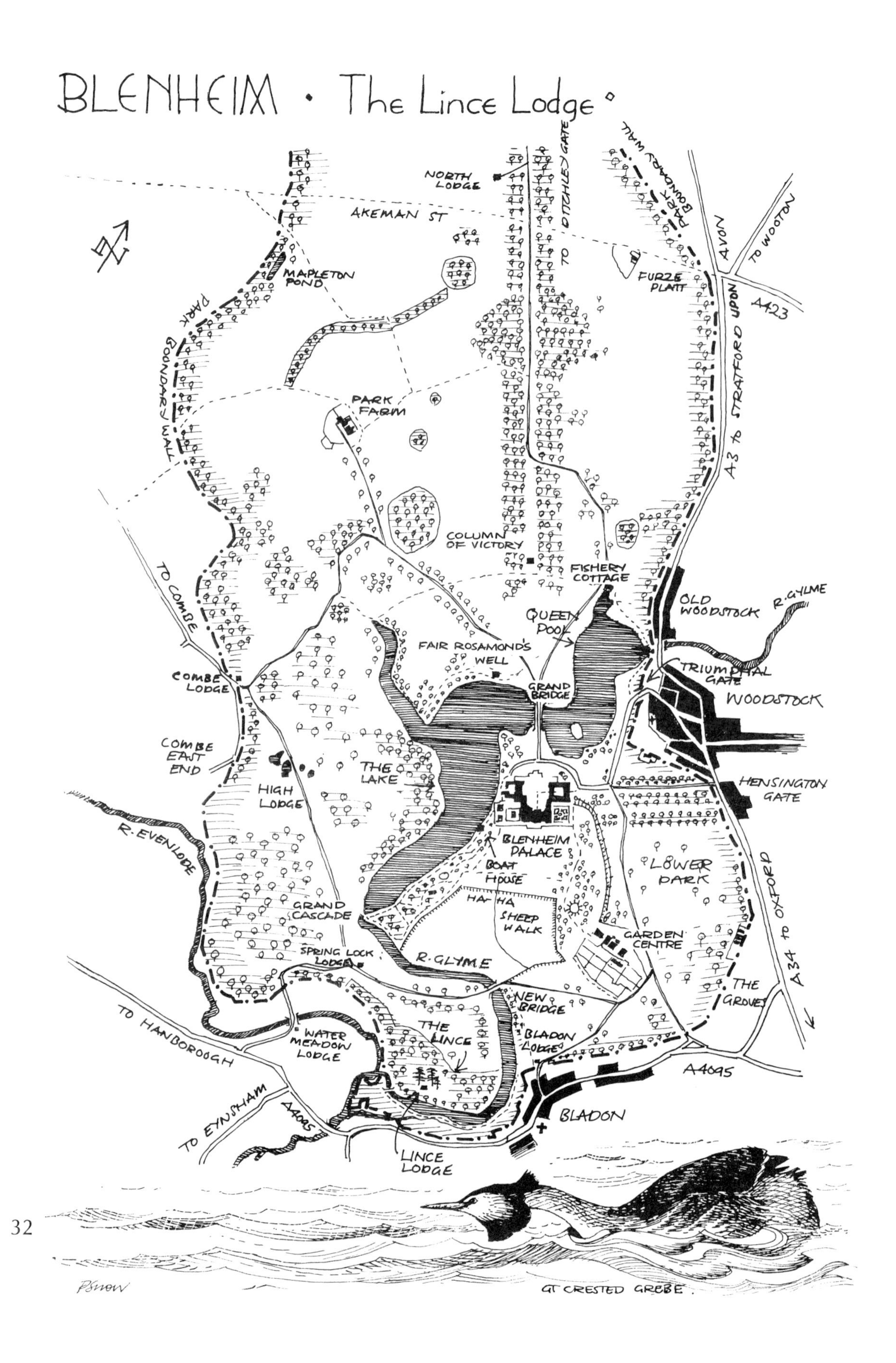
BLENHEIM · The Lince Lodge
NORTH LODGE
AKEMAN ST
TO DITCHLEY GATE
PARK BOUNDARY WALL
MAPLETON POND
FURZE PLATT
AVON
TO WOOTON
A423
A3 to STRATFORD UPON
PARK BOUNDARY WALL
PARK FARM
COLUMN OF VICTORY
FISHERY COTTAGE
TO COMBE
OLD WOODSTOCK
R. GLYME
QUEEN POOL
FAIR ROSAMOND'S WELL
COMBE LODGE
TRIUMPHAL GATE
GRAND BRIDGE
WOODSTOCK
COMBE EAST END
THE LAKE
HIGH LODGE
HENSINGTON GATE
R. EVENLODE
BLENHEIM PALACE
BOAT HOUSE
LOWER PARK
HA-HA
SHEEP WALK
A34 to OXFORD
GRAND CASCADE
GARDEN CENTRE
SPRING LOCK LODGE
R. GLYME
THE GROVES
NEW BRIDGE
TO HANBOROUGH
THE LINCE
WATER MEADOW LODGE
BLADON LODGE
A4095
TO EYNSHAM
A4095
BLADON
LINCE LODGE
GT CRESTED GREBE
P Snow

I stopped on the Grand Bridge to enjoy the magnificent view created by Capability Brown. A green woodpecker and a nuthatch were calling from the lakeside beeches that he planted over two hundred years ago. Numerous house martins were criss-crossing low across the lake in search of insects. These were the first I've seen this year and a number of them may well nest on the sides of the Grand Bridge. I drove on to the Lince where I left my car. The woods were echoing with the music of the chiffchaffs. I decided to take my usual circuit, down to the Cascade, up to the boathouse and palace then back through Grandpa's Garden and down to Bladon Water.

I stood on the Swiss Bridge below the Cascade. A pair of huge chubb were suspended in the clear current below my feet. I watched a family of coot feeding in the pool to the front of me. There were five chicks with their tiny rusty heads and red faces. This is an unusually large brood for Blenheim as the pike take most of them in the first few days. I once disturbed a nest of young coot at the Lince. Three chicks scampered off over the water. I watched in horror and amazement as the water erupted and an ugly pike took all three in turn.

The parent coot looks incredibly buoyant – like a black rubber ball – as it dives for vegetation on the bottom. Air is pushed out of the feathers by flattening them and a leap well clear of the water before submerging helps the coot dive down to as much as twenty feet.

The boathouse provides the perfect vantage point for enjoying the great crested grebes but also at this time of year the glorious greens of the beech and chestnut trees surrounding the lake.

In the early summer of 1906 an international crisis blew up as the Ottoman Sultan laid claim to the Gulf of Akaba. Edward Grey had only been Foreign Secretary for a few months and in his book *Twenty-Five Years* he includes the following charming passage:

> Another aspect of the Akaba trouble was peculiar and personal: I hesitate to describe it lest it should seem too trivial. It needs a digression that, to begin with, must seem quite irrelevant. The serious student of foreign policy had best perhaps pass over it unread.
>
> There are a few days in the first part of May when the beech trees in young leaf give an aspect of light and tender beauty to English

> country which is well known but indescribable. The days are very few; the colour of the leaves soon darkens, their texture become stiffer; beautiful they are still, but 'the glory and the dream' are gone. Unless Whitsuntide is unusually early, Sundays in the first half of May are the only days on which those who have business in towns can be sure of a whole day spent in the country at leisure. The first Sunday in May was a little too early for the perfection of the beeches in the country around my Hampshire cottage; the second Sunday in May was the perfect day. In my calendar it was known as 'Beech Sunday', a day set apart and consecrated to enjoyment of the beauty of beech leaves and to thankfulness for it. It was my habit on that morning, each year, to cycle to a beech wood some nine miles from the cottage. There I lunched once every year on that day at the foot of a certain tree. The wood was entirely of beech; the trees standing far apart, the grey bales grew straight and clear and smooth for some distance above the ground. High overhead the branches touched and made a canopy; the blue sky just visible here and there; the sunshine coming through the tender light green leaves; a breeze stirring them now and then, but very gently – such was the vision of what I had seen and known year by year that was present to me in the Foreign Office in the second week of May. I thought of it, looked forward to it, counted upon it.

I wonder how many of our present politicians would appreciate 'Beech Sunday'?

On my way back to the Lince I sat down under a clump of cedar trees by Bladon Water to listen to the reed warblers. They are not here in numbers any more as a good deal of the vegetation has been cleared as part and parcel of the construction of a cross-country course.

Between 1893 and 1919 my great grandfather was responsible for planting in and about Blenheim Park no fewer than four hundred and sixty five thousand trees. Between Bladon Gate and New Bridge he planted three lakeside clumps, hoping for the following effect:

> That a person passing the Bridge will first see a mass of copper beech, followed by another mass of grey glaucous cedars and again, beyond, yet another mass of copper beech. I believe that the combination of the two colours, the copper and the grey, ought to be most effective and picturesque.

The song of the reed warbler is much more restful than that of the sedge warbler. Edward Grey finds its song is more repetitive and has a steadier rhythm:

> The reed warbler's name is so literally descriptive of the bird as to be unimaginative and almost dull. It lives entirely in reed beds; it populates large tracts of reeds, such as are found in the Norfolk Broads, but wherever a rood or so of reeds grows we may expect to find a pair or two of these birds. Away from the reeds I have never found it; and they must be the common reeds with long thin stems; sedge or other kindred growths will not serve its purposes. It is quiet and soft in colouring and its song is a monotonous warbling, less varied but more melodious than that of the sedge warbler and

> pleasant to listen to. It sings continuously clinging to the stems of the reeds, among which it is invisible, except at a very short distance.

Grey paints a romantic picture of their riverside home:

> As the new reeds grow up green in May the reed warblers come and make their presence known. The time to listen to them is on a fine day in June, when there is just enough breeze to make a slight rustling in the tall reeds that blends with the continuous singing of the birds. Then we know the world in which reed warblers live, and we feel the spirit of it.

As I drove home through Woodstock at lunchtime, I encountered into my grandfather's old butler, Mr Wadman, and his wife and I took them for a drink at the Bear Hotel. Mr Wadman is now eighty-five and came to Blenheim in 1938. He reminisced about what a wonderful woman my grandmother Mary was – 'a real duchess', he said. She died of cancer at the young age of sixty-one when I was about eleven. I can remember the last time I saw her. She was bedridden in the Tower Rooms and I came back from fishing below the Cascade. I told her a breathless story about a large perch I had just lost. It was in exactly the same pool where I today watched the coot feeding their young. Thirty-five years have passed since then.

I have some vivid childhood memories of my grandmother. On one occasion when I was no more than five, she asked me to take a drink into the Smoking Room. A plump bald-headed man smoking a large cigar sat at the card table with an elegant lady who had a strikingly long aristocratic neck and wore her grey hair tied in a bun. My great grandmother, Consuelo Vanderbilt, was enjoying a game of bezique with Winston Churchill. In her autobiography *The Glitter and the Gold* she tells how as a nineteen-year-old American heiress she was forced into an unhappy marriage with my great-grandfather.

Sunday, 14 May

Sunny spells but still with a coldish wind although I am thankful to say it has now gone around to the west.

I heard my first Derbyshire cuckoo of the year as I went down to feed the ducks before breakfast. Still well over twenty ducklings at the table. The chick feed makes all the difference in this cold weather. There was a frost last night.

On my way down the valley I listened to two cock redstarts singing for the first time this year. It is a louder song than I expected and to begin with, not having located the bird, I put it down to a chaffinch. Later, I picked up *The Charm of Birds* to read what Grey says about the redstart's song.

> At Fallodon there are three or four pairs every season. I called a friend's attention to it there this year: he did not know the song and after listening for a while said that the first part of the song reminded him of the chaffinch. At that moment a chaffinch sang close to us, and we listened to the two birds: the contrast between the robustness of the voice of the chaffinch and the slender notes of the redstart destroyed all resemblance. The redstart's is a thin song, but there is

> something brisk and wild in its tone that gives distinction. The first notes seem to be uttered with ease; the last notes sound as if they caused the bird a little effort and uncertainty. I have once heard the song as far north as Sutherland before the end of April.

The first young moorhens have hatched on another nest at the far end of the enclosure. They are little more than dark balls of fluff. Like the coot chicks they sport a colourful head. Their beaks are pink with a yellow tip.

Moorhens have two or three broods a year and the young of the first brood will help feed the nestlings of the next. Grey describes the complex domestic life of the moorhen.

> Once a May young bird, having received a piece of bread from a parent, transferred it to the beak of another May bird which then fed one of the little July birds with it. In this manner the July brood was fed at second or third hand. Apparently it was against the rules for them to receive bread from a parent at first hand, for when a parent bird did for once put bread straight into the beak of a July bird, one of the May birds at once ran up, took the bread out of the beak of the infant and then replaced it there. 'Sheer red tape' was the comment of one to whom the story was related.

Stan White, our neighbour who takes the summer grazing, told me that a vixen had been found with cubs at Tissington and the earth had been gassed. This highly unpleasant but sometimes necessary activity will increase if hunting is banned. Stan said the area surrounding the earth looked like a battlefield, the ground being strewn with lambs' bones and chicken wings.

Tuesday, 16 May

A cold north-east wind again and wet with it. Another brood of mallard have hatched under one of my broodies. I found a half-eaten duckling outside the enclosure which must either be the work of a crow or a magpie.

A goldfinch is sitting on its nest at the end of one of the fan-like branches of our cedar tree on the lawn. Depending on which way she is sitting, one can either see a neat little forked tail or a lovely crimson head. Every year a minimum of two pairs will nest in this tree; additionally, they will choose a fruit tree in the walled garden. The nest is strong and neat and deep enough to retain the eggs and chicks in windy conditions. The walls of the nest are faced with moss and lichen and it is well lined with wool, fluff and feathers. This particular nest is about ten feet off the ground.

In *The Charm of Birds*, Grey quotes an enchanting passage about a goldfinch on its nest written by his wife, Dorothy.

> One of the prettiest nests ever found was a goldfinch's. It was in a yew tree and the outside of the nest was made of green lichen: the lichen you find on beech bales and wooden palings. The inside was incredibly soft to the touch, which was possible only by a very long stretch, so the bamboo ladder was fetched to get a clear sight of it. There it was found to be lined completely with dandelion 'clocks',

each little sphere detached from the many that make the full round of the puff. Another nest this time lovely in its environment was again that of a goldfinch. Holding my face deeply into a pyramid apple tree in full blossom in order to enjoy the light filtering through the mass of petals that clustered on the boughs so thickly as to shut everything else out, I became aware of the ruby mask of a goldfinch, sitting on her nest not ten inches away. She never stirred, happily I had insinuated myself very gently into this world of light. Neither did I withdraw hastily. I stayed long enough to see how the rose and gold of sunlit apple blossom could be deepened by the touch of red.

Thursday, 18 May

A lovely still sunny morning but with a sharp frost overnight. The woodpigeons are cooing restfully and a blackcap is singing in the walled garden wood. I found another goldfinch's nest in a climbing honeysuckle on a wrought-iron arch in the walled garden. It is at the opposite end to last year. We are very lucky to be visited by so many goldfinches in the summer. They are such an important part of the garden. They enrich it with their bright colour and constant happy twittering.

The woodpigeon is an underrated bird. It has a delightfully soothing song and an attractive grey plumage. It is also characterised by a rather laid-back display flight in which it goes into a sharp climb, gives two or three whipcracks of the wings and then proceeds on a downward glide. There is not much else relaxed about it as, being a bird which is constantly shot at, it is very wary of man. I have had some wonderful days in the past flighting pigeons into roost or on to kalefields in winter or over water (the Test at Laverstoke) or stubble fields in high summer, but I will never shoot a woodpigeon anywhere near my house because I enjoy its song so much in spring and summer.

Edward Grey also had a soft spot for this common British bird:

> It is one of the redeeming features, indeed a real distinction, of London that the woodpigeon can be observed there tame as well as free. It is the largest of our pigeons and very beautiful; it walks busily

and bulkily about the grass in the parks; there is an odd look in its eye that suggests perpetual astonishment. I have never seen one grow tame in the country in natural conditions; perhaps because it is a favourite object for everyone who shoots and because every farmer's hand is against it. Woodpigeons are blacklisted because of the damage done when they feed in large number on crops of tender green and of grain. It would be very sad if the race ever became extinct and of this, happily, there seems to be no danger.

I spent the morning in Sheffield and returned home at 2.00 p.m. and mowed for an hour and a half. A sunny afternoon with a light wind. I walked down the Bletch Brook around teatime. A cock pied flycatcher was singing in an ash tree by the hawthorn bank. This is only the second I've heard at Parwich Lees this year. The sedge warbler is still singing in the ditch behind the enclosure. This time it was joined by a handsome cock whitethroat looking very dashing in its grey cap and sporting a bristling snow-white neck.

A couple of years ago the Tissington Estate dug out the Bletch Brook below my land giving rise to a rather featureless V-shaped stretch of stream. One benefit has been derived from this exercise. They have fenced the brook on both sides to stop the cattle treading in the banks. This allows rough white grass and rushes to grow up unmolested by animals. A pair of whinchat were gently swaying on the stems of two large rushes. The whinchat likes moist uncultivated habitats with plenty of isolated bushes and fence posts which provide look-out points and song posts. When cattle were put on the north side of the valley a few years ago, they ate out the rough white grass and the whinchat disappeared. I have missed these attractive summer visitors and their return is to be celebrated. They are easy to identify as they have a distinctive pale eyestripe and a flush of pink or buff on their chest. Warde Fowler captures their charm in *A Year with the Birds*:

> The whinchat, for example, an abundant bird here every summer, gives the railway banks its especial patronage. The predatory village boys cannot prowl about their banks with impunity except on Sundays and even then are very apt to miss a whinchat's nest. You

WHINCHAT BY THE BLETCH BROOK

> may see the cockbird sitting on the telegraph wires, singing his peaceful little song, but unless you disturb his wife from her beautiful blue eggs you are very unlikely to find them in the thickening grass of May or June. And even if she is on the nest, she will sit very close; I have seen an express train fly past without disturbing her when the nest was but six or eight feet from the rails.

This book was written over one hundred years ago and the whinchat is sadly no longer abundant. A general tidying up of the landscape, land drainage and new farming practices encouraged by the Common Agricultural Policy have resulted in a severe loss of suitable habitat. The whinchat is merely one of a large number of birds that have suffered from an improvement in post-war farming methods.

On my way back the blossoming hawthorn bushes reverberated with the song of both willow warblers and garden warblers. When I arrived home I couldn't resist a peep at the goldfinch's nest so I took the stepladder into the walled garden. What struck me most was the minute size of the deep snug nest. Inside were five bluish-white eggs marked with reddish-brown spots.

Saturday, 20 May

The last of our summer migrants to arrive have finally made it. I watched one undertaking its acrobatic flycatching routine in the copper beech before breakfast. In the same way as I expect the curlew in Cheltenham week you can always rely on the spotted flycatcher to arrive in Cup Final week.

Although it is singularly silent and has no obvious colouring, the spotted flycatcher is a most attractive bird. The brown upperparts contrast with the buffish-white underparts which are neatly streaked on the throat and breast with dark brown. I always feel it is the most human of our garden birds. This is because of its alert upright posture and big 'spaniel eyes' that seem to follow you everywhere. At no time is this more noticeable than when the bird is sitting on the nest. It loves to nest in creepers on the side of a house but for one that lives in such close proximity to man it is decidedly edgy. It will always dart off its nest if you approach too close, clearly drawing on that great well of nervous energy it displays when flycatching. Like the robin, the spotted flycatcher will choose some of the most original places for a nest site. Every year one nests snugly behind a large hinge on a door in the yard. This just happens to be the door behind which Lucinda keeps all her imported flowers. It is opened and shut countless times a day, which seems to make no difference to this little bird. It darts off the nest and comes back within minutes.

Warde Fowler writes:

> This flycatcher is an excellent study for the young ornithologist. He is easily seen, perching almost always on a leafless bough or railing, when he may have a clear view, and be able to pick and choose his flies; and he will let you come quite close, without losing his presence of mind. His attitude is so unique, that I can distinguish his tiny form at the whole length of the orchard; he sits quietly, silently, with just a shade of *tristesse* about him, the tail slightly dropped and still, the head, with longish narrow bill, bent a little downwards, for his prey is almost always below him; suddenly this expectant repose is changed into quick and airy action, the little wings hover here and there so quickly that you cannot follow them, the fly is caught and he returns with it in his bill to his perch, to await a safe moment for carrying it to his young. All this is done so unobtrusively by a little greyish-brown bird with greyish-white breast, that hundreds of his human neighbours never know of his existence in their gardens. He is wholly unlike his handsome and livelier namesake, the pied flycatcher, in all those outward characteristics which attract the inexperienced eye; but the essential features are alike in both, the long wing, the bill flat at the base, and the gape of the mouth furnished with strong hairs, which act like the backward-bent teeth of the pike in preventing the escape of the prey.

Sunday, 21 May

Spotted flycatchers seem to be everywhere; there was one having a bath on the birdtable. I usually find at least two nest sites a year – I expect we have three pairs around the house and buildings. There seem to be more swallows around this year than usual. With their twittering song and colourful demeanour their presence enriches life in the yard as much as the presence of the goldfinches enriches life in the garden.

A chaffinch has built a nest in a climbing rose on one of our barns in the yard. The beautifully constructed nest is wedged against the wall in a half-moon shape and contains three furry nestlings. The experience of a small brood is paralleled by Grey:

> Every chaffinch's nest is a delight on account of its neatness; indeed each one seems neater than our recollection of previous nests. As described in our earlier chapter, there is a touch of the commonplace about the bird and its ways, but there is a real distinction and refinement in the nest: it surpasses all other nests that I know for neatness. I have never seen the cock chaffinch take any part in building the nest, or sitting on the eggs. One interesting experience of the resourcefulness of a hen chaffinch came under my notice. The bird had nested in the creepers on the cottage; it had been sitting for a few days on three eggs; one morning the nest was empty: some animal or bird had robbed it. Later in the day a hen chaffinch was flying industriously to and fro between the cottage and a place in a hedge some twenty yards away. The repeated flights invited closer attention; the bird was engaged in removing the empty nest piecemeal and reconstructing it in the hedge. Business in London prevented me from noting how many days were occupied in completing the nest in the hedge, or whether any new materials were used for it; but all the material of the nest on the cottage was removed and the bird again sat on three eggs in the reconstructed nest; it is curious that the clutch should have been so small in the first as well as the second laying.

In the afternoon a representative of the Derbyshire Wildlife Trust came over to check the sixty-eight nest boxes they have erected at

CHAFFINCH'S NEST IN THE ROSES

Parwich Lees. Birdsong is at its peak at this time in May and it seemed to me that every bird in the garden was singing its heart out.

The experience of the Wildlife Trust is that bird numbers are down this year and so it appeared with our boxes. We only found one pied flycatcher's nest with eggs, although I'm pretty sure there are two more singing males around. We also found two grass nests (either a pied or redstart) that had just been started. It's still quite early so you never know. In addition there were two redstarts' nests, one jackdaw and a stock dove in the kestrel box with two eggs. In total there were twelve great tits nesting in the boxes and ten blue tits. We opened up one blue tit box and the parent absolutely refused to come off her nest, the chicks probably having just hatched. She sank her head right down into the mossy nest. The interesting fact about the great tits was the size of the clutches. One nest box had eleven chicks and another twelve eggs – the latter heavily blotched at the wider end with red markings.

Tuesday, 23 May

I spent the day in our Leeds office and in the evening I drove over to play tennis with Andrew Sebire. Since moving to Derbyshire, Andrew has become a close friend and is solely responsible for getting me back into the saddle. He lives life to the full. He is a successful businessman who keeps a herd of pedigree Herefords at his pretty farm near Hartington. He really ought to found a Derbyshire Dangerous Sports Club, he has such a passion for hunting and skiing. It was a lovely warm still evening and we played until 8.00 p.m.

Before playing I walked down the Bletch Brook to the Tissington Estate's new pond. The pond was part of the drainage scheme. Although the brook has been dredged the valley floor is still a haven for wildlife.

While enjoying the activities of a cock reed bunting in a small willow bush, I noticed a curlew circling the meadows calling in an agitated fashion. It was not a normal display flight and the call was one I didn't think I'd heard before. A loud 'chee-chee-chee' rather like that of a green woodpecker.

The cock reed bunting is a good-looking specimen. He has a dark brown-streaked back and a most decorative head complete with black hood and white collar. He obviously had a nest nearby as he sat nervously on a branch flicking his conspicuous white-edged tail, his beak full of insects. The reed bunting was a great favourite with Grey.

> The cock reed bunting is very handsome, and the birds are common on ground that suits them, such as chalk-stream water meadows and reed and sedge growth. At Wilsford, where water meadows adjoin the garden with no fence to separate them, the reed bunting is a garden bird.

Although numbers have declined since Grey wrote, largely as a result of food shortages caused by the introduction of herbicides to control weeds, the reed bunting has successfully extended its habitat in recent years. It has now spread into drier areas, including hedgerows, conifer plantations and gardens. The latter remain less preferred habitats but will obviously be used to a greater degree when population numbers are high.

As I walked home I disturbed a pair of long-tailed tits in the Bletch

hedgerow. Judging from their persistent thin calls and stubborn refusal to depart they almost certainly had a nest in the vicinity. I failed to find it.

Wednesday, 24 May

Wet, misty and overcast. In the evening I walked down the Bletch again towards the Tissington pond – a pair of curlew were circling their territory and calling loudly. On the way home I found a linnet's nest with four tiny chicks in a single small hawthorn bush on the valley side. The female flew off the nest, the white sides to her forked tail conspicuous as she went. A good number of linnets come to spend the summer with us and they tend to nest in loose colonies in the small gorse and hawthorn bushes. With their musical twittering and natural beauty they brighten up the valley sides in the way the goldfinch does the garden and the swallow does the yard. Grey felt their appearance more than made up for a rather bland song.

> The song of the linnet needs close attention in order to hear the quality of some of its notes, which otherwise might pass unappreciated: it is well also to look at the cockbird through field-glasses. The linnet is thought of as a brown and not a brilliant bird; and so it seems as usually visible to the naked eye. A mature cock linnet, however, in his best plumage is very handsome, with glorious pink on breast and forehead.

Thursday, 25 May

My forty-sixth birthday. I had an early meeting in York and then went to our Leeds office. Finally I drove to Ambleside in the Lake District.

I look upon my birthday as the climax of the year's birdsong. From now on it will taper off into the relative silence of August. We must wait for another year before enjoying 'the Great Dawn Chorus' at its best. In his chapter on 'The Month of Full Song' (May) Grey quotes 'the best description of a Dawn Chorus I know', written by his late wife Dorothy:

> It is worthwhile to wake early during these days because of the Dawn Chorus. It opens with a few muted notes of thrush song. This sets the tits waking; they have no half tones. There are the sawing notes, the bell notes, the teasing notes, the festoon of small utterance that

> belongs especially to the blue.
>
> But you can hardly pick out the individual songs before the whole garden is ringing. There is the loud beauty of the thrushes. Seemingly further away, and in remoter beauty, comes floating the blackbird's voice. The notes are warm, and light as amber, among the sharper flood of song.
>
> The Dawn Chorus is like a tapestry translated into sound. The mistle thrush, with merle and mavis, perhaps the rounded note of an owl, these stand out like chief figures in the design. All the others make the dense background of massed stitches; except the wren; he, with resounding scatter of notes, dominates the throng.
>
> Then as suddenly as it arose, 'this palace of sound that was reared' begins to subside. One or two thrushes persist. The greenfinch goes on with his two modes of single utterance. Perhaps a linnet continues his husky song. He can be heard now. Then the sun rising flushes the water meadows and the snipe start drumming. The grass is all bent and straggled with its weight of cold dew.

Grey leaves us in no doubt that May was the month he liked above all others and that Wordsworth was his favourite poet:

> To all this must be added the full song of woodland birds; the long vibrating notes of curlews, the first fresh green of deciduous trees and geans with their abundant delicate white flower. Year after year all this loveliness for eye and ear recurs; in early days, in youth, it was anticipated with confidence; in later years, as the season approaches, experience and age qualify the confidence with apprehension lest clouds of war and civil strife, or some emergency of work, or declining health, or some other form of human ill may destroy the pleasure or even the sight of it: and when once again it has been enjoyed we have a sense of gratitude greater than in the days of confident and thoughtless youth. Perhaps the memory of these days, having become part of our being, helps us in later life to enjoy each passing season. In every May, with the same beauty of sight and sound, 'we do beget the golden time again'.

Friday, 26 May

I spent last night with Peter and Sue Jackson near Ambleside in the Lake District. They run the Heart of the Lakes holiday-cottage agency and are shareholders in my own Peak Cottages. Their home is only a few hundred yards from Rydal Mount where William Wordsworth lived for over thirty-five years.

Before breakfast I went for a stroll round Rydal Water where Wordsworth and his sister Dorothy walked so much. The nearby gardens were full of fragrant and vivid colour as the azaleas and rhododendrons were in full bloom. The water on the lake was like glass and the early morning sun shone on the hills up towards Grasmere. Cuckoos called in the distant hanging woods of beech and oak with their many shades of fresh green. There was still a carpet of bluebells under the mature trees which rang with singing warblers. It is so easy to understand why this part of England inspired the poets.

There are three warblers that I have yet to hear sing, the wood warbler, the lesser whitethroat and the grasshopper warbler (maybe I heard the latter once in Anglesey). Grey reminded me that the wood warbler should relish these woods:

> The wood warbler is well named. It is a bird of full-grown woods. It does not frequent gardens and shrubberies, as the chiffchaff and willow warbler do: it lives in big trees, especially beech or oak; so indifferent is it to bushes that it seems almost to prefer woods, where the ground is bare, as is so often the case under beech trees.

For a moment I thought I caught a snatch of song as described by Grey. 'The song is very remarkable: the bird has in fact two songs so distinct and unlike that nothing but clear and close view can convince one that the different sounds are made by the same bird. The song that is most frequent is the shivering or sibilant sound, as it is called in books.' It was this latter sound that I thought I was listening to, although I suspect I could easily have confused it with that of the wren.

Rydal Holme sits at the Ambleside end of the lake. There were four pairs of Canada geese grazing below the house with a total of twenty-two goslings – it is easy to see what a pest this bird is becoming. A drake goosander with two attendant females was diving at the water's edge; one of the females flew up into the fork of an oak tree. The house is situated beside the busy Keswick road and it is in the holly hedge that separates the two that a pair of long-tailed tits have built their nest. They couldn't have chosen a noisier spot. Wordsworth would certainly not have approved of the amount of traffic in the Lake District today, although he is indirectly responsible for it. It only took five minutes or so to find the nest which was situated in an impregnable position at the top of the hedge. The two parent birds were fidgeting nervously on the overhead telephone wires and uttering their thin call note as they carried little green caterpillars across the garden. The long-tailed tit's nest is a beautiful construction and one of nature's wonders. It is either placed low in an inaccessible thorn bush or prickly hedge, as was this one, or high up against a fork in a tree.

LONG-TAILED TIT & NEST PS.

Edward Grey tells us that if he had to give a prize for nest building among our common birds, he would give it to the long-tailed tit. On 2 January 1923 he gave an address to the School Nature Union in London on 'Pleasure in Nature' which is reproduced in his book *The Fallodon Papers*. In this address Grey gives a delightful description of the long-tailed tit's family life:

> It builds a most elaborate nest and the whole time taken for the building of the nest, the hatching of the eggs and the fledging of the young is a very long one – much longer than in the case of any other British bird I know.
>
> When I was in office I had a cottage in the country to which I went at weekends, and one Sunday morning before the middle of March I observed from the window a pair of long-tailed tits building their nest in a sweetbrier hedge. When I went out and looked at the nest it was then like an ordinary nest, cup-shaped. A long-tailed tit is not content with that, but it builds a nest like a bag with a hole at the top. Every week I went down there the building and business of the nest was going on. It so happened that 19th May that year was a Sunday and I was at my cottage. It also happened that this particular day, about noon, was the time when the young birds first came out of the nest. It also happened that I was standing close by the nest at the time when the little birds first came out of it. Thus you will see that this pair of long-tailed tits required about two months and a half from the time they began to build their nest to the time the young came out of it. During all these weeks, when I could be there, the nest was a subject of interest to me, and many of you living in the country may have the same experience provided that you will yourselves observe, and are able to induce other people to observe, the rule not to disturb or destroy.
>
> Long-tailed tits are particularly interesting from another point of view. The birds go in a company and the brood remains together all the autumn and winter, but early in March you will see the long-tailed

> tits in pairs, and if you will look closely you will see about that time that they have some little nesting material in their beaks, and if you watch them you will see them going to the nest and you can locate it. Sometimes it is rather high up in the fork of a tree, generally oak or ash, but as often as not it is only four or five feet from the ground in a gorse bush or ordinary hedge. Whether they think then that they are so small that you do not see them or whether they are so intensely busy in their work, it so happens that they are not at all shy, and you can stand at a distance of three yards from the nest quite openly and watch them build. You will see first one bird and then the other get into the nest when it is cup-shaped and make it round and smooth by rubbing its breast round and round against the wall of the nest. You will see it arch its head over the sides of the nest and pull some of the outside over and inwards, weaving it thus; and when the nest is completed outside, the birds will line the inside with feathers. Then if you like you can help in the building of the nest. If you can collect small feathers and put them close to the nest, you can stand near and see the long-tailed tits take the feathers that you put for them and use them in their nest building. When the young birds have fledged you can, without doing any harm, take the nest and examine it, because I have never known long-tailed tits use their nest a second time. I have been told that the feathers used in the lining of a long-tailed tit's nest have been counted and number more than nine hundred. That seems incredible; I have not yet verified it, but any of you can do so.

In his book *The Birdman*, Henry Douglas-Home tells us that his brother Alec, when writing his autobiography, included the statistic that there were over three thousand feathers in a long-tailed tit's nest.

Arrived at Brilley in Herefordshire at 8.00 p.m. to stay with the Bulmers after a seven-hour train journey from the Lakes. Exhausted, but not to be deterred, we went down to listen to Jools Holland and his band who were opening the Hay Festival.

Saturday, 27 May

It rained heavily in the night. A rather grey windy day. After breakfast I sat on the terrace enjoying the spectacular views across to the Black Mountains. Lucinda has taken the boys down to the Wye to watch the hundred-mile raft race that begins at Hay.

When you think of Herefordshire you think of cider, and when you think of cider, you think of Bulmers. David has worked at the family firm for forty years and he and Rosanna bought Brilley in the early seventies as a small farmhouse. They have created the perfect home. A large comfortable country house with a pretty garden and its own surrounding farms.

I must therefore offer an apology to dear Brilley, where I have spent many a happy time over the last twenty years, for choosing it as the context in which to write about the house sparrow. As I sat on the terrace, a garden warbler sang his heart out in the wild garden and spotted flycatchers busily moved about the countless creepers on the side of the house. What caught my eye was a pair of 'chatty' house sparrows mating on the slate roof and then disappearing into a hole in the tiles, presumably their summer home.

POSING MALE HOUSE SPARROWS

House sparrows are my least favourite birds mainly because they have little charm. They are noisy – they chirp but don't sing, they are boisterous, messy and on the whole rather colourless. At my childhood home, Kidmore End House in South Oxfordshire, they would always take over the nests of the unfortunate house martins. If they were diligent enough to build their own it was usually a mass of dried grass protruding from the ivy. Like the collared dove, they are very dependent on man and are often seen in numbers around farmyards. I do not regret their absence at Parwich Lees.

Needless to say Grey finds some good qualities in the bird, but perhaps only after digging a little!

> Several pairs of sparrows were always about; never would one of these feed while anyone was looking on; but as soon as I was behind a tree or had gone to a little distance, they would descend upon the food. Compared to other birds, they had the manners of thieves, and snatched surreptitiously. The sparrow is a very unattractive bird compared to others that are akin to it. What is there to be said in favour of it? This, to begin with: it is a bird, and, being a bird, it has feathers, and having feathers it has not been able to avoid a certain degree of beauty. The cock sparrow, if carefully considered, is a beautiful bird. Sparrows are also very affectionate to mates and nestlings. The cock sparrow takes a strenuous and devoted part in rearing the young. Then it must be admitted that sparrows are very clever birds; in one respect there is something uncanny about their cleverness. The hand of man is against them, and yet they take no trouble to conceal their nests. On the contrary, by excessive untidiness with feathers and straw, they thrust their nests upon man's attention; yet, in spite of this, sparrows thrive. How is it done? Chiefly, I think, by choosing situations for the nest that make man disinclined to go to it. A sparrow's nest can be discovered without search, but cannot be reached generally without trouble.

Grey felt there was no craftier bird in Britain:

> A man of business was once being sounded as to the capacity of other prominent persons in his own or allied industries in the north of England. 'What about X?' he was asked. 'X doesn't miss much,' was the reply. So it can be said of the sparrow, that it doesn't miss much. This faculty, combined with domestic virtue and a robust body, enables the sparrow to hold so very much more than its own in spite of man's antagonism.

In the afternoon I went down to the Hay Festival to listen to Jeremy Paxman speak about 'Fishing'. He did not quote from Edward Grey's *Fly Fishing*, which seemed strange as he wrote the introduction to a recent edition. He was quite human and rather nervous when it came to questions. He was asked a question as to which politician he would most like to go fishing with and which he would least. A satisfactorily evasive answer would have been an opportunity for bringing in Edward Grey!

Sunday, 28 May

After breakfast we drove up to the Bush, David's two-hundred-acre farm four miles to the west which is situated at 1,000 feet on the Welsh border. The approach is by way of narrow lanes with high banks and thick hedges. At this height the bluebells are still in flower on the verges. A cock yellowhammer was repeating its lazy song from the top of a telegraph pole. The breeding male is most attractive with a brilliant lemon head and a chestnut-streaked back. It is very much a bird of the hedgerows and as such we don't see it in the Derbyshire stonewall country. At my mother-in-law's home in Hampshire (Bramdean) its song can be heard up on the downs late into the summer when few other birds are singing.

W. H. Hudson writes a charming paragraph on the yellowhammer, when describing Selborne in his book *Birds and Man*:

> Mile after mile I trudged on without meeting a soul, where not a house was visible – a still, wet, desolate country with trees and bushes standing in water, unstirred by a breath of wind. Only at long intervals a yellowhammer was heard uttering its thin note: for just as this bird sings in the sultriest weather which silences other voices so he will utter his monotonous chant on the gloomiest day. It may be because he sung 'the yellowhammer in the rain' that I have long placed Faber among my best loved minor poets of the past century. He alone among our poets has properly appreciated the singer who never stops, but, pleased with his own monotony, shakes off the rain and sings on in a mood of cheerfulness dashed with melancholy:
>
> And there he is within the rain,
> And beats and beats his tune again.
> Quite happy in himself,
> Within the heart of this great shower,
> He sits, as in a secret bower
> With curtains drawn about him,
> And, part in duty, part in mirth,
> He beats, as if upon the earth.
> Rain could not fall without him.

The yellowhammer's song, 'a little bit of bread and no cheese', is well known. When one is sitting in the garden at Bramdean at the foot of the downs on a hot summer's day it is the drawn out 'cheese' that catches the ear. As in the case of the linnet, Grey felt that the song did not match its owner's appearance.

> The yellowhammer's song is continued very late in the summer, even into August. It is not a song of power or melody; its merit is in quaintness and familiarity: it draws attention to the bird when he is perched conspicuous on the top of a hedge or whin bush, and it is always worthwhile to observe through field-glasses the uncommon yellow head and the exceedingly rich brown colours of the back, for the mature cock yellowhammer is a very handsome bird.

At lunchtime we went over for a picnic by the River Arrow. Approximately twenty minutes' drive from Brilley, between Kington and Prestigne, the Bulmer family owns a hundred and fifty acres of mature woods and meadowland. The river rises above Brilley and flows into the Lugg which in turn flows into the Wye. We lunched in the fishing hut – as always when you want to have a picnic it poured with rain. In the afternoon the sun came out and so did the mayfly and the warblers. The woods of oak and ash were alive with the songs of willow warblers, chiffchaffs, blackcaps and garden warblers. Again the wood warbler was absent although there was a solitary singing pied flycatcher in a small alder by the river.

This valley is one of the prettiest pieces of Britain I know and it is the only place I have ever heard the notes of the female cuckoo. Grey's description of this unusual song cannot be bettered.

> The female cuckoo has notes in the breeding season that are as distinctive as those of the male among the notes of other birds; but these female notes are not a familiar sound, and, when heard, they are not known to be those of a cuckoo. They are somtimes called 'the water-bubbling notes' and I cannot improve on this description. They seem to me to be used solely as a mating call.

Tuesday, 30 May

Flew up to Aberdeen for a meeting in the morning and decided to go and lunch with old friends Jamie and Fiona Burnett who live at Crathes near Banchory. After lunch we went for a short walk along the river. I will always associate the Dee at this time of the year with flowering gorse bushes and the happy piping of oystercatchers and sandpipers.

Grey is expansive on the subject of the whin in May:

> Is the whole air ever so wonderfully and gratefully fragrant as when it is pervaded by the scent of the whin? New-mown hay or a bean field in flower are rare delights, but the flower of whin is best of all. The scent is fresh and invigorating and yet so rich and luscious that it suggests apricots: it is as if the apricot had been designed in order to transmute part of the excellence of the scent of whin into something that could be perceived by another sense than that of smell. At any rate both the scent and the fruit have this in common, that each is

> only to be known to perfection when warm in a hot sun. The whin is suited to the British climate, it needs no hot weather to enable it to flower and ripen its seeds. A cool summer does not discontent it; but it cannot endure extreme cold, and is grateful for our mild winters: it is essentially a plant for a gulf-stream climate. A stray flower of whin may be picked, so far as anything so prickly can be picked at all, on most bushes in every month of the year; but it is in May that every bush of whin is a glorious blaze of colour. Later in the summer, on a warm day, there is a sporadic ticking noise amongst the whins: it is the opening of the dry seed pods.

A pair of oystercatchers were piping noisily in a field above the opposite riverbank. In England, they are largely a coastal bird and you don't expect to see them on agricultural land. They must have been welcome companions to Grey on his many fishing holidays in Scotland.

> They are still about the river in May, but they are less noisy and restless than they were in March. They have eggs to attend to. These are laid on shingle, with no attempt by the bird to hide them; but their pattern is so cunningly devised that the whole bed of shingle is their concealment.

A sandpiper skimmed past me low over the water on stiff wings as it patrolled its territory.

The common sandpiper is one of my favourite birds and when I am fishing on the river in early summer it is a constant and noisy companion. Sandpipers are summer visitors from sub-Saharan Africa that come to breed on our upland rivers (their bobbing walk and white underparts make them one of our most distinctive small waders); they migrate through the centre of England as demonstrated by a sighting in my Derbyshire duck enclosure on 14 April 1990. The most memorable recollection I have of a sandpiper is of one sitting on Vanburgh's Grand Bridge at Blenheim on 7 September 1985. I had already seen a bird in late April that same year above the Cascade and the one on the bridge would have been moving back south on its long journey to Africa. I have only once come upon a sandpiper's nest and that was when I was fishing with my uncle at Castle Grant on the Spey and found one hidden in the river bank.

Grey obviously enjoyed their company on the river: 'Sandpipers give an impression of happy affection, as a pair flit about together, piping pleasantly as if each enjoyed the other's company.'

Wednesday, 31 May

The ash is finally coming out at Parwich Lees and this evening there was a mistle thrush in full song at the very top of the ash tree by the ha-ha. Somehow you don't expect to hear them sing at this time of the year. This is blackbird season and I associate the mistle thrush with a mild blustery day in February.

The hawthorn is looking lovely – snow white – and the yellow flag iris is coming out on the ponds. Grey wrote to his friend Captain Barton giving his views on the smell of the hawthorn:

> I love the smell, but it is very nearly a nasty smell, and it is clear to me that the hawthorn, being in nature pure and innocent and full of good intentions, has all but stumbled into a horrible mistake and made a mess of its smell. But it just hasn't.

Two sedge warblers were singing in the ditch behind the duck enclosure and a blackcap in the walled-garden wood.

The spotted flycatcher is nesting yet again behind the hinge on a door in the yard. She laid another egg today bringing the total to three rusty-brown spotted eggs to date.

I found another mallard's nest in the duck enclosure with four eggs. This probably represents a second clutch and belongs to one of the females whose eggs I picked up a month or so ago. There is plenty of cover now and of course natural food for the ducklings so I will leave any nests I find. I counted fifteen ducklings on the ponds all of which are developing well. I have another dozen with my bantams and two broods still to hatch.

JUNE

Thursday, 1 June

I left home for our Leeds office at around 6.15 a.m. As I was driving over Beeley Moor, just before Chesterfield, I watched a snipe 'drumming'. He was circling a marshy field in a slow, deliberate, undulating fashion. Although secretive birds, snipe become conspicuous in the breeding season as they display over their territories. The drumming sound is produced by their tail feathers during a sharp dive. I have often heard snipe drumming on South Uist when staying with Willie Russell at Drimore. In the early eighties, I used to go and help him with the lambing and the machair would echo with the sound, particularly on a still evening. I have only once heard a snipe drum at Parwich Lees and that was on 16 June 1990. The recent draining of the Bletch Brook makes a repeat unlikely. I thought at first the sound came from an animal, yet high up in the sky was a snipe. I watched it for about ten minutes as it continued to circle, intermittently diving steeply and fanning its tail with two protruding tail feathers.

Grey describes this strange experience:

> The other joy sound is the so-called 'drumming' of the snipe. It is said to be made by the outside tail feathers. I have not verified this statement but I do not doubt it. The sound is made during a prolonged joy flight. The bird flies round and round over a wide area at some height, and every now and then descends in the air at an angle and with accelerated speed; it is in the descent that the sound is made: indeed, this seems to be the whole object of the descending motion, for the bird then immediately recovers itself in the air and resumes its flight. The whole proceeding is one to be watched. The flight has a very happy appearance, but the 'drumming' seems to be performed by the bird in order to find vent for an exuberantce of

spirits that cannot be expressed by flight alone. The sound is that of a bleat rather than a drum, and in some places the snipe is called 'air goat' in consequence.

Although a widespread bird the snipe has been affected by modern farming techniques and particularly the draining of our wetlands. A discussion paper by the RSPB, 'The Reform of the Common Agricultural Policy – New Opportunities for Wildlife and the Environment' (July 1988), includes the following paragraph:

> Snipe are highly vulnerable to drainage because they need the water table to be within twenty centimetres of the soil surface. Breeding is invariably disrupted, if it starts at all, in drained grasslands. Snipe have disappeared from many breeding sites, particularly in the southern counties. A high proportion of the remnant population of about 3,700 pairs nesting on lowland wet grasslands in England and Wales now depend on a handful of protected sites. In the UK it is estimated that fifty per cent of lowland fens, valley and basin mires, and sixty per cent of lowland raised mires, have been lost or significantly damaged over the last thirty years. It is also estimated that the area of fens has been reduced by ninety-nine per cent since 1600.

One of the main beneficiaries of my little complex of ponds and water meadows at Parwich Lees is the snipe. They start arriving in September and drop in throughout the winter. They tend to breed on the higher ground and move down the lowland river valleys in the winter. At this time indigenous birds are augmented by huge 'wisps' of migrants which arrive on our northern shores from Scandinavia. These travellers seldom remain in one spot for long, suddenly deciding to move on, as if they knew they were being chased by the hard weather. Snipe are very susceptible to bad weather as they rely on their long bill for probing the damp ground for earthworms. The tip of the bill is covered by a very sensitive membrane which enables them to locate food well below the surface. When the ground freezes hard they congregate around fast-flowing streams and springs. They prefer to feed at night which explains why one often hears them moving overhead when duck flighting at dusk. Their high-pitched cry betrays them as they flight into their feeding grounds, hidden by the approaching dark.

A beautiful sunny evening with a fresh wind. Stan White came over to show me a pheasant's nest on the bank above the duck ponds. It was dangerously exposed in some rushes. She was sitting so tight she hissed at me; the cockbird was only a yard or two away. There were nine eggs which I successfully sat under a broody bantam. Another brood of bantam chicks has just hatched.

Saturday, 3 June

Lucinda and the children have gone to Mothercombe in Devon. It rained steadily for the first part of the morning. A blackcap sang throughout in the walled-garden wood as did a cock greenfinch. The wheezing notes of the latter reminded me of the little piece by Warde Fowler on the yellowhammer singing in the rain.

For sheer beauty, Grey puts the greenfinch in the same category as the linnet and the yellowhammer:

> So, too, the cock greenfinch is a fine bird – green as a parrot may be green, and with a touch of yellow. His song is made up of various chirpings, but it has one typical drawn-out note that is always to be recognised as unmistakably that of a greenfinch. This sounds like 'eeze' or 'breeze'; and I think of it as a welcome suggestion on sultry hot days. The greenfinch is a real grosbeak, with strong mandibles that make short work of the hips of sweetbrier and wild rose in autumn.

Something has destroyed the goldfinch's nest in the cedar tree; the disappointment is immense. It could have been a squirrel but the nest was right at the end of a flimsy branch; more likely a jackdaw or magpie. Grey experienced the same sense of remorse:

> At the Hampshire cottage the destruction of the nests in the little garden and the thickets of the adjoining chalk pit was heartbreaking. The nests that were known to be destroyed were, of course, nests that we had found and were watching: otherwise we should not have known of their fate. The proportion of those that came to grief was so large that in some years it seemed that the breeding season must be a failure. It never was so: there was always a good output of young birds from nests that we had not found. There was no reason to think that human mischief was to blame for the robbing of nests in this particular spot. There were stoats, weasels, rats, fieldmice and jackdaws, and these were enough to account for all the damage: but why did the particular nests that we found appear to suffer so heavily, while others, of which we did not know, prospered? It is probable that when a human being finds and examines a nest he leaves some track or trace that betrays the treasure. A bent twig or a misplaced leaf may catch the keen eye of a hungry jackdaw looking down from above. The thought thus suggested discouraged one from nest finding at the cottage, and in later years, I was content to be assured by ear that the birds were there.

I enjoy watching the pied wagtails gathering food on the newly mown lawn. They appear very tame; they rush about in a quite unconcerned manner pouncing on insects and filling their beaks with a mass of booty for their young. Even with a mouth full they still seem to manage their high-pitched 'swallow-like' call.

Sunday, 4 June

Arrived at Seahouses near Alnwick with Ian Herbert at 8.00 a.m. after a three-and-a-half-hour drive from Derbyshire. Ian has been a friend and colleague at work for ten years. Not only is he a very shrewd businessman but he is also a talented naturalist with a wealth of knowledge on birds and butterflies. Ian has recently been elected on to the council of the RSPB.

Seahouses was once a sleepy fishing village but is now a rather over-commercialised embarkation point for the Farne Islands. It holds many happy childhood memories. For a number of years in the fifties my parents took a house on the seafront with friends. As children we swam in the chilly North Sea, went lobster potting with Mr Donaldson and had picnics on the wild romantic Farne Islands. This group of dangerous rocky isles forms one of the most important seabird colonies in Britain and there is no better time to visit them than in early June when all the occupants are busy nesting.

A few miles to the south west of Seahouses lies the little village of Fallodon, the one-time country seat of Edward Grey. As our route took us past the lodge gates I couldn't resist a peep at his famous home. We drove down the long wooded drive for nearly a mile and there at the end we caught a glimpse through the trees of the two-storey redbrick house, rebuilt after the fire in 1917, and one of his large Wellingtonia trees. At some future point I must arrange a more formal visit!

Grey must have made many visits to the Farnes to enjoy the wildlife. In a charming passage in his book *Edward Grey and his Birds*, Seton Gordon describes one such excursion:

> The last expedition I made with Lord Grey to the islands was on Boxing Day 1932, when we sailed out to the Farnes from Seahouses to see the young grey seals. His sight was then very bad, and walking on uneven, seaweed-covered rocks must have been tiring for him. Yet he would allow no one to assist him, and I believe that, although he could not see the birds and could only, with difficulty, see the young seals that lay moaning on the rocks a few yards from him, he was glad to be on the low islands which he remembered in earlier and happier days.

No one was so greatly loved by the humble folk of Northumberland as Lord Grey, whom they preferred to call 'Sir Edward'. That was brought home to me on the day when we crossed to the Farnes. The fisherman who owned the boat told me, on our return passage, that forty-five years before, when he was a small boy, he and his mother were walking along the hard road towards Seahouses, the small fishing village where they lived. A dog-cart passed them, then stopped, and they saw that a lady and gentleman were seated in it. The gentleman asked them if they would like a lift. He, a small boy, had afterwards asked his mother who those people were, and she told him 'Sir Edward and Lady Grey'. The incident had remained in the fisherman's mind all his life, but he had never had an opportunity of speaking to Lord Grey until the day when he took us both out to the islands. He ended his story by saying to me, 'We think a terrible lot of Lord Grey in Northumberland.'

After breakfasting on Craster kippers we set off for Staple Island in the Outer Farnes – the latter immortalised by Grace Darling of the Longstone Lighthouse in 1850. As we closed on the island, the low cliffs and surrounding sea and airspace were occupied by a mass of auks, consisting of thousands of guillemots, puffins and razorbills. The little puffins with their tiny rapidly beating wings reminded me of individual propeller-driven aero engines. Puffins are universally loved because of their distinctive beauty. In the breeding season they have a conspicuous orange spot on their cheeks and a bill complete with all colours of the rainbow. Puffins nest in large colonies of old rabbit burrows and it is here that it is most enjoyable to watch them as they flight in from the sea with their bills full of sand eels. They have to run the gauntlet of patrolling lesser black-backed gulls. They eagerly await the returning puffins and then proceed to rough them up with a view to stealing their meal. Over a thousand pairs of these aggressive gulls nest on the Farnes and the wardens sensibly control them by pricking the eggs. Although the Farnes represent a stronghold for the puffin with about 35,000 pairs, numbers in Britain as a whole have declined since the war. Conditions away from the colony during the winter appear to be critical for the puffin and one can point the finger at an overfishing of the sand eel.

The two other auks that nest on the Farnes, although in widely different numbers, are the guillemot and the razorbill. There are seventeen thousand nesting pairs of guillemots and only two hundred and fifty razorbills. They have very distinctive profiles, forgetting the razorbill's unmistakably heavy bill. The guillemot is brown rather than black and is an altogether more elegant bird with a longer neck. The razorbill is more dumpy with a classic auk-like shape. The Pinnacle Rocks on Staple Island present an extraordinary sight. Thousands of growling guillemots packed shoulder to shoulder. They stand upright on the ledges like rows of tiny soldiers, each incubating a single pear-shaped egg which is clutched between its legs. Both birds take responsibility for the incubation and it is amusing to watch the perilous change-over procedure, when an enormous amount of shuffling about goes on. The unique shape of the egg was not lost on Grey:

Now let us consider guillimots' eggs. The birds lay the eggs on bare

> ledges of rock and breed in colonies or crowds. The breeding place is so open and notorious that every marauding gull must know the eggs are there. It is the dense mass of the guillimots that protects their eggs; for the purpose of protection the colour of the eggs can be of no use: yet nature has taken care to make guillimots' eggs very curious, elaborate and varied in colour and markings. The great danger to which each guillimot's egg is exposed is that of rolling off the bare ledge on which it is laid; there is a continual hustling and jostling in the crowd, as individual birds go and return. Against this danger the eggs are protected by shape; the small end is exceptionally small in comparison with the large end. The egg therefore, when disturbed, rolls round in one spot, from which, unless absolutely pushed in one direction, it will not roll away. The conclusion of the matter is that in many, if not in the majority, of birds the colouring of eggs has no protective value. If this was so originally, it is so no longer and it is only in some, not in all birds, that the colour of their eggs serves this purpose.

Another interesting feature of the guillimot is the occasional occurrence of the 'bridled' variety. We came across one pair that had a white ring around the eye and a white line running back from it over the sides of their heads giving the appearance of a pair of spectacles. Their frequency increases from south to north but the reason is unclear. One of these birds had brought in a sand eel for its mate and underneath the incubating bird you could see a tiny beak protruding from the single blue-green egg.

Other species that inhabit the inhospitable cliffs are the shag, kittiwake and fulmar. The shag are the most glamorous with a lovely iridescent greeny-black plumage and upturned crest. They sit tightly on their nests and if you get close they shake their heads disapprovingly and open their large yellow gape. They also sport a beautiful green eye and aside from the crest the best way to tell them from a cormorant is by their smaller size and lack of a white throat. There are five thousand pairs of kittiwakes on the Farnes. They have got great charm and are quite unlike the aggressive scrounging seagulls. They are pretty with a clear yellow bill and distinctive black wing tips. They are loving birds and greet their mates affectionately and with much commotion as they fly in from the sea. Then there is the fascinating fulmar with its extraordinary tubular hooked beak. A pair of birds were at their nest and were making a loud cackling noise, as they flirted together. The fulmar, along with the collared dove, is one of the great success stories of the bird world. One hundred years ago it bred only on St Kilda, but today there are over five hundred thousand breeding pairs in Britain. This increase is thought to have been triggered by a huge increase in the Icelandic population as a result of the greater availability of whaling and trawling offal as food. The St Kilda population has remained stable and still exists on a diet largely of plankton. Intruders at a fulmar nesting site are liable to be squirted with a foul-smelling oil which is ejected as a form of defence; rich in vitamins A and D, it is also used for feeding the young. If it gets on your clothes the smell lingers for many years!

After lunch we took the boat to Inner Farne on which is built a delightful little chapel which contains a memorial tablet to Grace Darling inscribed with some lovely verse by Wordsworth. Inner Farne presents you with one of the most exciting ornithological experiences imaginable and is a must for any child who is interested in natural history. Inner Farne is the only Arctic tern colony that you can actually walk on in Britain. The intruder is greeted by a crescendo of shrill sound ('kik-kik-kik') as thousands of these graceful little seabirds lift off their nests which are no more than scratches in the ground. There are over four thousand pairs of Arctic terns nesting on Inner Farne. It is rather like participating in an exotic Easter-egg hunt, as one after another little hollows present themselves along the pathway containing one, two or three green eggs with heavy brown markings. They are pretty birds with a sleek black cap and nape, a blood-red bill and similar coloured yet tiny legs. There are one or two common terns nesting in their midst and they are immediately recognisable by their longer legs and the black tips to their bills. The unforgettable experience is to receive a dive-bombing from these elegant yet bold little seabirds – although tame enough to be touched on their nests, if you venture too close they will dive down and draw blood from your head with their dagger-like bills. Having no hat I went some way to protecting myself by laying my umbrella across my head! Twice a year the Arctic tern sets out on a mammoth journey which takes it from its nesting grounds in the north to the wintering grounds in the Antarctic some ten thousand miles away and then back again.

Halfway up the island a gaggle of excited twitchers had their scopes pointed at the middle of the sandwich-tern colony. Elsie, the by-now-famous lesser crested tern, has returned for her twelfth year on the island to cross breed with her close cousin the sandwich tern. She has a ludicrously large yellow bill but otherwise seems identical to her mate. What she is doing in the northern hemisphere I have no idea. Nearby another pocket of ornithological activity was centred on two nesting pairs of rare roseate terns. They are quite beautiful with their long tail streamers and the subtle pink flush on their chests. The best way to distinguish them from their relatives is by their completely black bill. At regular intervals along the pathways unconcerned female eider ducks sat

brooding like sleepy sentries. One or two early broods had hatched out as we saw a crèche of fifteen ducklings, on a rock pool being attended by eight females. At this time of year the drakes keep their own company, forming small rafts on the sea. They are pretty birds with an attractive green wash at the back of the head yet when first seen close to they present a strange sight. The forehead has no bulge and joins the bill almost in a straight line. They also give the appearance of being blind as the eye is hidden by the jet black on the crown which contrasts with the snow-white lower down.

The view from Inner Farne towards the Northumbrian coast is spectacular. Sandy beaches, Bamburgh Castle and, to the north, Holy Island. A mysterious and historic landscape. In the distance a line of five gannets flew north, probably to the Bass Rock in the Firth of Forth, against a background of the romantic hills above Fallodon where I hunted with the Percy foxhounds at New Year.

Tuesday, 6 June

A grey and overcast Derbyshire day. I went for a short walk in the evening and saw both the male and female pied flycatcher emerge from their nest box on Tissington bank. Another pair of spotted flycatchers are building high up behind a drainpipe by the Sky TV dish. They always seem to return to the same nesting sites. The pair nesting behind the barn-door hinge now have four eggs. There are a good number of young blackbirds around which have successfully fledged in the relative safety of our barns and sheds.

Friday, 9 June

A lovely sunny day with a fresh wind. I think the weather is going to be kind to us for our party tonight. We are having a reception to launch Peak Cottages at Parwich Lees and William Astor, who is Under Secretary of State for Heritage and responsible for tourism, is giving a speech.

I went for a walk down the Bletch this morning. The wind was causing great 'waves' to run through the hay meadow and the surrounding countryside has become a green patchwork quilt. This is the season of silage making and the quiet hum of machinery can be heard from all points of the compass. The meadows are full of buttercups and cuckoo flowers.

Birdsong is definitely less intensive as parents are busy feeding their young. The willow warblers are still in good heart. Two birds in particular, the sedge warbler and whinchat, have stayed with us to nest, which is very satisfying. The sedge warbler is still singing in the ditch behind the duck enclosure. I watched a pair of whinchat sitting on a fence down by the Tissington pond with their beaks full of insects. I sat a short distance from them for fifteen minutes but they refused to betray their nest. Redstarts were 'hooeeting' frantically in the hawthorn and nervously flicking their pretty rufus tails. The drake mallard have gone into eclipse and look a rather pathetic sight among all the beauty of 'flaming June'.

The young pied wagtails have left their nest and are being fed on the lawn by their parents. They are much lighter and have shorter tails, but they flick them just as vigorously. The young goldfinches in the walled garden will fly any day now and another chaffinch is sitting in a climbing rose on the west wall.

Sunday, 11 June

In the afternoon I drove over to Bakewell to meet some members of the Derbyshire Wildlife Trust. The rain had ceased and the sun made a feeble effort to come through as we set off into Manners Wood behind the old railway station to try and detect a singing wood warbler. This large wood, which is owned in part by the Chatsworth Estate and in part by Haddon, provides the perfect habitat for wood warblers – lots of mature beech, sycamore and oak with little ground cover. Needless to say, everything else was singing except the wood warbler.

I was comforted by Grey's entry in the 'Fallodon Green Book' dated 28 May 1893: 'I listened in vain in the favoured place for a wood wren; we haven't heard one on the Itchen either.'

The bird has two calls; for a few moments we thought we could have been listening to the less frequent song – a single mournful 'pieu' call, repeated at intervals. Grey describes this unique characteristic in *The Charm of Birds*:

> The other form of song is one clear and very plangent note, repeated in gentle succession as often as nine or ten times. The bird no doubt expresses the same feelings by this as by the other part of its song, but the impression made on a human listener by these plaintive notes is one of intense sadness: the tone is pathetic; there are tears in the voice. Sometimes a wood warbler will give these notes at no long intervals, though never so frequently as the shivering notes; at other times we may listen to these commoner notes repeated again and again, at very short intervals, and the bird will withhold the plaintive notes altogether. When this is so, we do not get a complete impression of the wood warbler, for it is the contrast between the two songs that is characteristic of the bird, and indeed remarkable among all birdsongs.

Tuesday, 13 June

Visited two companies in Leicestershire and lunched with the Llewellyns at Wymondham. A solitary skylark – no more than a speck in the sky – was singing high over the walled garden at 8.00 p.m. It took me some time to find him. We have surprisingly few skylarks singing in Derbyshire these days.

We have three pairs of spotted flycatchers nesting within fifty yards of each other. The one behind the Sky dish is now sitting and another has five eggs inside a slit in the barn wall within the walled garden.

Wednesday, 14 June

Drove to Suffolk after breakfast and visited two companies in the Ipswich area. I spent the night with friends near Debenham. We all drove over to Iken on the River Alde to have dinner with Paul Cooke and his wife. Paul is a talented businessman who has a passion for birds and conservation. He bought Stanney Farm because of its stunning location and in order to be able to pursue these interests. The property is

THE FOOD PASS: MARSH HARRIERS

around seven hundred and fifty acres and sits opposite Aldeburgh on a bend in the river. It is a natural haven for wildlife but one which he has improved immeasurably. New sluices have been incorporated into the dykes below the seawall to raise the water table. Artificial banks have been created for nesting sand martins and kingfishers and scrapes placed in the meadows to encourage the black-tailed godwits. Dead elms are left in place to encourage the woodpeckers and barn owls and nest boxes placed in the farm buildings to facilitate the latter's breeding success. Stanney Farm has its own small shoot and provides a fine example of how country sports and conservation can live in harmony together.

Before dinner we walked down to the seawall through the meadows which have recently played host to numerous nesting redshank, lapwing and oystercatchers. The main purpose of the expedition was to enjoy the flight of the breeding marsh harriers. Although there is now a substantial local population in coastal Suffolk it is a bird that is just about as foreign to me as the barn owl has sadly become.

Twenty years ago, the marsh harrier was on the brink of extinction in Britain with perhaps no more than a pair of birds nesting at the RSPB's Minsmere Reserve in Suffolk. There are now around one hundred nests in Britain and the reason for this improvement is quite simple. The days of mindless killing by gamekeepers have gone and most importantly pesticides have been banned. These worked their way up the food chain and had their most serious effect on the leading predators.

The New Atlas of Breeding Birds in Britain and Ireland states:

> Marsh harriers can be polygamous and the number of polygamous males has slowly increased over the last twenty years, with about fifteen per cent of all breeding males having two or more mates.

And so it is this year at Stanney Farm with one male feeding two females who have both nested in the thick reedbed below the seawall, no more than a few hundred yards apart. As we approached, both females soared

BARN OWL PS.

high above their nests and on two separate occasions we saw the male flying in with prey trailing in his talons. A third female – a rather scruffy looking specimen missing a number of her wing feathers – came in from across the river only to be ejected by the local birds from their territory. This demonstrated just what a common sight these birds have become along parts of the Suffolk coast.

The crowning moment was witnessing the ceremonial food pass. The male and female are easily told apart. The female has a creamy coloured head and the male a broad patch of grey on the inner wing. Both birds are otherwise dark brown. We watched the male flying in low with prey for nearly a mile. As he approached the female she carried out a half-somersault and received the gift of what looked like a dead moorhen from her mate. The transfer always takes place in mid-air – the male then returns to his hunting duties and the female flies back to the nest.

It was in these same reedbeds at Stanney that I saw for the first and only time a pair of bearded tits. In December 1993, Paul and I were taking a leisurely walk around the farm after shooting when I heard an unfamiliar metallic call – 'pting'. We then saw the unmistakable cockbird, with long tail and a pale blue-grey head marked by a black facial stripe. The bearded tit is in fact misnamed as its 'beard' looks much more like a moustache. Scientists have also decided that the bird is not related to the tits, but to the thrushes. This species is almost certainly increasing its range in Britain after it was nearly exterminated by the cold winter of 1947. The current population is thought to be around five hundred pairs after an expansion in the 1960s caused by immigration from newly created polders in the Netherlands.

We walked back to the house past a large open redbrick barn in which Paul had placed a nest box for the barn owls. As we entered, startling a handful of stock doves, a barn owl ghosted out across the meadows. This part of coastal Suffolk is one of the remaining strongholds of the barn owl in Britain. Although they are difficult to survey accurately as they are largely nocturnal and not particularly vocal, Paul believes he has a minimum of three pairs on his farm. Numbers have dwindled as agriculture has intensified since the war. All over the country hedges have been ripped out and ditches filled in to create large fields suited to modern machinery. Sometimes the only rough grasslands left lie along roads and, as a result of their being low-flying hunters, over three thousand barn owls are killed by cars every year. I have never seen a barn owl in the Derbyshire Dales (although there are plenty of old barns) and I suspect this is because of a lack of rough grassland. Every inch is grazed or cut for silage. Grain is now stored in rodent-proof bins in sealed barns which deprives these owls of their severe-weather food source. In the past pesticides undoubtedly played an important part in reducing barn owl numbers, but now that their use has been restricted, the population is probably beginning to recover. I have two overriding memories of nesting barn owls. When we were living at the Lince I would often see the 'white owl' gliding spookily among the ancient oaks in the High Park at Blenheim. On 17 November 1985 the beatkeeper took me to see three chicks still in their nest in a hollow oak. This demonstrates just how long their breeding season is and what a considerable duration the young spend in the nest. The other memory concerns a summer holiday we had with my cousin Ian Beith at his family home near Agen in the south of France. A pair of these owls were nesting in a slit in a barn wall very close to the house. All night long our ears were ringing with the hissing of the young as the parent birds brought food to the nest site.

Two other birds encountered on our walk warrant a mention here. A single avocet was feeding in shallow water on the far side of the seawall. The avocet has been adopted as the logo of the RSPB and with its striking black-and-white plumage and upward curved bill it is now familiar to thousands in Britain. It represents one of our great success stories for conservation and recolonisation, so much so that there are now over five hundred pairs breeding. I think they are much more numerous than the RSPB let on as, when staying with our friends the Hughes Halletts at Decoy Cottage in wintertime, I have seen hundreds in the estuary opposite Iken church.

As you approach the house from the direction of Aldeburgh you pass a small wood that lost most of its mature trees in the great gale of 1987. All that is left are a few small trees and some hawthorn and elder bushes. Out of this green bower wafted the gentle purring call of the turtle dove – Europe's only migratory dove that winters in Africa. I have not come across any in the Derbyshire Dales, although I have often seen them just outside the kitchen window at my mother-in-law's house in Hampshire. It is a most attractive bird that is boldly marked with distinctive brown edges to the black feathers of its upperparts. Edward Grey found its song soothing and restful:

> The turtle dove is not a resident bird, and its notes are therefore looked forward to as a sign of arrival. This bird, I think, it must have been that suggested to Tennyson 'the moan of doves in immemorial elms'. The sound is like a crooning, with something of tenderness and affection in it. It is associated most pleasantly with warm still summer days in the south of England; there it is part of the summer, which would be very incomplete without it. The bird is quiet in its ways, but its plumage is rich in colour when it can be seen close at hand: and the row of white spots at the end are very conspicuous when the tail is spread in flight. Turtle doves as I know them in Hampshire and Wiltshire are fond of sitting on fields that are fallow and where the earth is exposed: presumably they find there some kind of food specially suitable to themselves.

AVOCETS : SUFFOLK PS

Thursday, 15 June

Arrived back in Derbyshire from Suffolk mid morning. Towards evening the weather broke at last and we saw some blue sky; it is, however, still cold for this time of year. The evening is always the best time to listen to the blackbird perform. Having played a set of tennis with Andrew Sebire over at Hartington, I took a walk in the garden around 9.00 p.m. specifically to enjoy the blackbird's song, knowing all too well that in a few weeks he will be silent for the next eight months. It was a windy night but the blackbirds were in fine voice, along with the song thrushes. Grey leaves us in no doubt as to how highly he rates the blackbird's song.

> One last word about the song. Let anyone who wishes to measure its value listen to the great dawn chorus in May; that half-hour before sunrise, when like morning stars all the birds sing together. Listen attentively and consider how the song of the blackbird gives tone and spirit to the whole. A dozen or more different species of birds are taking part, but it is the notes of the blackbird that the chorus could least spare.

There is another moorhen's nest with five eggs in a clump of reeds at the point where I feed the ducks. It is only a yard away from the nest I discovered in April. I'm sure its the same bird producing a second brood.

Friday, 16 June

I have finally heard my wood warbler sing! I got up at 5.00 a.m. and had a short walk in Manners Wood (east of Bakewell) before catching the 7.00 a.m. train from Buxton to our Manchester office. Within five minutes I came across a bird uttering what Grey refers to as its 'shivering or sibilant sound'. On the previous two occasions – in Manners Wood last Sunday and a couple of weeks ago in the Lake District – it does now seem likely I was listening to a wood warbler.

On Sunday it was performing its second song – the single melancholic call note 'pieu'. In the Lake District (which is its perfect habitat with hanging mature woodland), it was producing the shivering trill. It is now quite easy to understand why I confused this song with that of a wren, although the wood warbler's is slower, not so high pitched and doesn't seem to go on for so long. It is an unwarbler-like song and one I would place somewhere between a wren and a grasshopper warbler. I don't think we caught sight of this large yellowish bird as it was high up in the canopy.

W. H. Hudson gives a romantic description of this particular song in his book *Birds and Man*. He contrasts it with that of the chaffinch which he says is loud and intensely distinct.

> The effect produced by the wood wren is totally different; the strain does not contrast with, but is complementary to, the 'tremulous cadence low' of inanimate nature in the high woods, of wind-swayed branches and pattering rain and lisping and murmuring of innumerable leaves – the elemental sounds out of which it has been fashioned. In a sense it may be called a trivial and a monotonous song – the strain that is like a long tremulous cry, repeated again and again without variation; but it is really beyond criticism – one would have to begin by depreciating the music of the wind. It is a voice of the

> beechen woods in summer, of the far-up cloud of green, translucent leaves, with open spaces full of green shifting sunlight and shadow. Though resonant and far-reaching it does not strike you as loud, but rather as the diffused sound of the wind in the foliage concentrated and made clear – a voice that has light and shade, rising and passing like the wind, changing as it flows and quivering like a wind-fluttered leaf. It is on account of this harmony that it is not trivial and that the ear never grows tired of listening to it: sooner would it tire of the nightingale – its purest, most brilliant tone and perfect artistry.
>
> The continuous singing of a skylark at a vast height above the green, billowy sun-and-shadow-swept earth is an etherealised sound which fills the blue space, fills it and falls, and is part of that visible nature above us, as if the blue sky, the floating clouds, the wind and the sunshine, have something for the hearing as well as for the sight. And as the lark in its soaring song is of the sky, so the wood wren is of the wood.

Saturday, 17 June

A wet windy day which has put paid to a morning with the chain-saw. This must be the worst June on record.

A willow warbler sang continuously for the early part of the morning in the rough around the old tennis court. His song was as vigorous as if he had just arrived from Africa. I went to listen to him perform, knowing that he would soon be silent. There is something quite romantic about standing under wind-blown trees in the summer rain.

W. H. Hudson has a chapter on 'The Secret of the Willow Wren' in his book *Birds and Man*. This little bird played an important part in his summer:

> He is a sweet and constant singer from the date of his arrival until about the middle of June, when he becomes silent for a season, resuming his song in July and continuing it throughout August and even into September. The late summer singing is, however, fitful and weak and less joyous in character than in the spring.

What really touches Hudson is the feeling that there is something human-like in the willow warbler's song:

> Now this arrangement of its notes, although very rare and beautiful, does not give the little song its highest aesthetic value. The secret of the charm, I imagine, is traceable to the fact that there is distinctly something human-like in the quality of the voice, its timbre. Many years ago an observer of wild birds and listener to their songs came to this country and walking one day in a London suburb he heard a small bird singing among the trees. The trees were in an enclosure and he could not see the bird, but there would, he thought, be no difficulty in ascertaining the species, since it would only be necessary to describe its peculiar little song to his friends and they would tell him. Accordingly, on his return to the house, he proceeded to describe the song and ask the name of the singer. No one could tell him, and much to his surprise, his account of the melody was received with smiles of amusement and incredulity. He described it as

> a song that was like a wonderfully bright and delicate human voice talking or laughingly saying something rather than singing. It was not until some time afterwards that the bird lover in a strange land discovered that his little talker and laugher among the leaves was the willow wren. In vain he had turned to the ornithological works; the song he had heard, or at all events the song as he had heard it, was not described therein; and yet to this day he cannot hear it differently – cannot dissociate the sound from the idea of a fairy-like child with an exquisitely pure, bright, spiritual voice laughingly speaking in some green place.

After a good fall of rain the birds often reciprocate with a fine burst of song. So it was today as I walked down the Bletch Brook before lunch. A cock whitethroat sang lustily from the top of a hawthorn bush in the Bletch hedge. His white throat becomes very conspicuous, bristling as he sings with his little mouth wide open. From the bottom of the hedge the sedge warbler gave me a short, jerky jingle, just enough to declare his presence. Downstream at the Tissington pond the cock whinchat was 'chatting' away on his normal fencepost, looking most serene with his orange chest and striking white eyestripe.

In the evening I took Robin and Marcus rabbit shooting and a pair of wheatear flitted around the old lime kiln, conspicuous by their snow-white rumps.

Wednesday, 21 June

Midsummer's Day – a beautiful sunny evening with a fresh breeze. I always think this is a rather sad day in the calendar, as from now on the evenings will get shorter. In addition, birdsong is distinctly on the wane; it was eerily quiet in the garden when I arrived home.

I left early in the morning for Leeds and a collared dove was cooing monotonously from the willow tree in the walled garden. The odd bird turns up with us in the summer, no doubt to sponge off the corn I put out in the yard for the ducklings and young bantams. Their relative scarcity results from the fact that we have few evergreen trees, which they prefer as nesting sites.

The dramatic spread of the collared dove is one of the most interesting ornithological phenomena of this century. In the 1930s in the last years of Edward Grey's life, it was restricted to Turkey and the Balkans. By 1955 it was first reported breeding in England and today there are over two hundred thousand pairs in Britain.

W. H. Hudson wrote in his chapter on Grey's cottage in *Hampshire Days*:

> During the month of July 1900 the swift was the most abundant and most constantly before us of all our Itchen Valley birds. In the morning he was not there, we had the pigeons then, all three species, ring dove, stock dove and turtle dove – being abundant in the woods on the opposite side of the valley – and from 4 o'clock to 6 was the time for the morning chorus, when the still air was filled with the human-like musical sound of their multitudinous voices mingled in one voice.

There was no collared dove present when Grey and Hudson spent happy hours on the banks of the Itchen. The ring dove referred to, so called because of the white collar around its neck, is the woodpigeon. As you would expect the collared dove also wears a collar around his neck, but it is black and white and goes only halfway around.

In fact all members of the pigeon family have prospered and increased their range since the turn of the century, largely due to new methods of arable cultivation. The real catalyst has been the introduction of fodder crops which remain green over the winter, like kale and turnips; no longer do they have to rely on natural food, such as acorns and beech mast.

The collared dove found a niche that was not occupied by any other bird and quickly exploited it. It became a 'hanger-on' to man – a classic case of a 'sponger'. It is completely associated with human habitation – always to be found in gardens, parks or on village greens, always on the look-out for a free meal of some sort. It is invariably there when the chickens are being fed or nosing around the barn in the farmyard. It is rarely seen in open country or on stubble fields like its close cousins. A main reason for its astonishing spread must be its long breeding season and multiple brooding. *The New Atlas of Breeding Birds* states: 'Robertson (1990) recorded a mean of 3.8 clutches per pair a year, with some pairs recording up to five broods.'

Yesterday I visited two businesses in County Durham. I was driving past the Wildfowl and Wetlands Trust's Washington reserve so we called in to meet the curator. I was on the council for two years in the late eighties and I have thoroughly enjoyed my visits to Slimbridge, Martin Mere and Arundel. The Washington reserve is on the edge of a built-up area and is surprisingly large, covering some hundred acres of diverse habitat, including ponds, woodland and the River Wear.

Thursday, 22 June

Woke up just before 4.00 a.m. to a song thrush in full song outside my bedroom window. If it had been a month or so earlier he would have been conducting a much larger chorus. The repetition of each loud phrase prevents confusion with the blackbird or mistle thrush.

Song thrush numbers have declined over the past twenty years. Before the war they were more numerous than blackbirds, but now the situation has reversed Most people find this sad as I suspect the song thrush is preferred. It is the more attractive of the two with its spotted chest and light brown plumage. Over the year it sings for twice as long as the blackbird, but against this must be set the beauty of the blackbird's song.

There has been much written about the decline of the song thrush, putting it down to such things as the overuse of slug pellets in gardens and the wider application of pesticides. In fact the favoured food are earthworms and caterpillars. Snails are only taken later in the year when the former are in short supply. The increase of hard winters in the seventies and eighties certainly did not help the thrush population. They are less tolerant of low temperatures than blackbirds and a good number move southwards every winter. The main reason for their decline is the fact that the blackbird is the more dominant species. The blackbird can often be seen robbing the thrush of its meal once the latter has cracked a snail open. Blackbirds tend to occupy the best nest sites and chase the more gentle song thrushes from their territories.

When I left for Birmingham at 7.00 a.m. a blackbird was still singing in the walled garden and a little owl was sitting on the telephone wires on the Alsop road demonstrating its diurnal habits.

Friday, 23 June

Having spent the night in London, I got up at 5.00 a.m. to take the train to Oxford and arrived at Blenheim at 7.00 a.m. It was a beautiful high-summer morning so I decided on a brief walk in the Park before setting out for Derbyshire.

It was an hour full of nostalgia – ten summers have now passed since we left the Lince. I took a sharp right through the Triumphal Arch towards the Fisheries *en route* for the Grand Bridge. Just before you reach the Fisheries (a keeper's cottage) there is a low arched bridge where the River Glyme flows into the lake. A few yards out a kingfisher sat on a small branch protruding from the water. The brilliant iridescent blues and oranges of the plumage are quite breathtaking – this is Britain's most exotic-looking bird. We spent forty months in total at the Lince and in all that time I only recorded fourteen kingfisher sightings in Blenheim Park. I think its most charming characteristic is its tendency to hover like a humming bird before diving when no suitable perch is available.

In his book *Birds and Man*, W. H. Hudson relates a popular delusion whereby people think they can immortalise all this beauty by a visit to the taxidermist.

> A man walking by the waterside sees by chance a kingfisher fly past, its colour a wonderful blue, far surpassing in beauty and brilliancy any blue he has ever seen in sky or water, or in flower or stone, or any

other thing. No sooner has he seen than he wishes to become the possessor of that rare loveliness, that shining object which, he fondly imagines, will be a continual delight to him and to all his house – an ornament comparable to that splendid stone which the poor fisherman found in a fish's belly, which was his children's plaything by day and his candle by night. Forthwith he gets his gun and shoots it and has it stuffed and puts it in a glass case. But it is no longer the same thing: the image of the living sunlit bird flashing past him is in his mind and creates a kind of illusion when he looks at his feathered mummy, but the lustre is not visible to others.

Looking west from the Grand Bridge, I counted four pairs of great crested grebes. A pair fished right below me, quite unconcerned by a flat-bottomed fishing boat; both were in their summer dress and conspicuous by their beauty, with erect 'ears' and russet heads. The birds in the distance looked like little snowballs as they lolled on the lake exposing their gleaming white breasts and flanks. On the Woodstock side of the bridge a group of around thirty mute swans glided around the island. There is no doubt these birds are on the increase again and will shortly reach pest-like proportions.

As I drove up to the Lince two fox cubs ran into a field of newly turned hay and a muntjack scuttled across the drive. These miniature deer escaped from Woburn over thirty years ago and have spread like wildfire. They have little to recommend them and are not even attractive.

I walked from the Lince down Bladon Water to New Bridge and on past Rough Piece to the Cascade. I then crossed the stepping stones above the Cascade and made my way back past Spring Lock Cottage. Yellow lilies were coming out along the lower lake and white lilies on the main lake. Along the waterside grew a mass of cow parsley and purple comfrey. The copper beeches and the giant cedar trees looked

glorious in their new growth. There was only a trickle of water coming over the Cascade but how I wish Capability Brown could have been here to see it all!

Birdsong has diminished significantly. The odd chaffinch, chiffchaff, blackcap and goldcrest were singing. At this quieter time it is the song of the wren that stands out. It sings in nearly every month of the year and for such a small bird its song is startlingly loud. The tits have been silent for some time now as they have been busy feeding large clutches of young. I heard one member of the family – the coal tit – several times today. It produces a distinctive repeated call ('tee-chu'), similar to the great tit, but more high pitched. They are quite common in the Park as a result of a liking for evergreen trees.

Until this morning I had never seen a grebe fly. As I approached New Bridge on Bladon Water I surprised a dabchick. It did not dive but took off for a few yards with its long legs dangling behind. It looked like an effort of a pioneer aviator in the early part of the century.

Arrived back at Parwich Lees mid-morning to a glorious summer's day with a refreshing north wind.

Saturday, 24 June

Grey and overcast with the fresh north wind persisting. Someone once said, 'We don't have a climate, just weather.' On a brighter note, the roses at the front of the house (Buff Beauty) and the wild dogrose covering the hawthorn bushes are looking magnificent.

After breakfast I took the boys for a 'bird walk' to see how many were still singing. The odd willow warbler and chaffinch are still in song. Two birds in particular attracted us. The Lees pond is surrounded by a large nettlebed and for weeks now a cock whitethroat has been performing his jerky song – today was no exception. Last year I can picture another whitethroat singing late into the summer in a large chestnut by the road in front of our holiday lets. Again, there was a substantial nettlebed under its song post. A whitethroat nests about eighteen inches above the ground and a bed of thick nettles provides the perfect habitat. I heard as many blackcaps singing today at Parwich Lees as all season. One sang in the old tennis court, one in the hawthorn bank and another in the Bletch hedgerow. Perhaps they were experiencing a short period of exuberance having just completed their nursery duties and not yet having to contemplate the long journey south. I was reminded of a passage in *The Charm of Birds*:

> On the other hand, I have noticed in certain birds a revival of song in the latter part of June, which is continued into July. In the Hampshire chalk-pit, where a pair of blackcaps nested every year, it was noticeable that the song would become very infrequent for some days in the latter part of May or early June. The birds were then engaged in feeding the young: while this was so, whether before or after the young left the nest, there was little time or energy to be spent on song. There would come a time in the latter part of June when the chalk-pit blackcap repeated his song from dawn to dusk. I have noticed in the same place a similar slackening and revival of song on the part of the wren and the chiffchaff.

When we arrived at the Tissington pond the usual family of whinchats were present; this time they were accompanied by a young bird. They are very nervous and not great songsters. As soon as you get close to them, they become quite anxious and start their agitated 'chatting' call. W. H. Hudson, writing in his book *Nature in Dowland*, suggests the whinchat's song is underrated:

> The whinchat's song is even less well-known or less regarded than that of its more conspicuously coloured relation, the stonechat. Thus, William Borrer, in his *Birds of Sussex*, expresses the opinion that this species has no song; yet he had spent eighty years of his long life in a rural district where the whinchat is fairly common, and had been a lifelong observer of the birds of his county. It is in fact a low gentle song that cannot be heard far, and when other birds are singing it is not regarded. The song is a warble of half a dozen notes, and is hardly longer than the redstart's song, with which it has been compared. But it is not like it. The whinchat's best notes, though low, have a full, sweet, mellow quality which makes them comparable to the blackbird or blackcap. The redstart's best and opening note is bright, yet plaintive, and reminds one at the same time of two such unlike songsters as the swallow and the robin.

The Prime Minister has called a leadership election and the Foreign Secretary, Douglas Hurd, announced his retirement yesterday. In today's *Times* leader he is being compared to Sir Edward Grey in that both men practised 'good old-fashioned diplomacy'.

> A certain whig-liberal aura about Mr Hurd has prompted comparisons with Sir Edward Grey, the even more durable British Foreign Secretary from 1905 to 1916. This can be misleading and not only because Mr Hurd has circled the globe like Puck, whereas Sir Edward left British shores for the first time on official business only in 1914 for the Paris Conference that attempted, futilely, to avert world war. The lights which Sir Edward famously remarked then went out all over Europe were rekindled during Mr Hurd's tenure. Nothing has been more central to his concept of British foreign policy than the conviction that Britain's active engagement is indispensable to the successful restoration of peace and stability in the European Continent.

Sunday, 25 June

The boys and I walked over to Shaw's Farm after breakfast through the Bletch meadows. The meadow pipit is an aptly named bird. It is either associated with lush buttercup-strewn meadows, as it is with us, or with the high heather-covered moorland. In neither case is the bird left unmolested. On the lower ground its nest is a favourite target for the cuckoo and on the higher ground it is the victim of the merlin.

Meadow pipits are migratory and come to spend the summer with us. Their sharp call note is easily recognised and characteristic of a hot June day in our valley. They have a delightful territorial song flight whereby they glide down to a nearby stone wall or fence post, with wings spread and tail slightly cocked, uttering a trill of continuous 'pheets'. Grey describes this attractive ritual:

> The meadow pipit is a bird that, being gifted with only a small song, displays it to the best advantage; it ascends to no great height – perhaps twenty feet or so – and then descends like a little parachute, singing as it comes down. Here again the song is evidently part of a joy flight and when one is salmon fishing in early spring in moorland country, meadow pipits make a minute but perceptible contribution to the happiness of the day.

We went to lunch with an old Cambridge friend whose family owns a very attractive farm at Croxton Abbey near Alton Towers. After lunch we walked around the grounds of the old Cistercian abbey and a chiffchaff sang with the zest of late March, giving weight to Grey's theory that there is a short revival of song after the breeding season.

Tuesday, 27 June

In the heat of the day birdsong is very sparse. The reed bunting is singing down by my duckponds and he will continue late into the summer when so many other birds are silent. His song is not very musical and takes the form of a monotonous accelerated squeak. Edward Grey was evidently very fond of it:

> In spite of his noble appearance the reed bunting has a rather paltry song: it suggests to me the ascent of steps, the first two or three being mounted sedately and the last taken trippingly. In the plenitude of song in May and early June the reed bunting's contribution would not be missed, if he happened to be absent or silent, but in July by a chalk stream I should miss him very much; there he prolongs the season of song.

The reed bunting is a common sight in the damp hedgerows of Derbyshire from March onwards. Come colder weather 'at the back end' of summer, they tend to move south on to lower ground and join up with marauding flocks of finches in the fields.

W. H. Hudson informs us that the reed bunting was a frequent visitor to the surrounds of Grey's cottage.

> Here by the Itchen, where we have all four buntings, I find the reed bunting – called black head or black top – is, after the cirl, the latest singer. He continues when, towards the end of August, the corn bunting and yellowhammer become silent. He is the poorest singer of the bunting tribe, the first part of his song being like the chirp of an excited sparrow, somewhat shriller, and then follows the long note, shrill too, or sibilant and tremulous. It is more like the distressful hunger call of some young birds than a song note. A reedy sound in a reedy place, and one likes to hear it in the green valley among the wind-rustled, sword-shaped leaves and waving spears of rush and aquatic grass. So fond is he of his own music that he will sing even when moulting.

A blackcap was in full song in the walled-garden wood until 10.00 p.m.

We found another goldfinch's nest in a clematis on the yard wall. It was deserted, contained one egg and was beautifully lined with pheasant feathers.

HOBBY, SWALLOWS & H. MARTINS.

Thursday, 29 June

The hottest day of the year so far. We've been turning the hay and will bale it tomorrow. I spent the day in our Leeds office and came back around teatime. As I drove up from Chesterfield towards Beeley Moor a hobby flew high over my car. It bears a superficial resemblance to a kestrel but has longer and more sickle-shaped narrow wings. The tail is shorter than that of a kestrel and such is its agility in flight that it is able to catch swifts. This was my third sighting in Derbyshire which proves that this particular raptor is gradually increasing its range northwards. The first time I saw one at Parwich Lees was in August 1992 when it was flying high over the valley and being mobbed by swallows and martins. It put on a breathtaking aerobatic display and then, in an instant, it was gone. Hobbies take prey on the wing, both small birds and insects. They can be seen taking a dragonfly in their claws and then holding it to the beak to eat without pausing in flight.

The hobby winters in Africa and is a summer visitor to Britain, where it frequents heathland such as the New Forest.

Friday, 30 June

Another sweltering day – I stayed at home to help with the haymaking.

I sat in the garden listening to the birdsong just as it was getting dark (10.00 p.m.). At the end of the day the background noise is provided by the cooing of woodpigeons, the 'chukking' of my friendly cock pheasants up at roost, and the high-pitched single calls of the recently fledged spotted flycatchers. I thought that by now the blackbird had fallen silent but a single bird gave a rather poor finale from a high beech beside the walled garden. The flutey notes of the blackbird have rather surprisingly been replaced by the song of a most energetic and persistent blackcap.

There is no doubt that the star turn at present is the thrush. You appreciate him at this time of relative silence, particularly as he sings until it is nearly dark. He was a real favourite with Grey.

> The thrush has a variety of notes, but the order in which he gives them is improvised. We may listen to a thrush for a time without hearing the notes we most desire, for some of his notes are much less agreeable than others; a musical phrase resembling 'did-he-do-it?' may be repeated two or three times and then abandoned for some other notes. Probably if birds were to be regarded as endeavouring to please us by song, the thrush should be put first among British birds. He does not rank in the very highest class for quality, but he certainly comes high in the second class. His is undoubtedly a major song, and owing to the number of thrushes, their persistent singing and the many months in which they are to be heard, we hear more of their song in the South of England than of any other bird, except the robin. In song the thrush seems to be working very hard to please, and he succeeds. His song, too, can give a very pleasant impression of quiet contentment as well as of exultation.

Edward and Dorothy Grey kept a 'nature notebook' down at their Hampshire cottage. There is an entry by Grey from 28–30 April 1894 which refers to the song of the thrush:

> A nightingale's song is the most wonderful but the most imperfect of songs. The long notes are divine, but they come seldom and never go on long enough: the song continually breaks out with a burst, which promises a fine full spell, but it is always broken off in the most disappointing way. A blackcap's song, which comes next in quality, is short enough, but it seems flushed in a way that no part of a nightingale's ever does, and one can't help thinking with some satisfaction of a good, steady old thrush singing right through from the beginning of February to the middle of June.

The Cottage Book was printed privately in 1909 and had 137 pages.

A family of linnets flew into the copper beech just after lunch – no doubt to evade the blistering heat. They squeaked and wheezed happily as they flitted playfully under the shady canopy.

JULY

Saturday, 1 July

The weather has broken but it is still very dry. We gathered all the hay in successfully but we now badly need rain.

The spotted flycatchers are everywhere, doing what they do best, toiling to quench the insatiable appetites of their expectant young that sit in the trees and call loudly.

One wonders where all the tits go in summer – in the winter months they completely take over the garden; but I saw four today giving themselves a bath on the birdtable – a great tit and a blue tit with two young.

We filled the pheasant feeder in the hawthorn bank and found another pheasant's nest in the long grass in which eggs appear to have been hatched successfully. There were a number of willow warblers still in song. Drove around to the lime kiln where a family of wheatear were sitting on the adjacent wall. They obviously do stay and nest with us.

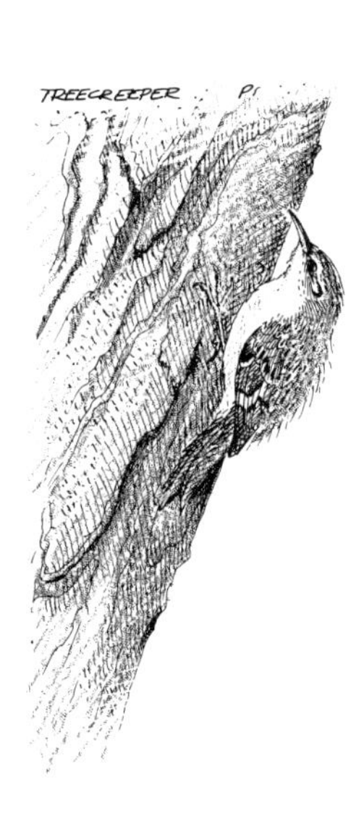

I have noticed treecreepers flying into the horse chestnut tree by the ha-ha for some days now but have failed to locate the nest. Today we found a recently fledged treecreeper on the inside of the sitting room window which we released and it flew off unharmed. The nest is likely to have been in a crack in the tree or behind loose bark. A few years ago they nested in between a gritstone gatepost and the garden wall. They are the most delicate birds with a thin down-curved bill and sophisticated claws to facilitate climbing. They rarely climb downwards and, once up, will fly down to the base of another tree and start again. The treecreeper is beautifully streaked with buff and it has a rigid pointed tail which, like a woodpecker, it uses for support as it climbs a trunk. It is a bird that is easily overlooked and more often heard than seen. My first encounter with a treecreeper is clearly etched on my mind. It was on 20 April 1985 when we were living in Blenheim Park. We were walking from New Bridge back to the Lince when, on a tree in the middle of Laurel Bank, a slight silvery flash of movement caught my eye. The treecreeper reminded me of a little mouse as it shuffled up the trunk.

Monday, 3 July

A lovely evening but much cooler. I am feeding about sixty mallard, which consist of both those reared under bantams and the 'wild birds'. I found two dead ducklings in the water that had been decapitated. I think the culprit could well be a tawny owl. They must be using the big enclosure posts as perches.

Three moorhen have hatched in the little 'island tuft' where I feed the ducks. I picked up one of the chicks and put it back in the nest; it is black and fluffy with a bright red beak. Another was just pushing its beak through the eggshell.

Birdsong is thin. I did, however, hear a few notes from a dunnock, willow warbler, garden warbler, blackcap and sedge warbler. The only regular performers now seem to be the wren and the cheerful goldfinches.

I got very close to Sir Richard's white hare. He has in fact got a brown head and only a 'white jersey'. He was with two of his more conventional friends.

Wednesday, 5 July

At Parwich Lees even the thrush now seems to have fallen silent, having moved into his midsummer moult. The joyful tinkling of numerous families of goldfinches in the garden trees is never far away, which keeps the spirits up. Grey describes the goldfinch in July in his chapter 'From Full to Least Song' and it is perhaps my favourite passage in *The Charm of Birds*:

> Goldfinches are happily very common in all chalk-strewn valleys that I have known, and doubtless in many other places. There were twelve nests in one season lately in one Hampshire garden of no unusual size; they make liveliness in July, when so many other birds are becoming dull. They are restless, always flitting about, and the fine gold on the wings is conspicuous as they fly; they are thus lively to the eye both in colour and in movement: and the young birds have this conspicuous yellow on the wings, so that they contribute to the vividness of the charm from the moment they are fledged, though their heads are plain and without the rich crimson of mature goldfinches. The song is rather trivial, a tinkling sound, but happy; and as the birds are so constantly on the move, now in one place and now in another, the garden is always being enlivened by them. Indeed, goldfinches give a touch of lightsomeness to the heaviest day in July. They suggest to me what the ash does among trees. July is the month in which to appreciate the ash. When the leaves of oak and beech are dark, impenetrable to sunshine, and stiff, almost stubborn, to the breeze, then observe a fine ash. The leaves are graceful on long stems, and are stirred by a gentle air, and the foliage is so open that the light seems rather to permeate and be welcome than to be excluded. With the early spring green and bright autumn colours of other trees the ash does not compete; even in bareness its stout branches tipped with black buds are without the grace of other trees in winter; but in midsummer it has a gracious presence. No day in midsummer can be unrelievedly heavy if there are goldfinches in the garden and ash trees in the field beyond.

In Derbyshire the ash does very well on the limestone. At Parwich Lees we have a large ash tree on the lawn that is alive with the happy song of goldfinches all summer long.

Thursday, 6 July

My mother-in-law, Jean Hastings, has had a serious stroke at her Hampshire home and is in a deep coma in Winchester Hospital. I drove down to join Lucinda at Bramdean after lunch. As I sat in the garden in the evening, listening to the lazy song of the yellowhammers up on the downs, I felt an overwhelming sense of sadness at the emptiness of the place. My father-in-law, Robin, died over five years ago and now the lights surrounding Lucinda's last links with her childhood seemed to be dimming.

Friday, 7 July

I got up at 6.00 a.m. and drove the eight miles or so from the house at Bramdean through the little village of Titchbourne to the site of Edward Grey's cottage at Itchen Abbas. All that now remains is an ivy covered brick chimney and a scattering of foundation stones. The village itself lies a few miles upstream of Winchester.

It was at Titchbourne, on a summer's morning in 1910, that Grey and Theodore Roosevelt commenced their famous 'Bird Walk' down the Itchen valley and then on into the heart of the New Forest. Although Roosevelt was a past President of the United States and Grey our incumbent Foreign Secretary, the two had never met. Roosevelt specifically asked the Foreign Office to arrange this excursion so that he could familiarise himself with British birdsong. United by a love of birds, both men became firm friends and remained so for the rest of their lives, corresponding on a regular basis.

The historic city of Winchester – King Arthur's capital – is dominated by its ancient cathedral. Among my earliest recollections are enjoyable hours wandering around the cathedral and the adjacent Close whilst weekending at Dean with my cousins, the Beiths.

Little did I know at the time that a decade or so later I would participate in two memorable services at Winchester Cathedral which would result in an enduring bond of affection with this magnificent building. In December 1983 Lucinda and I were married in the choir stalls and six years later I read a poem by Dorothy Wellesley at Robin Hastings' memorial service. The cathedral is the regimental chapel of the Rifle Brigade and as Robin was one of their most distinguished wartime offices, we were lucky enough to have the use of it.

In the 1870s Edward Grey was at school at Winchester and it was here that he first developed his lifelong interest in fly fishing and his love for Hampshire. It would almost certainly have been along the banks of the Itchen that he became interested in birds, sharing many a peaceful moment as he cast his fly upon those clear chalk-stream waters.

In 1890, when married to Dorothy, Grey built a little cottage overlooking the river at Itchen Abbas directly opposite Avington, the house of his cousin, Lord Northbrook. It was to this idyllic refuge that Grey would escape from the Foreign Office. He obviously could not travel north to Fallodon every weekend and for the best part of thirty years (the cottage was burned down in 1923) he spent some of his happiest days beside the Itchen, relaxing, fishing and enjoying the birds.

On 14 August 1901, Grey wrote the following letter to Dorothy:

> It's one o'clock and I have just got here and I feel as if my heart was too full and might burst; the place is so sacred. I move about it in the most touching way. I feel as if I must keep coming in every half hour to write to you. I have been on the bridge and eaten my figs on it and thrown the stalks into the river. I can hardly breath for the sacredness of the place. It is very strange that you aren't here, stranger than I thought; but I suppose it wouldn't be so strange to you, as I am so often away. What wonderful days you must have without me!'

The site of the cottage has become a place of personal pilgrimage and whenever I stay at Bramdean I drive over to walk in the valley. Ninety-five years ago this month the celebrated naturalist W. H. Hudson arrived for his summer holiday at the Cottage, as it was called. The Greys were close friends of Hudson and he in turn inscribed his book *Hampshire Days*, written in 1903, to 'Sir Edward and Lady Grey, Northumbrians with Hampshire written on their hearts'. Hudson dedicated two chapters of this book to his experiences at Grey's cottage in the summer of 1900. He writes as follows:

> They had told me about their cottage, which serves them all the best purposes of a lodge in the vast wilderness. Fortunately in this case the 'boundless contiguity of shade' of the woods is some little distance away, on the other side of the ever green Itchen valley, which narrowing at this spot, is not much more than a couple of hundred yards wide. A long field's length away from the cottage is the little ancient rustic tree-hidden village. The cottage, too, is pretty well hidden by trees and has the reed and sedge and grass-green valley and swift river before it, and behind and on each side green fields and old untrimmed hedges with a few old oak trees growing both in the hedgerows and the fields. There is also an ancient avenue of limes which leads nowhere and whose origin is forgotten. The ground under the trees is overgrown with long grass and nettles and burdock; nobody comes or goes by it, it is only used by the cattle, the white and roan and strawberry shorthorns that graze in the fields and stand in the shade of the limes on very hot days. Nor is there any way or path to the cottage; but one must go and come over the green fields, wet or dry. The avenue ends just at the point where the gently sloping chalk down touches the level valley and the half-hidden, low-roofed cottage stands just there, with the shadow of the last two lime trees falling on it at one side. It was an ideal spot for a nature lover and an angler to pitch his tent upon. Here a small plot of ground, including the end of the lime tree avenue, was marked out, a hedge of sweetbriar planted round it, the cottage erected and a green lawn made before it on the river side and beds of roses planted at the back.
>
> Nothing more – no gravel walks, no startline geraniums, no lobelias, no cinerarias, no calceolarias, no other gardener's abominations to hurt one's eyes and make one's head ache. And no dog, nor

> cat, nor chick, nor child – only the wild birds to keep one company. They knew how to appreciate its shelter and solitariness; they were all about it, and built their nests amid the green masses of ivy, honeysuckle, virginia creeper, rose and wild clematis which covered the trellised walls and part of the red roof with twelve years' luxuriant growth.

In the summer of 1893 Dorothy Grey wrote a letter to her husband from their London house and sent it down to the House of Commons. It contains references to two people from very different worlds who probably had more influence on the lives of Dorothy and Edward Grey than any others, Haldane and Hudson. Dorothy had just undergone a long discussion with Haldane as to whether Grey should resign and go and live at Fallodon. It ends:

> I wonder if you will see him in the House tonight and what he will say to you. He told me he had had a talk with you today which had been nicer than of late. It's funny to write and tell you all this but I may be gone to bed when you come. I shall read more Hudson tonight and store it up for you like honey.

As I walked down the lime avenue towards Grey's bridge, a fox cub ambled across the entrance to the chalk pit opposite the cottage. In the distance I heard the odd burst from a blackcap or chiffchaff but it was the wrens and the woodpigeons that were the main performers. It is only at this time of the year when most birds are silent that you might guess the wren is Britain's commonest bird. A kingfisher flashed across the river towards Avington. Although the woodland birds were relatively silent the river still provided its special music: the chatter of the reed warblers, the whinnying of the dabchicks and the abrupt calls of the moorhen and coot.

Hudson writes of his July holiday at the Cottage in *Hampshire Days*:

> The best vocalists had ceased singing: the last nightingale I had heard utter its full song was in the oak woods of Beaulieu on 27 June; and now all the tree warblers and with them chaffinch, thrush, blackbird and robin had become silent. The wren was the leading songster, beginning his bright music at 4 o'clock in the morning, and the others, still in song, that visited me were the greenfinch, goldfinch, swallow, dunnock and cirl bunting. From my seat I could also hear the songs in the valley of the reed and sedge warblers, reed bunting and grasshopper warbler.

Saturday, 8 July

Spent last night with Lucinda at Jean's bedside. She has terrific spirit and fights on although she is very ill.

I woke up at 4.30 a.m. to a dawn chorus provided by wrens and woodpigeons. A solitary thrush was in fine song. I'm sure that thrushes and blackbirds sing just that bit longer in the south of England. Grey thought so:

> I should say that the thrush after his midsummer silence begins to sing again in October and continues to sing in mild weather till the next mid-July. On Sundays in November in the south of England,

> when I have been out for a walk with lunch in pocket, a thrush has, by his singing, decided the choice of a spot for luncheon. Indeed in the south of England a thrush has only little more than two months in the year of complete abstinence from song.

When I arrived at Bramdean on Thursday, I heard a very short scratchy performance from a blackbird. They have been silent for some weeks now and will not sing again until next March. Grey adored the song of this otherwise uncharismatic bird.

> I have, however, heard a blackbird singing well in St James Park in July, even late in the month, if my memory is correct. Why this should have been so it is not easy to guess. It may have been a bird, let out from a cage, that had not mated and escaped the exertions of the breeding season, and thus retained its vigour and delayed the moult. I remember being rather resentful that a London park should continue to have the privilege of blackbirdsong for some weeks after the birds had become silent in the country.

We went over to Arundel for lunch with the Balfours which from Bramdean involves a lovely drive across the downs past Goodwood. They are very dear friends; Roddy and I used to 'mess together' at Eton and Tessa is an old family friend going back to my Oxfordshire childhood. They have a charming house at Burpham with spectacular views across the Arun valley to the Castle. The house overlooks the southern end of the Amberley Brooks which provide perfect habitat for many different species of both migratory and nesting birds. In early summer the damp meadows and dykes echo with the song of nesting redshank and reed warblers. Burpham Lodge is of particular interest if you enjoy watching swifts. The house is a pretty flint Victorian rectory and its high deep eaves play host every summer to several families of nesting swifts. I can watch these birds for hours as they scream playfully in groups around the house and then fly directly up under the eaves through the smallest aperture.

They are fascinating birds that arrive with us to nest every year from Africa. They are a totally aerial species and unlike their close cousins, the swallows and martins, they never alight on the ground. They may well

travel over a million miles in their lives and think nothing of flying hundreds of miles in a day to feed in the right conditions, catching anything up to ten thousand individual insects in the process.

One of the best descriptions of the swift is found in Henry Douglas-Home's book *The Birdman*. He designed special nest boxes for them and fixed them on his house in the Borders. Henry was the brother of Prime Minister Alec Douglas-Home who writes the forward to Jan Karpinski's book on Edward Grey, *Capital of Happiness*. Henry tells us how he first studied the swift while at school at Eton where, from his bedroom window, he would enjoy their screaming aerobatics around the fives courts. He noticed how they would cease playing as it became dark and then circle higher and higher into the sky until they disappeared from sight.

> Swifts do everything in the air because of their inability to perch. Their circling to high altitudes at night is just one example of this. The intriguing mystery I witnessed at Eton had been solved some years before by aircrews on night reconnaissance over the Western Front in the First World War. They reported seeing parties of them as high as ten thousand feet asleep on the wing. And that is how they roost, drifting, buoyed by the updrafts for the few hours of summer darkness sometimes to heights of over three miles above the earth. Not every swift roosts in this way. In the breeding season I have noticed that nesting birds will often creep into their nesting boxes for a two- to three-hour siesta of an early afternoon. They have to be airborne to survive, which explains why they spend the shortest time of any migrant in this country, being assured of the best of the weather and the maximum amount of sunlight and insects. They are to the skies what the ocean wanderers – albatross, shearwater and petrel – are to the seas, but unlike them the swift cannot rest at will. It can crawl into crevices or on to ledges, it can cling to vertical rough surfaces, but to fly again it must be able to fall free. Its minute feet are too frail to support the weight of its body. A swift on the ground is almost helpless. To fly it must have a height to topple off. In this dependence on the air it would seem to be the most evolved of any bird, the least land based, the most efficient in flight – the most tireless as well as the fastest. It is airborne for most of its life. It feeds in the air, mates in the air, drinks by swooping to water and gathers nesting materials in the air.

His study of swifts in their nest boxes produced some interesting results.

> I soon realised how subject they are to weather and how extraordinary are the depths of their resources in combating its ill effects. The first thing I noticed was that if the temperature dropped to near freezing, as it can do in the north in May, all the adult birds would disappear, sometimes for as much as four days. Research has shown that these journeys occur when local insect food becomes scarce. Swifts in this predicament will travel unimaginable distances in search of warmer weather. Radar has revealed that a Border bird for instance thinks nothing of making a round trip as far as the Baltic in a

single day to gather flies, and since they are capable of speeds of up to 100 mph this may not be the limit of their daily range.

Douglas-Home tells us how the young birds adapt to adverse weather conditions in their own way.

> I came across apparently dead and abandoned young lying in the boxes, motionless and stone cold. I was to discover that this too was caused by insect shortages. The birds were not dead but in suspended animation in the expectation of the return of their parents from one of these lengthy food forays. As with the eggs, when I actually watched a female perform the manoeuvre of tipping them overboard, I happened to be there when a parent bird returned with the fruits of its wanderings: a congealed ball of flies about the size of a marble swelling its throat. In half an hour it had warmed and cajoled its young into a state of full consciousness.

Tuesday, 11 July

Jean died peacefully on Sunday without regaining consciousness. We are busy organising the service of thanksgiving at Bramdean on Friday.

In the afternoon I escaped for a few hours to walk at Needs Ore. The gulls are still there in force but there are few waders about, only a splattering of curlew, oyster catchers and redshank. There was a solitary wader asleep on a mudbank by the creek which we found difficult to identify but settled on a greenshank. It was darkish with a distinctive white V on its back and was noisy in flight.

Grey and Hudson would have been amazed by the distinctly Mediterranean sight of two white egrets standing motionless on their long legs in a shallow flash on the Blackwater Meadows. These little snow white herons are increasing their range northwards as a result of a series of mild winters. They are still quite rare but can be seen on the south coast at all times of the year, although they have yet to nest with us in Britain. The horrid Canada geese are in moult and when we approached too close they all scampered off to the river with their heads held low.

Thursday, 13 July

I drove over to the Cottage before breakfast for a short walk by the Itchen. It was a journey tinged with sadness as after the funeral we will probably be selling the house at Bramdean and visits to this part of the world will presumably be few and far between.

A green woodpecker flew from the lime avenue into an ash tree in the chalk pit, laughing as it went. It is the loud ringing laugh that has earned it the popular name of 'yaffle'. I caught a glimpse of its beautiful crimson head high in the foliage. I was unable to distinguish the sex; both male and female have a crimson moustache.

In his chapter on the Cottage in *Capital of Happiness*, Jan Karpinski states: 'The brick chimney still stands amidst a mass of greenery, the old avenue is still there, so too are the birds.'

The latter is not altogether true. A number of birds well known to Grey and Hudson in Hampshire are either very rare or no longer present in the county.

When W. H. Hudson was sitting under his lime tree at Edward Grey's cottage on that sweltering day of 21 July 1900, he specifically mentions the cirl bunting as one of the half a dozen birds that visited his shady paradise. He also tells us of an encounter with a cock cirl bunting on his way to the cottage while travelling between Winchester and Romsey:

> I did not know that I was in a district where this pretty species is more numerous than in any other place in England, as common, in fact, as the universal yellowhammer, and commoner than the more local corn bunting. Here in July, August, in the course of an afternoon's walk, in any place where there are trees and grass fields, one can count on hearing half a dozen birds sing, every one of them probably the parent of a nest full of young.

The cirl bunting was a common bird in southern England during the nineteenth century, as witnessed by comments in Kelsall and Morris's book *Birds of Hampshire and the Isle of Wight*. In it they quote Mr Meade Waldo:

> I should consider the cirl bunting a characteristic Hampshire bird, certainly in the districts with which I am best acquainted. It is a common inhabitant of all the surroundings of the New Forest, although it does not penetrate much into the forest itself; its favourite haunts seem to be wooded fields, with a certain amount of high hedgerow timber, from the top of which its monotonous trill, somewhat resembling the first part of the song of the yellowhammer, may be heard from March to November.

The turning point in the fortunes of the cirl bunting may have come around the beginning of the century. Grey certainly suggests this:

> There was no cirl bunting's nest there [the Cottage] in any subsequent year [subsequent to 1900]. Cirl buntings, which had been plentiful in that region, became scarce; and for some years I have not heard a cirl bunting within earshot of the place.

A research project undertaken by the RSPB in 1988 points to the real decline setting in some forty years later with change in agricultural practices after the Second World War. The cirl bunting relies very heavily on open stubbles for sources of winter feed. After the war, with moves away from mixed farming to intensive cereal production, cereal crops were planted in the autumn and no winter stubbles were left. In the old days and more recently during the agricultural recession between the wars, stubbles were left as rough grazing for sheep and would have produced vast amounts of seeds from annual weeds. In the 1960s, with the advent of modern herbicides, stubble fields were 'cleansed' with the resulting loss of food for the cirl bunting. There is, however, hope for the future; the RSPB has proved that with selective conservation and the cooperation of a small group of farmers, this pretty bunting can not only survive as a breeding bird in Britain, but also increase in numbers. As a result of their conservation programme, unsprayed winter stubbles enclosed by thick hedges, particularly in the smaller fields of Devonshire, have played host to flocks of up to forty cirl buntings all winter.

There is a school of thought that suggests the cirl bunting may have arrived in this country only at the tail end of the eighteenth century with the advent of warmer weather. The cirl bunting is essentially a Mediterranean bird and today southern England represents the northernmost limit of its range, the point where the yellowhammer takes over. The cirl likes southward-facing slopes on chalk escarpments, particularly at the border of the chalk downlands and the lower farmland. The only time I have heard one sing is when on holiday near Agen.

The theory that the cirl arrived in Britain towards the end of the eighteenth century is based on the surprising fact that Gilbert White completely omitted the bird from his *Natural History of Selborne*. It was discovered as a breeding bird in 1800 by Montagu down in Devon. W. H. Hudson writes in *Hampshire Days*:

> And as at Selborne and Farringdon, so I have found it in most places in Hampshire, especially in the southern half of the county; the cirl is the village bunting whose favourite singing place is in the quiet churchyard or the shade-trees at the farm; compared with other members of the genus, he might be called our domestic bunting. The yellowhammer is never heard in the village at Selbourne, to find him one has to climb the hill and go out on to the common, there he can be heard drawing out his lazy song all day long. How curious to think that Gilbert White never distinguished between these two species, although it is probable that he heard the cirl on every day during the greater part of his life.

The cirl bunting can easily be confused with the yellowhammer, both in appearance and song, but it seems hardly likely that this was the case with such a talented naturalist as White. The cock cirl is like a brightly coloured yellowhammer but plumper and with a shorter tail. The most noticeable difference lies with the cirl's conspicuous black chin and eyestripe and colourful chestnut flanks. Needless to say Hudson found its repetitive song easy enough to distinguish:

> The song is not quite accurately described in the standard ornithological works as exactly like that of the yellowhammer, only without the thin, drawn-out note at the end and therefore inferior – 'the little bit of bread, but without the cheese'. It certainly resembles the yellowhammer's song, being a short note, a musical chirp, rapidly repeated several times, but the yellowhammer varies his song as to its time, the notes being sometimes fast and sometimes slow. The cirl's song is always the same in this respect and is always a more rapid song than that of the other species.

Maybe it was not until the arrival of warmer summers and milder winters at the end of the eighteenth century that the cirl bunting spread north across the Channel and as a result Gilbert White did not confuse this pretty bunting with the yellowhammer. We shall probably never know.

What we can be sure of is that the trend noticed by Edward Grey at the beginning of the century continued and we are left with only around two hundred and fifty pairs in this country. The cirl is a sedentary bird, which in winter flocks with other seed-eating finches in the fields, and is very susceptible to hard winters. The very cold winters of 1962–3 and 1970–1 combined with an increasing contraction in their source of winter feed had a devastating effect on numbers and as a result their only real stronghold is now in Devon, the bird having become very rare in Hampshire. The cirl has been dangerously affected by habitat removal in more ways than one. Hudson refers to the cirl as our domestic bunting; and it was perhaps more commonly known as the village bunting. Their nests were often to be found in spacious gardens and the removal of trees and hedgerows from our rural villages as they have expanded in linear fashion has no doubt adversely affected them.

An entry in Edward Grey's *Cottage Book* for 22 May 1902 reads thus:

> I went with Dorothy on Tuesday to be shown a stone curlew's egg – we spied and stalked and crept and saw a stone curlew standing by a ragged lonely whin bush on the down like a sentinel. As we got nearer it trotted off with the skip of a ghost in the evening light, passed the nest and disappeared. In the nest we found one egg and one young bird hatched since the day before which lay flat and uttered. Both the egg and the bird are coloured to match chalk flints that have been a long time among mole heaps.

When Grey made this entry in *The Cottage Book* the stone curlew was well on its way to becoming a breeding rarity in Hampshire. Today there are probably only around a hundred and fifty breeding pairs in Britain and they are mostly confined to the East Anglian brecklands. R. Bowdler Sharpe in his edited version of *Selbourne* (1899) hinted at their decline:

> I have seen many pairs on Salisbury Plain and the occasional pair on the downs above Avington but near Selbourne the species is much less plentiful than it was in Gilbert White's days.

He goes on to tell us what a certain Professor Bell wrote (around 1880):

> I have occasionally heard its cry late in the evening as it passed at considerable height above the village, but in thirty years I have never seen one alive or dead.

Almost a hundred years earlier, Gilbert White wrote in his Selbourne diaries:

> I wonder that the stone curlew should be mentioned by writers as a rare bird; it abounds in the champaign parts of Hampshire and Sussex and breeds I think all summer having young ones I know very late in the autumn.

The real decline has taken place in the last forty years as a result of changes in farming practices. My father-in-law, Robin Hastings, would tell me how his King Charles spaniel, Rupert, would chase 'the thick-kneed bustard' on the chalk downs above Bramdean in the 1950s. As soon as these chalk grasslands were converted to arable farmland the bird vanished. The stone curlew frequents dry stony ground with sparse or short vegetation mainly overlying chalk. Like its close cousin the lapwing, it must have a short sward for feeding. On farmland, spring-sown crops may become too dense by early summer and it will therefore

STONE CURLEWS at NEST

need to move to nearby grassland with its chicks. Many crops are today sown in winter and are therefore unavailable as a nesting site in early spring. Rolling the ground and crop spraying will also lead to nest destruction. Disturbance by farmers is not a recent phenomenon; as Gilbert White wrote in 1768:

> It lays its eggs usually two but never more than three on bare ground without any nest in the field so that the countrymen in stirring its fallows often destroys them.

There has been a general decline in mixed farming in the south of England which has adversely affected the stone curlew. It has a particular liking for sugar beet or maize which remain open until midsummer and are close to feeding grounds on pasture. Between the wars, during the agricultural depression, some suitable marginal land, no longer cultivated, saw a small increase in stone curlew numbers; however, the drastic reduction in the rabbit population in the 1950s as a result of myxomatosis allowed scrub to develop and engulf downland sites. For the stone curlew it has been downhill ever since.

The stone curlew is a summer visitor arriving as early as March and leaving in October. British birds winter in Spain, France and North Africa and White stated that they were the earliest of our summer arrivals along with the chiffchaff and wryneck. A few birds sometimes overwinter in southern England which may well explain the 24 January 1774 entry in the Gilbert White *Journals*: 'Stone curlews still appear on Temple Farm.'

The stone curlew takes its name from the terrain it frequents and from its thin high-pitched 'coor-lee' call similar to that of the curlew. As mentioned earlier it is a member of the plover family so the name is rather misleading. It is a strange looking creature and perhaps even rather 'spookie', as suggested in Grey's *Cottage Book* entry. The 'thick-kneed bustard' is a more appropriate name as its long strong yellow legs and prominent yellow eye give it a distinctive look; the name 'bustard' also throws up connotations of a grassland-loving bird that spends most of the time on its feet rather than on the wing. The large prominent eye indicates a bird that moves and feeds at twilight or later and its eerie cry is often heard at night. It moves with a slow deliberate gait with its back hunched like a deformed old man.

The stone curlew has declined drastically in numbers over the past hundred years. In the late 1930s Yorkshire lost the last of her breeding population when the total number of British pairs was around fifteen hundred – today the number has declined to a tenth of that. There is, however, some good cause for optimism. The cooperation of farmers and careful management of certain grassland sites by conservation groups may reverse the bird's decline. In addition, and perhaps most promising of all, the recent moves to cut back cereal production and set aside arable land, should have a beneficial effect on this unusual bird in the long term.

In *Hampshire Days*, W. H. Hudson describes the old chalk pit by Grey's cottage:

> Yet it was a great place but a few yards away at the side of the old lime trees and in the small protecting fence. The entrance to it and its wide floor was on a level with the green valley, while at its upper end it formed a steep bank, forty feet high. It was doubtless a very old pit with sides that had the appearance of natural cliffs and were overhung and draped with thorn trees, masses of old ivy and traveller's joy. Inside it was a pretty tangled wilderness; on the floor many tall annuals flourished – knapweed and thistle and dark mullien and teazel, six to eight feet high. Then came good-sized trees, ash and oak, thorn, bramble and elder in masses. It was a favourite breeding place of birds of many species; even the red-backed shrike nested there within forty yards of human habitation, and the kingfisher has safely reared his young, unsuspected by the barbarous waterkeeper.

I have a vivid childhood memory of a ghoulish picture of a red-backed shrike. The bird was sitting on a gorse bush and gloating over the corpse of some unfortunate fledgling which it had impaled on a sharp thorn. The red-backed shrike is also known as the 'butcher bird'. It acquired this unattractive name as a result of a tendency to 'larder' its victims. The shrike, like the fox, will kill more than it requires and store the surplus on the spikes of a thorn bush. Tennyson writes in his poem *Maud*:

> For nature is one with rapine, a harm no preacher can
> heal;
> The mayfly is torn by the swallow, the sparrow
> speared by the shrike;
> And the whole little wood where I sit is a world of
> plunder and prey.

The main diet of the red-backed shrike consists of larger insects such as beetles, dragonflies, butterflies and grasshoppers. It will also take more substantial prey such as frogs, lizards and young birds. It is a bird of open heathland and commons with scattered bushes and trees which offer a good vantage point for spying prey. The bird is quite hawk-like in behaviour, it will fly fast down hedgerows, swoop, carry prey in its feet and hover.

This beautiful shrike, which is a summer migrant, has sadly become a very rare bird in Britain over the last fifty years. Even though it bred in most of the southern counties of England around the turn of the century, it has always been thinly spread. Gilbert White considered it a scarce bird and procured one on 21 May 1768, which, in a letter to Pennant in the *Natural History of Selborne*, he says:

> might easily have escaped notice had not the outcries and chatterings of the whitethroats and other small birds drawn attention to the bush where it was.

The decline of the red-backed shrike has really taken place since the Second World War; in 1952 there were three hundred breeding pairs but by 1971 the number had declined to eighty-five. The last recorded breeding pairs nested in East Anglia in the late 1980s.

The most widely quoted reason for their decline lies with the climate. While there has been an overall improvement in the weather during the present century, summers have tended to be wet and windy with a resulting shortage of flying insects, which represent the red-backed shrike's principal source of food. East Anglia is the driest part of the country and least affected by our maritime climate, which could explain why the red-backed shrike made its last stand in the Norfolk Brecks. Other factors in its decline must be the huge increase in the use of insecticides and the accelerating loss of our heathland habitat. Another reason which must be taken seriously is the damage done by egg collectors; their eggs vary extensively and are therefore much sought after, as evidenced by Grey:

> One or two species have the misfortune to be variable in the colour of their eggs; clutch after clutch is then taken by egg collectors that they may have examples of every type of egg of this one species represented in their collection. The tree pipit suffers from this misfortune and it is said that the number of clutches of tree pipits' eggs to be found in a single collection is sometimes infamous. The red-backed shrike is reported to suffer in the same way, but the only eggs I have found of this bird have been of one type. It is a curious type: the ends

of the egg are without markings, but a zone or girdle of thick-set spots goes round the egg not far from the larger end.

It is obvious from the writings of White, Hudson and Grey that the red-backed shrike was never a common bird in Britain; however, just over a hundred years ago it was breeding within yards of the Cottage. Today it is in all likelihood lost to us forever as a breeding bird.

Sunday, 16 July

Arrived back at Parwich Lees yesterday afternoon following Jean's funeral on Friday at Bramdean Church. We had a lovely service followed by a lunch for close friends.

It has 'greened-up' a little but it is still very dry and the ponds are lower than I can remember.

I went to church at Alsop this morning and a blackbird entertained us from the churchyard. A song thrush was also in fine voice in our garden before breakfast. It just shows there are no hard and fast rules as to when they cease singing, although most blackbirds have been silent for well over a fortnight now.

This afternoon I took advantage of a rare shower of rain to go for a walk down the Bletch – the flies were terrible. The willow warblers and blackcaps have fallen silent and the only warbler that made its presence known was a whitethroat from deep in the hawthorn bank. On my return I flushed a young pheasant from the long grass. Another cheeper flew off over the hedge, as the agitated mother ran around me in circles, calling angrily. It's good to see some wild birds.

This is an excellent time for wild flowers. I find the harebell particularly attractive, which does well on our limestone banks. Also the wild geranium (meadow crane's-bill) which is very common by the roadsides in July. Both are a pretty sky blue.

Wednesday, 19 July

We are taking advantage of the dry weather and improving the drainage in the bottom meadow – the JCB is here for the day.

Stan White told me he saw a brood of young partridges on his Tissington farm last week. We have the odd pair most years, but I've only seen them on one occasion this year. When flushed they take off in low fast flight with a whirring of their rounded wings. They are pretty birds with an orange head and throat and the male has a distinctive chestnut horseshoe on his chest. The time I enjoy them most is at dusk when they sit on the high bank across the valley uttering their harsh grating call.

The common partridge has been one of the main victims of modern farming techniques and there is every danger that it could eventually diminish in the same way as the corncrake. It has been in serious decline since the 1950s and its population is now one fifth of what it was at its height at the turn of the century. The partridge began proliferating with the advent of hedgerows in the eighteenth and nineteenth centuries as a result of the Enclosure Acts. Their population probably peaked from 1880 to 1914 when gamekeeping was widespread. You only have to read *The Diary of Colonel Peter Hawker 1802–1853* to note how common the bird once was.

For the first five to six weeks of their lives young partridges live entirely on insects. As a result the indiscriminate use of herbicide and insecticide sprays in the 1960s and 1970s had a devastating effect. The chicks rely on insects that live both in weeds and cereal crops for their survival. In addition hundreds of miles of hedgerows have been ripped out to create larger and more productive fields. Hedgerows not only provide invaluable nest sites for partridges but also shelter numerous weeds on which life-supporting insects thrive.

Like the grouse, the partridge is a good example of where shooting and conservation go hand in hand. There are certain pockets around the country where the grey partridge is still relatively strong and these often coincide with well-managed shooting estates. On such farms you are likely to find unsprayed conservation headlands around the edges of fields to generate insect life for young birds. And stubbles are left unploughed for longer to provide a source of food for birds over the winter season.

The grey partridge is thriving in certain upland regions. The hill partridge is a tough little bird that lives on the marginal land between the heather moorland and the valley meadows. This area of 'white grass' would have at one time played host to blackgame. I have had great fun in the past waking up partridges at Arkengarthdale in Swaledale and Allenheads in Northumberland. Why do these little hill partridges do so well, when their counterparts in the south and on the low ground are vanishing? I think there are four reasons. Little silage is cut which means no sprays are used and nests are not damaged early in the season. Secondly, vermin is controlled. The partridge has two main enemies, the fox and the stoat. Keepers contain the foxes on the hill and down in the valleys they 'tunnel trap' for stoats along the stone walls. The third reason is maybe the most interesting: these hill birds are shot, but not over-shot, which tends to break up the coveys. This in turn cuts down interbreeding which can result in a surfeit of weak birds. Finally, it is important to top up their natural food source with wheat in winter, as when snow is on the ground, mortality can be high.

Partridges have great charm, not least because they are both sociable birds and excellent parents. They are strictly monogamous and pair early in the year with coveys breaking up by the end of February. For protection the covey will roost in a semi-circle facing into the wind.

GREY PARTRIDGE : DERBYSHIRE PS

The female sits very tight on her nest and like other gamebirds gives off no scent while incubating. When the young have hatched they are carefully tended by both parents. Grey describes how on first sight of danger the old birds will attack or lead off their enemy by feigning a broken wing.

> I came quietly and suddenly upon them; the young were in down, without a feather; flying was out of the question for them and the covey disappeared at once into the impenetrable brambles – all but two of the little birds: these adopted the alternative concealment of squatting on the open grass. I stood still, with these two birds at my feet, and waited to see what the next move would be. There were slight movements in the brambles, and little sounds that suggested consultation between the old birds. The little birds outside remained motionless. After a few minutes one of the old birds, with great fuss and *éclat*, burst out of the brambles three or four yards in front of me, and invited pursuit by the usual manoeuvre of pretending to make frantic efforts to escape and to be unable to fly. My intention being to keep my eyes on the little birds at my feet, I did not stir limb nor head; but so sudden and noisy was the old partridge's burst from the bush, that for one instant my gaze was diverted; in that one instant the two little birds at my feet disappeared: they were gone without my seeing them go; all was quiet in the brambles, nothing to be seen or heard of the covey except the single parent trying to decoy me away. Their manoeuvres were crowned with success by my withdrawing.

Thursday, 20 July

There are two late nesters in the walled garden. Five young wrens with characteristically thin decurved bills were poking their heads out of the domed nest. It is lodged in between a rack on the wall for garden tools and one of the implements hanging there. The nest has been in the potting shed for many months now and I thought it was unoccupied. This is proof that the male builds several 'cock' nests, one of which is chosen by the female and lined by her. In the winter these nests are used as communal roosts.

A woodpigeon is sitting on its nest about twelve feet up in an apple tree. The nest is a flimsy platform of twigs and you can see the white eggs through the bottom. When the squabs hatch they are fed on pigeon's milk for a good month before they fledge.

Sunday, 23 July

Arrived at Tarbert (Argyll) to take the ferry to Islay – *en route* for Jura – at noon, after a three-hour drive from Lanark. Lucinda has gone down to Hampshire to organise her mother's house so I am left with two yelping Jack Russells and a couple of over-excited boys.

We had an uneventful crossing. The sea was choppy, but the sun shone and we spent a good deal of time on deck. The birdlife was relatively unexciting, probably because it is rather early in the year. We normally go on holiday to Jura a month or so later. At that time when you pass Gigha and move well into the Sound of Jura, the sea is littered with families of guillemots and razorbills which have recently left their clifftop nesting grounds.

Aside from the odd gannet that swept so close to the stern of the boat that you could clearly see its bright yellow head, the star performers were the shearwaters and fulmers. Both birds have long thin wings which allow them to glide effortlessly for thousands of miles as they wander the oceans. They are aptly named birds. Shearwaters remind me of trapeze artists as they twist and turn on the air currents. They vanish into the troughs of the waves skimming the water with their wing tips as they go. When their underbellies catch the sun, they appear black one minute and snow white the next. The Manx shearwater is a bird of the open seas which only alights on land to breed and even then at night to escape the marauding black-backed gulls. They nest deep in rabbit burrows which echo with their spooky wailing cries as they call to their mates rafting out at sea. This eerie choir has given rise to many a good ghost story. The shearwater has an amazing in-built navigation system. A bird from the Welsh island at Skokholm was released in Boston in the US and took just over twelve days to return the three thousand or so miles to its burrow.

We arrived at Port Ellen just after 3.00 p.m. and drove the short distance across Islay to Port Askaig, the pretty little fishing port where you catch the ferry to Jura. After a five-minute crossing and a forty-minute drive north you reach Tarbert Lodge, the Jura home of the Astor family. The estate was bought in 1919 from the Campbells of Jura by William's grandparents, who themselves lived at Cliveden. The main house on the estate was originally Ardlussa, at the north-east end of the island. Tarbert was then just a small lodge but it has been extended at various times since the last war; it occupies a lovely position sitting above the bay. William was at the Lodge to meet us and we immediately took off for Glenbatrick, their 'summer house' on the west coast.

As we went down the drive to the boathouse, a pair of buzzards glided gently on the wind, the underside of their wings appearing quite white from the ground. They are easily recognisable by their chunky size, soaring flight and a characteristic mewing call that carries considerable distances. There have been buzzards at Tarbert for as long as I can remember and I have been coming to Jura for twenty-five years. Neil McInnes, the head stalker, says that today there are around eight pairs on

JURA • The Tarbert Estate
SCARBA
GULF OF
CORRYVRECKAN
CORPACH
YOUNG
GOLDEN EAGLE
& THE PAPS OF
JURA
ARDLUSSA
JURA
COLONSAY
SHIAN
TARBERT
BOAT
HOUSE
ORONSAY
RUBH'
an t-SAILEIN
THE
NARROWS
LOCH
TARBERT
GLENBATTRICK
CAIRIDH MHOR
RUBHA
A MHAIL
PAPS
OF JURA
SMALL ISLES
CRAIGHOUSE
FEOLIN FERRY
ISLAY
PORT
ASKAIG
JURA
HOUSE
LOCH
GRUINART
SOUND OF ISLAY
(RSPB)
McARTHUR'S
HEAD
PSnow

the Tarbert Estate alone (approximately twenty thousand acres). Their fortunes in the past were closely linked to gamekeeping and the availability of rabbits. Although they would find it hard to resist a brood of young pheasants, their diet consists largely of rabbits and carrion. In the early 1950s with the advent of myxomatosis their range contracted significantly. This was made worse by chemicals used in sheep dips as they turned to carrion to survive. This in turn made them susceptible to poisoned baits put down by gamekeepers. Although there is a small winter shoot at Tarbert today, this was not so in the past. Thus they were not persecuted by the gillies. On Jura their staple diet of rabbit is supplemented by a plentiful supply of adders. Between August and December in the stalking season, they will join the hoodies, ravens and golden eagles on any convenient grallock. The culling of the red deer on Jura provides an important source of food for a number of the island's largest birds.

BUZZARDS P.S.

With less oppressive and more enlightened gamekeepering, coupled with a resurgent rabbit population, the buzzard is increasing its range from its traditional strongholds in Scotland, Wales and the West Country.

A normal boat journey from the Lodge to Glenbatrick takes about forty-five minutes. Once out of the cosy anchorage and through the narrows you are out into Loch Tarbert. You pass Cairidh Mhor (the loch where we fish for sea trout) and then move out into Glenbatrick Bay. It is a journey of breathtaking beauty and full of interesting wildlife. The narrows on the edge of Loch Tarbert present the best chance of seeing one of Jura's most charismatic birds – the peregrine falcon. Each year a pair nests successfully at this remote spot, bringing off on average three chicks every two years.

When out on the hill with Neil I always enjoy hearing him talk about Jura birdlife. He has two vivid memories of a peregrine 'stooping' on its prey. On the one occasion his dog flushed a woodcock near his house and a peregrine appeared from nowhere to carry it off. The other was even more bizarre. They were fishing from a boat on the Ardlussa Loch and a blackcock flew along the bank only to be ambushed by a waiting peregrine.

Monday, 24 July

There can be few more beautiful spots on the west coast of Scotland than the little walled garden at Glenbatrick. The west coast of the island is totally uninhabited and the house that was once used by stalking parties and their ponies is today occupied for summer holidays in July and August. It is snugly wedged between the sandy shore and the raised beach, its dry stone walls built of smooth round boulders carved by the action of the sea over thousands of years. Inside the house, portable gas cylinders provide both light and hot water, and each room has a welcoming coal fire. The thick stone walls are insulated with seasoned pine and attractively edged in sea shells.

If you look directly east up the great glen you are confronted by staggering beauty. Its rugged sides run up to nearly two thousand feet and in the distance, directly above the raised beach, are the towering Paps of Jura, today capped in cloud. These are products of the Pleistocene Ice

Age, which only receded some fifteen thousand years ago, when the English Channel was formed. This is not long when you think that man has been on earth for several million years. The deep U-shaped glen, the smooth form of the Paps and the characteristic raised beaches are all by-products of the glaciers. The ice gouged out the glen, rounded and smoothed the hard quartzite rock of the Paps and then, when it melted, caused the sea level to rise which in turn created the raised beaches.

To the west you gaze out across the beach to the little seal-inhabited islands which provide a safe anchorage for our boats, then across Rubh' an t-Sailein point and away to Colonsay and Oronsay in the far distance. Aside from Glenbatrick, the scenery of the north-west coast of Jura is the loveliest on the island. It runs from Rubh' an t-Sailein at its southern point right round to Barnhill at the north end (where George Orwell wrote *Nineteen Eighty-Four*), and consists of miles of rugged shoreline with sandy bays, huge caves and spectacular waterfalls.

Glenbatrick Bay provides a perfect staging post for many waders on their long journey from their breeding grounds in the Arctic to their warmer winter quarters in the Mediterranean or Africa. When the tide is full you hear the distant cry of an oyster catcher, redshank or curlew, but when the tide recedes to expose the muddy seaweed a typical 'wader gathering' soon develops.

Although it is still early for the main migration southwards a small flock of dunlin were busy feeding at the edge of the shore before breakfast. They were probing in the seaweed along with some pied wagtails eager to feats on any disturbed insect life. Dunlin are incessant feeders that constantly prod the sand, and are agile in flight, darting this way and that. They flit back like dainty butterflies as a wave threatens to break over them. They were in their summer plumage looking most dapper with their jet-black tummies. The one wader you can be sure of seeing on Glenbatrick beach, and which often enjoys the company of the dunlin, is the ringed plover. As the tide turned in the evening and the first bed of seaweed was exposed, a group of eight came skimming in across the bay from their roost to gorge themselves on the tideline. They are not so active as dunlin and tend to pause between a series of fast pottering runs. In flight the bird gives a lovely soft evocative call, 'too-lee', and displays a distinctive white wing bar. This little plover is the master of camouflage. It needs to be as it nests on open shingle beaches. The ringed plumage blends perfectly into a surrounding of sand, stones and shells and unless you are aware of the eggs you will find them impossible to spot among the pebbly background. I have found their nests at Needs Ore along with those of the oystercatcher. The wardens wire them off to avoid the eggs being crushed. Statistics show that over sixty per cent of ring plover nests in Britain are unsuccessful with the figure rising to eighty-five per cent on the east coast.

We spent the morning at Cairidh Mhor where we failed to rise a fish. A whitethroat was singing in the bracken behind the fishing hut and a common sandpiper did a quick circuit of the loch, piping loudly before it vanished. Both were new to me on Jura; no doubt because we are here a month earlier than usual. When we normally come in August the sandpipers have finished nesting and are on their way south.

Tuesday, 25 July

A beautiful day with a strong south-east wind. A pair of choughs were playfully working their way along the raised beach uttering their characteristically shrill cries. Choughs were re-released on Islay in the 1960s and soon spread to Jura, where they are now established on the cliffs in the south west. The chough is a relation of the jackdaw with a long thin curved crimson beak. It used to be called the Cornish chough but it no longer occurs in the south-west peninsula, with its strongholds now being on the south-west coasts of Ireland and Pembrokeshire. Only around a thousand pairs now breed in the British Isles.

After breakfast I walked along the beach towards the mouth of the river and high in the sky I heard a deep, rapidly repeated duck-like 'kwuck'. There are few sounds more evocative of Jura than that of the red-throated diver. It is a bird more often heard than seen, because it tends to fly home to the hills from fishing trips at sea at a great height. Unlike the black-throated diver which prefers to frequent large lochs where it can also feed, the red-throated nests by the side of small hill lochans and will fly off to fish in the sea every day.

After searching the sky for some time I was able to make out a tiny shape with a long neck and pointed wings. This diver attracted the name 'raingoose' because the locals thought that its call was the harbinger of rain and bad weather. The red-throated diver is quite common on Jura and it is not unusual when approaching Loch Tarbert by boat to see one

take off from Glenbatrick Bay. A pair of black throats once nested on Loch Reig Beag but this is rare. Our most beautiful diver is the great northern which we rarely see in its glorious breeding plumage as it nests in the far north. A good number come and winter in the area of Loch Tarbert.

There are an estimated fifteen hundred pairs of red throats in Britain – ten times the number of black throats. Human disturbance and predation are the main causes of breeding failure, but there is a general concern that the population as a whole is being affected by declining fish stocks and a loss of breeding sites to forestry.

Wednesday, 26 July

A swelteringly hot day. I finished my book on Jackie Fisher in the sun and took the boys to swim under the waterfall in the river. We then tried the sea which was colder but very invigorating.

I swam out to one of the little islands in the bay. They offer panoramic views in both directions. The Lodge, already dwarfed by the raised beach, looks like a miniature doll's house against a background of the great glen. Inquisitive seals barked and frolicked in the seaweed like playful puppies. Oystercatchers piped angrily from their rocky roost and unseen in the heavens a red-throated diver ominously warned of changing weather. Across the bay from deep within the bracken a yellowhammer monotonously beat out his lazy tune. Another sure sign that we are visiting early this year.

There are few interesting waders stopping off in the bay – we are just that little bit too early. The main attraction was a group of around twenty-five noisy oystercatchers who have made the bay their summer home. They feed among the rocks, sand and seaweed at low tide and roost on the islands when the tide is up.

It is not hard to develop an immediate affection for these colourful birds. Their crowning glory is a bright red eye and bill which contrasts sharply with the pied plumage – after these delights their pink legs are a bit of a disappointment. Although you cannot tell the sexes apart, you can differentiate the young birds as they have a dark eye and a black tip to their bill. The noisy piping calls of the adults are territorial. The birds waddled along the sand calling loudly; with their hunched backs and hesitant gait they reminded me of little old ladies.

The oystercatcher is Britain's most successful wader with the indigenous birds increasing at a steady rate. The name is now a misnomer as they have spread up the river valleys and taken to a diverse food source. The coastal birds continue to take shellfish such as cockles and small crabs, but those that have moved inland have joined farmland birds such as rooks and lapwings in probing for earthworms.

Nobody knows why they have moved inland; perhaps it was human disturbance but this must be considered unlikely as the process started over a hundred years ago, when Edward Grey was fishing his Scottish rivers. Their success has probably been just a classic case of adaptation. If they probe for lugworms on the shore why shouldn't they feed on earthworms in the river valleys?

Thursday, 27 July

Another beautiful day but with less wind going round into the south. In the morning we fished at Cairidh Mhor where William, with a little help from his godson Robin, caught a five-pound seatrout on a spinner. This is probably the most prolific loch on the island. The top end of a small bay was dammed by William's grandfather and by way of a series of concrete pools and 'ladders' the fish can run up at high tide. When there is enough water the fish will continue up to the two bigger lochs higher in the hills.

As we left Glenbatrick for Cairidh Mhor a pair of common terns with one young bird were perched on the rocks. These birds have become very rare on Jura. I heard a tern squeaking out in the bay yesterday, but it is some years since I have seen them on Jura. Neil said it was the first time he had sighted a tern this year. They suddenly left the island about eight years ago. They used to nest in their hundreds on the islands in front of the boathouse. Neil told me, 'I looked for the arrival of the terns on 12 May as surely as the stags break out on 22 September each year.' I think the most likely reason for their absence is a scarcity of food. Their staple diet, the sand eel, is currently being indiscriminately hoovered up by the Danish fishing fleet off our northern coasts.

Sitting by the fishing hut at Cairidh Mhor, I watched a sparrow hawk try unsuccessfully to take a meadow pipit above the loch. As you would expect in this wild and mountainous environment most birds of prey are represented on Jura. If the peregrine is our most spectacular hunter, then the hen harrier is our most ruthless. This year I have not seen one on the island almost certainly because we have spent our time at Glenbatrick which lies in the heart of the 'deer forest'. Like the buzzard, the hen harrier is a bird that prefers to frequent the lower ground and the young conifer plantations on the east side of the island. It is a long-winged, long-tailed bird of prey which glides systematically over the hill with its wings held in a shallow V. You can well understand why the sportsman dislikes it. It criss-crosses the hillside in a methodical fashion, killing everything it comes across, particularly grouse. It is a very diligent bird. There are very few grouse left on Jura because of both the lack of suitable heather and the number of predators. I can remember shooting twenty brace on my first visit to Jura in 1972 and we have hardly shot a bird since. The crofters have overgrazed the low ground ('the flats') on the east of the island and good young heather is very scarce. The harriers have been forced to look for food elsewhere and as a result the smaller bird population on the island is suffering.

Hen harriers are very beautiful birds that have a conspicuous white rump. The male bird is a distinctive dove-grey and from a distance can look quite gull-like. I was staying with Willie Russell at Drimore in South Uist in the early 1980s and was on his tractor going down the drive when a cock harrier flew past. I had a preconceived idea that all birds of prey were brown and had absolutely no idea what it was. Neil had the same experience on Jura in the 1950s. His first sighting demonstrated just how rare this bird had become through persecution. It had been forced to retreat to a stronghold in the Outer Hebrides and at this time was just beginning to move out. Today it has spread

throughout Scotland and down across England. There are now probably up to eight pairs on Tarbert alone. Imagine what damage they can do to the wildlife. This year Neil said that he didn't think there were so many pairs on Tarbert. Maybe the increased harrier population is no longer able to support itself? Nature's cycle is constantly turning and as Grey writes in *The Charm of Birds*:

> It is often so with anything specially interesting observed in nature: hopes are raised and then disappointed, or it may be the reverse: there is an increase and decrease, ebb and flow, waxing and waning.

In the afternoon we swam in both the river and the sea at high tide. A wren sang lustily from the raised beach behind the house and a cock whinchat perched prominently on a spray of bracken 'chatting' loudly, conspicuous by his white eyestripe and buff chest.

Friday, 28 July

I was to have gone stalking with Neil but down came the mist. Also early in the seeason the stags are very high up so we decided it was not worthwhile. A major disappointment was missing the chance to see a golden eagle. There are now three pairs on Jura, but at one time there were almost certainly more. A pair always used to nest above Cairidh Mhor until the sheep were taken off that part of the island. *The New Atlas of Breeding Birds* tells us:

> Watson (1989) measured population parameters in nine areas of the Highlands and Islands and related differences to land use and ultimately food. They showed that density was related to the amount of carrion available in late winter, and thus highest densities occurred in Western Scotland where sheep carrion were particularly plentiful.

On Jura there is little natural food as the grouse and hare are scarce. The deer are well culled and there are few sheep on the hill. A combination of these factors keeps eagle numbers down in an ideal terrain. Jura is Gaelic for 'deer island' and there is no doubt that the red deer provide their basic diet. Last year Humphrey Wakefield shot three stags in the 'park' at Tarbert Lodge and we dragged them off the hill in the afternoon. Two eagles appeared within the hour and soared over the grallocks. They have telescopic eyesight.

Another bird which enjoys a free meal on the grallock of a red deer is the raven. About this time of year they start moving in from Mull and other islands to take advantage of the additional food source. If the call of the red-throated diver brings memories flooding back of fishing on the Oisedale or boating at Glenbatrick, it is the harsh croak of the raven that is so evocative of a day's stalking high up in the glen.

After lunch the boys and I went with William in the boat to pick up Norman and Rosemary Lamont from Port Askaig on Islay. In spite of a difficult period in office as Chancellor of the Exchequer he jovially says 'politics is still the greatest game in town'. He loves birds and is a knowledgeable ornithologist. He was thrilled when William took him down to the narrows in the boat and they sighted both adult peregrines over the nest site – 'so close that we saw the black moustache'.

We arrived back on a very low tide and there was a typical wader-gathering at the mouth of the river in the bay. At least twenty-five ringed plover, three dunlin, six redshank and a single turnstone. The turnstone is chunkier and bigger than the dunlin and ringed plover. It moves around the seaweed turning over little stones in search of insects and small crustaceans. This particular bird was in its lovely summer plumage – a rich chestnut brown and black which formed a dazzling tortoiseshell pattern.

In past years when we have visited in late August or early September I have seen more interesting waders in the bay. Last year a group of ten knot sat on the rocks by the mouth of the river. Initially I thought they were purple sandpipers because they were so tame. However, they had giveaway greenish legs, and one of the birds had a slight russet hue on its chest. They fluttered their wings in a dainty fashion and one or two of them were 'swimming' in the water like phalaropes.

In 1993 I saw a party of nine little stint on the shore. They are very dunlin-like, although an inch or so smaller and with a shorter beak. They are busy little feeders that suck continuously rather than probe. You can approach very close as they can be quite tame and you will see a white-bellied bird with a russet neck and markings similar to those of a hen pheasant. The first time I saw one at Glenbatrick (11 August 1992) a pair rose at my feet and surprised me by their tiny size.

On 4 September 1986 a solitary bar-tailed godwit visited the bay. It is more of a tideline bird than its cousin the black-tailed godwit and has shorter legs. It is the only straight-billed brownish wader with a white V on its back and it does not have the unmistakable black-and-white wings and dangling legs of its black-tailed relative.

Saturday, 29 July

Our last day as we leave tomorrow morning for the ferry home.

Aside from the pied wagtails there are two small birds that are frequent visitors to the little garden at Glenbatrick. A family of wheatears have been flitting around the dunes for most of the week but now seem to have moved south. They are one of the first migrants to arrive and among the earliest to depart. Rock pipits are exclusively coastal and search for food among the seaweed and rocks. Unlike our own meadow pipits at home which move south in winter, rock pipits are resident and do not move far from their territories. They are darker and larger than their close cousins.

I walked down to the shore before breakfast. There were two small yachts moored in the bay, otherwise I could have been the only person in the world. A pair of duck were nosing around in the seaweed at the mouth of the river. I knew at once that they were common scoter. I had seen them on two of my last three visits to Jura and there was no sign of the telltale profile of the eider duck. The common scoter is in fact a misnomer as they are quite rare, particularly at this time of the year, with only about a hundred pairs nesting in Scotland. The favoured habitat is a small lochan in the Flow Country, but around thirty pairs nest in nearby Islay. This solitary pair are probably an outlying family unit. As with many of our seaducks and divers, numbers are augmented from the north in winter when you are more likely to see them around our coasts and on inland reservoirs. The common scoter is a classic seaduck which appears in large rafts just out at sea; their preference is for feeding in shallow water (three to five metres) with a sandy bottom where they search for marine molluscs. The male bird is our only totally black duck while the female is brown with pale cheeks. They have saucy pointed tails and give the impression of great buoyancy in the water. They can be distinguished from their near relation, the velvet scoter, by the lack of a white wing bar in flight.

I cannot leave Jura without mentioning the corncrake which is facing extinction in Britain. It has been declining drastically for well over fifty years and its plight should have provided an early warning of how modern farming techniques were going to ravage our bird populations. I have never seen or heard a corncrake although I have spent a good deal of time in their last bastion, the Hebrides. They are common in the

Outer Hebrides but I have always been there at the wrong time of year. The corncrake is a summer migrant that arrives in April from south of the Sahara. It looks like an English partridge and is a secretive bird that keeps well hidden among thick cover in moist grassland. It can best be detected by its unusual croaking call.

The older farmers cannot remember hearing a corncrake in our valley in Derbyshire since the 1930s. A number of changes in our farming practices have led to its disappearance. Mechanisation destroys more nests than traditional scything and the introduction of new species of grass has led to earlier grass cutting. More recently a move from making hay to cutting silage has resulted in even earlier cuts. In northern Scotland the conversion of meadows to permanent sheep pasture has certainly led to a general decline in numbers.

Edward Grey comments on their decline in *The Charm of Birds*:

> The voice of the corncrake is now seldom heard in many places where it used to be common. No one can assert with truth that the sound is melodious; it is in fact very harsh; but it used to enliven many an early summer night in the field adjoining the garden at Fallodon and I regret that it is heard no more. Occasionally there is still a corncrake to be heard farther off but both here and about the Hampshire cottage the bird has in my recollection become rare as a breeding species.

The corncrake is still heard on the machair in the Hebrides where agricultural techniques are splendidly antiquated. On Jura it used to be a frequent visitor to the crofts of Knockcrome and Ardfernal on the east coast until even they, aided by large EC grants, upgraded their farming practices. The crofters will tell you that they still hear the odd bird calling on a cloudy night in summer; however, the future looks bleak for this strange yet charismatic visitor. Studies have shown that they are now threatened in their winter quarters and a 1991 RSPB survey concluded that there were only four hundred and seventy calling males left in the country.

ST ENODOC CHURCH, TREBETHERICK, CORNWALL. PJ.

AUGUST

Tuesday, 1 August

As if a twelve-hour drive from Jura on Sunday was not enough, yesterday evening I drove down from our Leeds office to Bramdean in Hampshire. There is still so much to organise at the house following Jean's death and we are going to Glyndebourne tonight for a performance of *The Queen of Spades*.

The beautiful weather continues with I suspect a plentiful harvest in prospect. The countryside looks more like a Mediterranean scene with the southward-facing hills burnt off into a parched brown.

I was up at 7.30 a.m. and went for a short walk by Edward Grey's cottage on the Itchen. Dabchick were whinneying from under the banks of the reedy river and, high up in the lime avenue, laughter from one green woodpecker was answered by another. It struck me that the great tits had started singing again following their silence during the rigours of the breeding season. They vanish in spring and early summer but today great tits were calling from all points. I even heard the distinctive higher-pitched song of a coal tit from across the river towards Avington.

I sat in the garden at Bramdean after breakfast on yet another scorching morning. In this weather, not unnaturally, it seems to be the lazy song that stands out. When not shuttling to and from the water trough to quench their thirsts, innumerable pigeons maintain a gentle cooing. Then there is the wheezing of greenfinches and yellowhammers from the hedgerows up on the downs. The soft piping of unseen bullfinches wafts down from the copse behind me. Overhead in the large silver birch is a noisy immature green woodpecker that had earlier been on the lawn prospecting for ants. They do well in this part of Hampshire and unlike their cousins, the spotted woodpeckers, they spend a good deal of time on the ground. Their exotic colouring and infectious laugh make them one of my favourite British birds.

Thursday, 3 August

In the evening I released a brood of my young mallard on to the Tissington village pond. They seemed happy enough nosing around in the fresh weed on the crystal clear water. A grey wagtail bobbed and flicked its tail on a stone wall by the water's edge. It has probably left its breeding ground on one of our fast flowing limestone rivers and is now making its way south. For sheer beauty the bright yellow on the underside of its rump places it in the same class as the green woodpecker. This delicate wagtail was Warde Fowler's favourite:

> All the spring and early summer the grey wagtail was among the noisy becks and burns in the north, bringing up his young under some spray-splashed stone, or the moist arch of a bridge; in July he comes southwards and from that time till December or January is constantly to be seen along Cherwell and Isis. He is content with sluggish water if he can find none that is rapid; but the sound of the falling water is as surely grateful to his ear as the tiny crustaceans he finds in it are to his palate.
>
> For some time last autumn [1884] I saw him nearly every day, either on the stonework of the weir, or walking into its gentle waterslope or running lightly over the islands of dead leaves in other parts of the Cherwell; sometimes one pair would be playing among the barges on the Isis, and another at Clasper's boat-house seemed quite unconcerned at the crowd of men and boats. It is always a pleasure to watch them; and though all wagtails have their charm for me, I give this one the first place, for its matchless delicacy of form and the gentle grace of all its actions.

Later in the evening I went down to the valley to feed the ducks where an expectant gathering of around sixty mallard greeted me. There was a glorious sunset at the end of another tropical day. The odd willow warbler was singing in the hawthorn but with little of the sweetness of May.

Back at the house the spotted flycatcher that nested behind the hinge of the barn door has brought off two young in a second brood. At the top of a large sycamore in the park a female great spotted woodpecker, identifiable by the lack of a crimson nape, repeated her sharp 'tchick' call before disappearing into the setting sun.

Sunday, 6 August

The heatwave continues – it has been sweltering all weekend. I walked down the Bletch before lunch. A heron lazily took off from my duckpond calling harshly. When I arrived at the Tissington pond further down the valley the whinchat family were still in residence. On a hot silent day in early August the tinkling of goldfinches is everywhere as they feed acrobatically on the thistle stems. The woodpeckers are still fairly vociferous. A green woodpecker laughed loudly from the top of a large ash tree by the duckpond and the female great spotted has been back twice to the sycamore by our house.

As I walked home I heard the sharp churring call of a mistle thrush. After the breeding season mistle thrushes leave their individual territories and take to foraging in open country in family groups. These flocks can often be as large as fifty and at a distance can be confused with fieldfares. It is still a couple of months too early for the latter to arrive from Scandinavia. Today a party of around fifteen mistle thrushes were feeding on the berries of the mountain ash in the hawthorn bank plantation.

Thursday, 10 August

The family has left for Cornwall so after spending the day in our Leeds office I drove to North Yorkshire to spend the night with the Becketts (my sister and brother-in-law) at Rievaulx.

The drought continues – the beech trees at Parwich Lees have gone quite brown. It was a beautiful evening with a cloudless sky and a cool east breeze. Rick and I went for a walk ending up on the terraces above the abbey which was bathed in the evening sun. The west side of the valley was in deep shadow with the setting sun just catching the tops of the ash trees. They appeared almost white as their slender leaves turned in the wind.

What a contrast to my walk here in early May. Aside from the screaming of a pair of jays and the crashing of three fallow deer through the dense undergrowth the woods at Greencliffe Hagg were totally silent. There was not even a wren singing and it is still just too early for the autumnal song of the robin.

The jay is a bird of the oakwoods and therefore one that we rarely see at home. In autumn jays pluck the acorns from the trees and fly off and bury them in the ground. We have just four mature oak trees at Parwich Lees and the only time I have seen them was in October 1994 when they were doing exactly that. In *A Foot in England*, W. H. Hudson unerringly describes their chilling call.

> A little later a jay screemed at me, as only a jay can. There are times when I am intensely in sympathy with the feeling expressed in this ear-splitting sound, inarticulate but human. It is at the same time warning and execration, the startled solitary's outburst of uncontrolled rage at the abhorred sight of a fellow-being in his woodland haunt.

The jay is one of our more decorative birds with a distinctive white rump, bright blue wing coverts and a pinkish-brown

JAYS

chest. At a certain time of the year they become ruthless predators and during the nesting season take the eggs and young of other birds. Apart from the damage they do, they are shy birds and their slow undulating flight makes them hard to hit. Outside the breeding season they move about in small groups and often fly in a line one after the other. If you shoot a jay overhead you should always be ready for another following. I was once 'back gun' in a wood shooting with an old Cambridge friend, Alastair Campbell, at his home Everlands in Kent, and I shot three in this fashion. Even the famous ornithologist Warde Fowler has little sympathy for them:

> And I shall only mention in passing the jays, the magpies and the crows, those mischievous and predatory birds which probably do more harm to the game in a single week of April or May than the beautiful mice-eating kestrel does during the whole year. They all rob the nests of the pheasants and partridges, both of eggs and young; and when I saw one day in the wood the bodies of some twenty robbers hung up on a branch, all belonging to these three species, I could not but feel that justice had been done, for it is not only game birds who are their victims. A large increase of these three species would probably have a serious result on the smaller winged population of a wood.

Sunday, 13 August

Blenheim day! (Interestingly enough 1704 was also the year in which the Wood family built the three-storey redbrick mansion at Fallodon which was destroyed by fire in 1917 and then rebuilt by Grey.) Arrived in Cornwall yesterday after an exhausting train journey from Derby to Bodmin via Newton Abbot. We are staying with friends in a rented house overlooking Daymor Bay near Polzeath which is on the north coast.

I have just eaten breakfast with a large group of herring gulls at my feet. I suspect that 'seagulls' are most people's least favourite category of bird; they certainly are mine. They are noisy, aggressive and great scavangers. Herring gulls haunt fish quays, picking up offal and refuse. Local-authority rubbish tips are a real favourite, attracting flocks all year round on the coast.

When a free meal is in the offing herring gulls become quite tame. Then even these most unattractive birds develop a charm and beauty of their own. At close quarters the herring gull is a handsome specimen. The adult bird is pearl grey in colour with pink legs and black wing tips. Most interesting is the large yellow downward-curved beak. Not as threatening as a black back's but nasty just the same. The bill incorporates a red dab on the lower mandible. When only a few hours old, young chicks exhibit the begging behaviour so characteristic of many birds. They peck at the parent's bill, concentrating their efforts on this red patch on the lower side. This is an inborn automatic reaction and the parent is stimulated to regurgitate a mass of partially digested food which is then fed by the adult a morsel at a time to the young.

There were two first-year birds in my breakfast party. They have little to recommend them, being a drab spotted pale brown with dark tails and wing tips. Because young herring gulls are brown and become progressively paler as they mature, it is possible to work out their age much more easily than with most birds. Their cousins, the black-headed gulls, have now lost their sooty caps which they acquire in the nesting season.

Later in the morning we hired bicycles and rode the five miles or so from Wadebridge down to Padstow along the Camel Trail. It used to be the old railway line which opened for passenger traffic in 1899 and closed sixty-eight years later. A tragically short life for what Sir John Betjeman described as the most beautiful train journey he knew. At low tide the Camel Estuary is a favourite place for many different species of wading birds and the trail makes an excellent vantage point for enjoying them. When I made the same journey in August 1990 there were greenshank and green sandpipers feeding on the explosed mud and sands, but today only large flocks of curlew and oystercatchers. In all I saw about half a dozen little egrets, which just goes to show how common they are becoming on our shores in southern England. We are still, however, waiting for them to breed.

Wednesday, 16 August

We have had a highly enjoyable few days holiday with beautiful weather and plenty of good surfing. I heard a chiffchaff sing yesterday and this morning an unseen whitethroat gave a few scolding 'churrs' from deep within the garden hedge. As I sit in the early morning sun with a fog horn monotonously calling, the sea mist gently rises from the estuary to reveal golden stubble fields on the far side; the robins have commenced their autumnal song. At the bottom of the garden a coal tit calls intermittantly from a small copse of fir trees. Left for home on the train at lunchtime.

Saturday, 19 August

Back in Derbyshire the drought continues. The fields are brown and my ponds are nearly dry. I am now feeding the mallard in the pond on the Tissington bank where there is more water.

Aside from the constant tinkling of playful goldfinches the garden is very silent; even the wren is now quiet. Happily, the robins have started singing again; Grey was most grateful for this small mercy:

> These are very silent months for birds; even those that sing through July do not continue through August, though several are to be heard early in the month. There is nevertheless some interest even now, for the last of the spring songs can be heard to overlap the first of the autumn. The robin has been silent since early in July and he begins again early in August. His first autumn song should be noticed before the last undefatigable wren has decided to rest its voice and before the yellowhammer's song has ceased. Willow warblers will utter a subdued and infrequent song – its 'shadow' song, as a friend aptly calls it – but unmistakably authentic.

The robin's autumnal song is a thin warble and a little on the sad side. Maybe this is something to do with the surrounding silence. You are reminded that the summer is nearly over. That the warblers will soon be packing up and the cheerful goldfinches will depart south. I associate the song with weather changes: misty, dewey, autumnal mornings with the leaves blowing off the trees. The song produces a slight twinge of 'butterflies in the tummy'. Not as bad as going back to school but the same touch of emptiness you feel when friends leave for London after a weekend with you in the country.

Because of its red breast the robin has always occupied a special position in the hearts of Englishmen. It is also very confiding and sings more than any of our birds. The robin is a classic example of a bird that sings to establish and maintain a territory. It is extremely territorial and will aggressively defend its 'patch' from the late summer onwards. Grey thought there was a difference in the quality of the robin's song between autumn and spring:

> In autumn the song has something thin and acid in its tone. The 'bitter note of the robin' was the comment of a friend, as we passed close to a bird singing in October. In spring the song seems more vigorous: it is worthwhile to stand close to a good robin and listen attentively: some notes of fine quality will be heard. In April, when thoughts are turned towards summer warblers, I have even heard one or two notes in a robin's song that prompt the exclamation 'black-cap'! In estimating the difference between spring and autumn songs allowance must be made for the human mood and expectation of the mind. In autumn when 'the warm sun is failing, the bleak wind is wailing and the chill rain is falling, the nipped worm is crawling' and the sun is getting lower and the days shorter, our own minds are attuned to a minor key, and we find it in the robin's song. On a warm April day, when the sap is rising and we are full of anticipation, with ears a-tiptoe for the first note of the blackcap, we judge the robin's song differently. 'We used,' said a Conservative who was cutting my hair soon after the war, 'we used to think Mr Lloyd George everything that was bad. Now we admire him. Is it he or is it we that have changed?' And so I ask, listening to a robin in spring and comparing the impression remembered of the autumn, 'Is it the song or is it I that have changed'?

Tuesday, 22 August

Drove from Parwich Lees to spend the day on Anglesey. I picked Philip Snow up in Conway and then we drove over to view his exhibition on 'the island'. We arrived at Lucinda's farm at Valley at midday where we met officers from the Welsh Office as we are entering into an ESA (Environmentally Sensitive Area) scheme. You receive grants for farming in an 'ecologically sensitive' fashion which suites our conservation plans as the RSPB are in the process of acquiring eighty acres of bog on which they will raise the watertable and plant reedbeds.

It will not be long before we attract nesting marsh harriers. As we were talking to the ESA officials a female marsh harrier soared overhead, her creamy crown distinctive in the scorching sun. For one magical moment a pair of buzzards mobbed the harrier high in the sky whilst a few hundred yards away a Snowdonia Mountain Rescue helicopter practised its hovering within feet of the parched fields!

Lake Traffwll was alive with wildfowl. A gaggle of two hundred noisy greylag geese glided over the glassy water escorted by a few pochard, teal and a number of tufted duck. The latter were in the middle of their moult and looked grimey in appearance. Among them a sight which would have been totally foreign to Grey and Hudson – a flock of around twenty ruddy duck.

I will never forget my surprise at the first sight of this bird in the wild. It was on 26 July 1987 and I was looking westwards across the Blenheim Lake from the Grand Bridge. There, below me, was an extraordinary looking cinnamon duck with a pale blue beak and a stiff black tail. In the late 1950s a group of around twenty unpinioned young ruddy ducks escaped from the Wildfowl Trust at Slimbridge. These North American 'stifftails' have spread rapidly and built up a local feral population of around three thousand five hundred pairs. Ruddy ducks prefer small lakes surrounded by emergent vegetation in which they build their nests.

The Wildfowl Trust are currently worried about the ruddy duck competing with the less dominant white-headed duck which could lead to the latter's extinction. As a result Anglesey has been chosen for a controversial pilot scheme to cull ruddy duck numbers. *The New Atlas of Breeding Birds* states:

> Indeed there have already been five breeding records on the continent. This has serious implications for the small population of the white-headed duck. There have now been around eighty sightings of ruddy ducks from the Andalucian breeding grounds of the white-headed duck where male ruddy ducks are dominant over male white-headed ducks. In consequence, hybrids between the two species have already been observed. Similar hybrids at the Wildfowl Trust are fertile. It is likely there will also be a high degree of niche overlap between the ruddy duck and the white-headed duck, causing direct competition.

Thursday, 24 August

We have arrived to spend a few days' holiday with David and Rosanna Bulmer near Ledmore in Sutherland, which is just north of Ullapool. Their house, Keanchulish, is situated on Loch Kanaird roughly equidistant from the two places. This is true Highland country, wild and desolate with mountains over two thousand feet and large wind-tossed lochs. It is the natural home of the black-throated diver and ptarmigan. Although the deeply contrasting Flow Country lies some way to the north east the country also plays host to nesting waders such as greenshank, dunlin and golden plover in spring.

Along with the golden eagle, osprey, peregrine and nightingale, the black-throated diver is one of Britain's select band of charismatic birds. It is quite rare; a bird of beauty that has a mysterious and even frightening call, appropriate to these inhospitable surroundings. A pair of black throats need a territory of at least three hundred and fifty acres. They prefer large sheets of water complete with islands where they can both breed and fish. Their cousins, the red throats, on the other hand, nest on small lochans high in the hills and then fly down to the sea to feed. This pattern makes the black-throated diver much more susceptible to disturbance by man. They are sensitive birds and as such are not successful breeders. If you go within a hundred yards of a nest by boat the female will slip off her nest and into the water. With three large lochs of well over five hundred acres David has three pairs at Ledmore. Today we fished the smallest, Loch Urigill, for brown trout and saw a single bird in the water. Although the RSPB placed a floating island on a small bay in the loch as an inducement to nest, this pair failed to bring off any young. On account of its rarity and poor breeding success the black throat has been the focus of considerable conservation attention in recent years. Although these divers tend to select lochs that do not undergo significant changes in water level, their nests are often susceptible to flooding, hence the idea of the small floating island. Black throats are also only found on lochs with an abundance of small prey needed for the chicks: fish of less than two inches in size – minnows, sticklebacks,

brown trout and Arctic charr. Colonisation by pike of black-throated divers' lochs represents a serious threat to the species.

If you are fortunate enough to get close to one of these birds what strikes you is their elegance and beauty. As with all divers they lie very low in the water and sometimes all that can be seen amid the choppy waters is the head on the periscope-like neck. This presents a glorious sight, the dove-grey head contrasting with the black and white lines and jet patch on the throat. Their natural beauty is best described by Niall Rankin in *Haunts of British Divers* (1947):

> The delicate lines of the grebe are hard to equal, the erectile crest and ruffle adding a touch of real beauty, but the finely contrasted colouring of the diver's plumage is one to be marvelled at. The top of the head, cheeks and back of the neck are of the softest dove-grey. The whole of the upperparts of the body and the wings are black save for four patches of white barring, one on either side of the back at the base of the neck and one large patch on each wing. Both wings carry a few white flecks as well. But it is the head-on view of the bird that is more impressive. Below the eyes the grey fades into black which is continued down the whole of the front of the neck, except for a narrow band of white feathers just below the chin – like a miniature pearl necklace – until it ends in a sharply divided line above the pure white of the breast. Separating the black panel of the front of the neck from the grey on the back of it is a series of delicate stripes, alternating black and white, which run vertically down the side of the neck, then curve sharply backwards to be lost in the grey. The whole of the underparts are white. Below the black of the throat a second series of similar stripes starts on either side of the upper breast, part of which sweeps round to join the black of the upperparts, while the remainder ends abruptly against the white of the breast. There is no difference in plumage between the sexes.

I have never heard the haunting call of the black-throated diver. Both divers have wailing cries in the breeding season as well as a deep quacking call when flying high overhead. When lying in my bath at Keanchulish yesterday evening, I heard what I am sure was a red-throated diver: a loud deep 'qucking' so reminiscent of Jura. This is understandable as Keanchulish is on the sea and although red throats are more abundant on the east coast there are birds in the vicinity. What confused me today was hearing the same call up on Loch Urigill – the home of the black-throated diver. Was it the latter with a similar cry or a red throat flying high from its home in the hills and out to sea to fish?

Grey found the black-throated diver's call quite spooky.

> A very extraordinary noise is made by the black-throated diver. It suggests to me the crying of a child in agony; it is often made at a great height in the air. As this peculiar and painful noise ceases after the breeding season, it is, I suppose, a joy sound on the part of the bird. Whether the flight is a joy flight I have not been able to observe. I have only seen and heard black-throated divers at the very end of the breeding season, on the rare occasions when I have been fortunate enough to get to western parts of the Highlands for

seatrout fishing in July. The red-throated diver has similar habits, but the cry, though very frequent at the same season, is not so strange.

Saturday, 26 August

Left Keanchulish for the hill shortly before breakfast to walk up the grouse over pointers. As we departed it was low tide and a small flock of common gulls were sunning themselves on the shingle. As far as seagulls go they are attractive little birds. Although they have the same dove grey plumage and black wing tips as the herring gull, they are a smaller and more elegant version. They have short green legs and do not have the threatening yellow beak complete with red blob that characterises the herring gull. Together with the kittiwake they are my favourite gulls. The attendant oystercatchers are uncharacteristically quiet at this time of the year.

As you approach the hill near Ledmore junction you drive through a mile or so of young plantation owned by the Forestry Commission. A buzzard hovered in the wind, the underside of its wings an attractive snow white. A female hen harrier glided over the rough heather ready to strike at anything that moved and conspicuous by her white rump and V-shaped wings. This particular bird had a distinctive lime-green 'tag' under her wing. Interestingly enough a few years ago I saw another harrier with a similar, yet crimson, tag. It is obviously the policy of the RSPB to tag a number of chicks when they are still in their moorland nests. As we reached the parking area on the brow of the hill a merlin shot low past the Land Rover. This small falcon is the size of mistle thrush and unlike some of its larger cousins poses no threat to the grouse. In fact it is suffering in the same way as the grouse from the enormous increase in forestry planting since the war. As we have seen forestry provides a safe haven for a wide variety of vermin and predators which venture out to attack the grouse. Forestry also encroaches on the young heather not only vital for the survival of the grouse but also the favoured habitat of the merlin, in which during summer they pursue the wretched meadow pipits. The survival of the merlin depends on the continuation of

WESTER ROSS : POINTER & GROUSE PS

grouse shooting. If trees and sheep take over, the heather disappears then so do the grouse and the merlin. It is only by continuing to shoot grouse that we will most effectively manage and protect the heather-covered moors that are rapidly becoming such a scarce resource.

We were four guns on the hill and walked from eleven in the morning through to five in the afternoon. We saw over a hundred grouse and shot nine brace. It was joy to watch the pointers working, ranging left and right, they didn't seem to miss a bird. Just as we were retrieving the grouse from the first point we watched a merlin kill a meadow pipit. The little falcon twisted and turned with the speed and agility of its larger relation the peregrine.

I have only shot grouse over dogs once before and that was staying with Bill and Cherry Palmer at Latheron in Caithness. As Grey describes in *The Charm of Birds*, later in the day when the dogs are tired they will occasionally point a meadow pipit rather than a grouse.

> They are very common in heather country and though so small and, except when in song flight, so insignificant in their ways, they evidently have a strong scent. To the nose of a pointer or setter, a moor must seem pervaded with the smell of meadow pipits and when grouse are scarce a dog will vary the monotony of finding no grouse by pointing a meadow pipit or 'tit lark' as it is often called. The scene is only too well known to everyone who shoots grouse over dogs. The pointer becomes rigid and earnest as if a covey of grouse were in front; the guns, if there are two, draw together and advance one on each side of the dog, which, encouraged by the keeper, moves forward with intense caution. At length a 'tit lark' flits unconcernedly out of the heather, the dog relaxes and wags its tail in a depreciating manner, as if asking us to excuse the joke since it is such a small one; and then, as if doubtful how the joke be taken, starts off again in quest of the scent of grouse. Thus in one way or another the little meadow pipit mixes itself with memories of Highland sport.

Monday, 27 August

The starlings have packed up again. There is a big flock that feeds among the seaweed at low tide and then roosts in the Keanchulish garden. It is composed of juveniles that are particularly striking as they are moulting into their first-winter spotted dress. They still have their dull brown heads, but their beautiful greeny black chests are covered with distinctive white spots. The spots on the first-winter birds are more conspicuous than on the adults, although their feathers will soon wear away to produce a darker spring plumage. Starlings are very noisy birds, especially when in one of their communal roosts. The song is a mixture of whistles, rattles, clicks and notes stolen from other birds.

Like the dunnock, it is easy to underestimate the starling. From a distance it appears a rather scruffy nondescript bird and it is not an 'obvious' songster. As I have suggested above, at close quarters and at certain times of the year its plumage is most colourful. From December onwards, the bill turns yellow and in spring the legs turn from a dark brown to a reddish colour. Pale feather tips weaken to reveal glossy colours beneath. The song is not musical but it commences early in the year (January) and is famed for its variety. Needless to say, as with the house sparrow, Grey saw the starling's point:

> When thrushes do not sing it is the most valuable and conspicuous event in bird music during the autumn and winter: every evening about sunset a starling, or a little party of them, sits on the top of a bare tree and gives a variety performance; some notes are their own, others are plagiarisms more or less close to the original; some are perfect imitations. The note that seems to me to be peculiarly the starling's own is a very clear boyish whistle; with this are all manner of other sounds – poultry noises, the chatter of sparrows, the cry of a peewit – one never knows what is coming next. Some of the notes are very pleasant, even beautiful, and are a delight to hear.

At Parwich Lees I have heard the starling imitate the green woodpecker and curlew. Grey had a similar experience:

> Where curlew breed, the spring notes of the curlew are a very favourite imitation. Nobody but a curlew can make that wonderful sound; but this does not deter the starling from attempting it, and the resemblance of the imitation to the original is sufficient to make us thank him. The starling is like a gramophone amongst birdsongs and it has chosen some of the best of which to make records.

Like the dunnock the starling lays a delightful blue egg, but unlike the dunnock the starling is a hole nester and therefore you would expect the egg to be a bright colour. Mysteriously odd eggs can be found on the lawn. It is not known whether they are laid there or removed from the nest by an intruding bird.

We had another exhausting day on the hill with the dogs. The grouse were again high up and we didn't get our first point until lunchtime. Maybe this had something to do with the fact that a golden eagle soared over the hill as we started the day. It is so much bigger than a buzzard with a wing span of nearly seven feet. We finished the day with a very creditable nine brace. When we returned to Keanchulish a solitary female common scoter was pruning herself in the bay, identifiable by the brown plumage and cocked tail. Her pale cheeks were visible at long range through the binoculars.

Wednesday, 30 August

Back in Derbyshire after a week at Ledmore. About a hundred yards from our house there is a small pond on the southward-facing bank of the valley. Today it has no more than the merest trickle of water in it as a result of the drought. As I walked down to feed the ducks in the evening a bird that looked like a large house martin propelled itself into the sky, uttering a high-pitched 'klu-eee-weet' cry. It had a distinctive white rump with a dark body and a twisting corkscrewing snipe-like flight.

In late summer I always look forward to a green sandpiper dropping in at my ponds for an overnight visit on the way south. August is the main month of movement but I have seen a bird pass through as early as 8 June and as late as 26 September. Birds moving north seem to take the more direct coastal route rather than moving down the central spine of the country as on their return. I am convinced that the early visitation was an unmated non-breeding bird on the return journey from its Scandinavian breeding grounds to its winter quarters in tropical Africa. Green sandpipers move north to their nesting sites much earlier than April and early May. When *en route* they tend to prefer their own company or to travel in small groups of two or three, and like to stop at small isolated ponds and woodland streams.

These visitors reminded Grey that autumn was around the corner:

> October is the month when the coming of these common winter birds is the most noticeable about our homes, but the movement of birds to us from the north begins long before the summer is over. In most years, on some day early in August, a bird flies up from the edge of one of my ponds. It is larger than a common sandpiper and it utters a cry that is more sharp and piercing than that of a redshank; sometimes there are two or even three birds and they may settle again, but generally there is only a single bird and it flies away with a sharp and repeated cry and is heard and seen no more. It is a green sandpiper. The bird has not been proved to nest in Britain; the bird at my pond has not spent the summer there. August is too late for it to be going north; the bird is therefore on its way south. It is said that the first birds to come from nothern breeding places are old males. Presumably they are birds that have not paired or have taken no part in rearing their young. Their strength has not been impaired by domestic cares; they are free from home duties and they come south before the young birds are ready for their journey or the breeding birds have recovered and are free. Probably this green sandpiper is an old male. I have come to look for the appearance of one early in August as the first notice at Fallodon of autumn migration and winter birds.

Grey is incorrect to say that the green sandpiper has not been proved to nest in Britain; it was recorded nesting in Westmoreland in 1919 and much later (1959) in the Spey Valley. It is the only wader that nests in a tree, usually favouring the old nest of a song thrush or sometimes a squirrel drey. It is a passage migrant but with the warm winters of recent years an increasing number appear to be wintering in the south of England. In fact Warde Fowler had this experience a century ago:

GREEN SANDPIPER: P. LEES. PS

> Both kinds (common and green sandpiper) come in spring and late summer, but the green sandpiper is much more regular in his visits and stays with us, in autumn at least, much longer. A stray pair found their way here last winter in a hard frost, and rose from beneath my feet as I walked along the Evenlode on 24 December.

They are now a relatively common sight in the Itchen Valley over the colder months and I often see one bobbing nervously on the Alresford cress beds or rocketing into the wintry sky from the banks of the tiny Titchbourne brook.

Thursday, 31 August

Left Parwich Lees for our Leeds office at 6.15 a.m. I had to stop on the little road behind Parwich Hall as a covey of twelve English partridges were gritting in the middle of it. They took off over the stone wall with a whirring of wings. In Derbyshire it is quite unusual to see a covey at all, let alone one with ten young birds. It has been a very hot summer with an abundance of insects. The Derbyshire hills are never going to be the perfect habitat for partridges because of the almost total absence of root and cereal crops. However, we have no shortage of thistles and nettles on our limestone grass and these are good plants for a surprising number of insects and beetles. Although a certain amount of 'topping' is undertaken in late summer, sprays are not used to any great degree.

The main enemy of the partridge in Derbyshire is the forage harvester; two cuts of silage are taken each year, the first early in the summer. The grass cutters destroy not only the nests of the partridge but also kill the hens themselves as they sit tightly on their eggs. Hedges are replaced by stone-walls in the hills so they will tend to nest in the long grass. In addition, because of the lack of large estates and gamekeepers, the partridge has to cope with a wide variety of predators – crows, stoats and foxes being the worst offenders – and there is no local foxhunt to keep the latter in check. An increasing problem is that of human disturbance, particularly here in one of our most popular National Parks. Walkers often do not keep to footpaths and let their dogs run loose. Any future government policy of unlimited access will exacerbate the problem, especially in the nesting season.

Generally speaking, across the country as a whole, the future is looking a little bit better for the English partridge. The introduction of 'set-aside', whereby certain cereal crops are taken out of production, has to be a move in the right direction. Sprays are used sparingly and topping only undertaken at the end of the summer, thereby encouraging a good population of broad-leaved weeds which result in high insect levels vital for chick survival. Aside from this, it is the small handful of well-run shooting estates that offer the English partridge the best hope for the future. Two of the most important initiatives are to leave unsprayed headlands around field edges and to undersow cereal crops with grass and clover. The headland is the most important part of the field; it is the arable area adjacent to hedge bottoms where partridges nest and rear their young. Undersowing crops means that fields are left untilled after combining for grazing, which results in an additional food source for the partridge over the cold winter months.

SEPTEMBER

Saturday, 2 September

We stayed with Janie and John Haddington at Mellerstain in the Borders and shot their moor in the Lammermuirs. Mellerstain is one of the great Adam houses, with both father and son having played their part. The elements were against us. With a north-westerly wind and heavy rain all day, we packed in after one drive in the afternoon. Even so we saw an encouraging number of grouse which will form the basis of a good stock for next year and we shot just short of thirty brace.

Country sports are a great aid to conservation and a benefit to indigenous wildlife as they preserve and develop some of our most effective landscape. Nowhere is this link more obvious than with grouse shooting. As more and more of our heather uplands have disappeared beneath commercial forestry, conservationists are now realising how vital grouse moors are to the survival of our uplands.

Grouse depend on heather for ninety per cent of their diet so it is vital for the heather to remain healthy. It is essential that a moor is not overgrazed by sheep. They eat out the young heather and the white grass soon returns. Landlords should always try and reduce the number of sheep on their moors and just as importantly they should undertake a rotational burning of the old heather (the optimum cycle is ten years) whereby the coarse old heather is burnt in strips allowing the nutritional young shoots to come through alongside the taller growth which in turn provides cover for the newly hatched chicks. This young heather also provides the perfect habitat for such diverse birds as the merlin, meadow pipit, hen harrier, peregrine, curlew, golden plover, redshank, wheatear, ring ouzel, dunlin and short-eared owl. The only real economic alternative to a grouse moor is commercial forestry and these tightly packed rows of pine and spruce encourage predators and destroy the grouse's natural breeding grounds. Keepers control predators, particularly the foxes, and this benefits other ground-nesting birds like the partridge and the golden plover. In the past keepers tended to be too hard on peregrines and hen harriers but a more enlightened policy by landlords in recent times has changed this practice. It must still be remembered that too many hen harriers can quickly destroy the economic viability of a grouse moor, and this in turn will lead to the disappearance of the heather moorland. Without heather moorland there will be no grouse. It is all a question of balance.

It is now generally agreed among the RSPB and other conservation bodies that without moorland being specifically managed for grouse, the heather declines, and the whole range of wildlife associated with it slowly disappears.

Monday, 4 September

Glen Affric, Inverness. Drove up from Mellerstain yesterday evening with Andrew Sebire and we spent the night at the little hotel in the village of Tomich. Tomich was built in the latter part of the nineteenth century as the estate village for Guisachan which was acquired in 1854 by the first Lord Tweedmouth. He was in the habit of taking sporting estates in the Highlands every year and among his favourite were Guisachan and Affric. My friend Andrew Sebire has recently taken a ten-year lease on West Affric for the deer stalking from the National Trust. Affric, which is not far from Loch Ness, is one of the most beautiful glens in the Highlands and is also a stronghold of the indigenous Caledonian pine.

Some months ago Andrew and I hatched a plan to make a brief visit to Affric before the stalking started in earnest, so I could try and shoot my first ptarmigan. Before breakfast we set off in the car to look at the ruins of Guisachan House and the impressive Home Farm steading. Guisachan is of particular interest to me on two accounts. Edward Grey used to spend summers there at the turn of the century, and his hostess was my great-great-great-aunt. In Trevelyan's biography of Grey there is a photograph of Winston Churchill, Haldane and Edward and Dorothy Grey on the drive at Guisachan dated 1901. Edward Tweedmouth was First Lord of the Admiralty from 1905 to 1908 and part of Asquith's

Liberal government when Grey was Foreign Secretary. In 1873 Lord Tweedmouth's son Edward married Fanny Spencer-Churchill, daughter of the eighth Duke of Marlborough. She died quite young in 1904 and we visited her granite memorial, a Celtic cross, that stands on the highest point of the present farm estate above the hill lochs. Guisachan is now a rather mysterious ruin. The estate was sold in 1908, a year before Tweedmouth died, and it has gone downhill ever since. It is sad that this splendid house with so many interesting associations had such a short life.

At around 10 a.m. Andrew and I started up the hill at South Affric (owned by the Forestry Commission) in search of our ptarmigan. The ptarmigan is a bird of the high mountains and is seldom found below 2,500 feet. It replaces the grouse above the heather line. Its food consists of the green tops of the blueberry and crowberry and it regularly feeds in the early morning when it seeks lower grounds maybe 1,000 feet off the high tops. It is a beautifully camouflaged bird that melds into its surroundings as completely as the ringed plover does on the shoreline.

We only saw two single birds all day. It can be very easy to walk ptarmigan territory and it is possible to trip over the birds before seeing them. They are difficult to flush as they prefer to escape by hiding themselves and crouching flat among the broken stoney ground. They are often oblivious to humans as they come across so few in their mountain lair. The first bird I saw was surprisingly wild. It peeled away from the screes about fifty yards to my left, appearing completely white. It gave the false impression of being in its winter colours as it swung away showing its belly and the underside of its wings. I finally shot a single bird just below a cairn on the 2,800-foot contour. It was a young cock in its summer plumage. A glorious mottled grey-black back with white wings and chest, which allowed it to blend perfectly into the screes and lichens of the moutainside. The winter colour change to white with the arrival of the snows helps with their survival. They are a favourite quarry of the golden eagle, particularly in areas like Affric where sheep carrion is scarce. The gillie told me that there were not so many eagles about since the sheep had been taken off the hill. Breeding success is hit

by heavy summer snow and rain as well as predation. *The New Atlas of Breeding Birds* states:

> At Cairn Gorm crows were attracted to the high ground by food scraps dropped by tourists and have greatly reduced the breeding success of the ptarmigan by robbing many eggs.

At 8.30 p.m., after an excellent dinner in the Tomich Hotel, I fell on to the Inverness-to-Crewe sleeper contemplating an unforgettable day. Before I went to sleep I read the chapter on the ptarmigan in *British Gamebirds and Wildfowl*. Here is a paragraph:

> Driving ptarmigan is seldom practical owing to the difficult nature of the ground they frequent, but in some places in Scotland where it is possible and has been attempted, fair bags have been made and as many as sixty brace killed in a day. They are best shot over dogs and as their pursuit is generally undertaken in fine weather when grand views can be obtained from the highest ground, even an off-day after ptarmigan, when only a few brace are found, is generally a delightful experience.

Thursday, 7 September

Rain at last in Derbyshire, and an inch or so of water is back in the ponds, which is perfect for the teal. A group of ten arrived overnight. They leapt vertically from the water and then turned, dived, glided and climbed in the dark sky around the valley. They often visit us at this time of the year when they move down from their moorland nesting sites. They are quite common visitors, especially if I have a pair of pinioned birds in my collection.

Another visitor at this time of year is the lesser black-backed gull. As I drove back from our Leeds office a large flock was feeding in the fields behind Parwich. You cannot get much further from the sea than Derbyshire and it seems strange to see them deep in the country. Whether it is the beginning of their winter migration to the Atlantic coasts of Iberia and North Africa I do not know. There is an increasing trend for these birds to overwinter in Britain like their close relation the herring gull. *The New Atlas of Breeding Birds* states:

> The large-scale cull in the moorland colony at Abbeystead (initially claimed to be to improve water quality but clearly having more to do with sporting interests) may be partly responsible for the decline in number at Walney.

This would seem an unproven statement. I have mentioned earlier what damage the lesser black backs are capable of doing to the puffin population on the Farne Islands. At Abbeystead there is no real evidence that they directly harm the young grouse. The real problem lies with the damage they do to the habitat. Over the years thousands of pairs of nesting lesser black backs had led to the destruction of hundreds of acres of heather moorland. Tonnes of gull droppings had turned the hill into a lunar landscape. As a result the grouse disappeared from the immediate vicinity of the colony.

Saturday, 9 September

Yesterday was a sad day. We drove Robin to Oxford for his first day at prep school (Summerfields). This meant I had to miss two days' grouse shooting at Abbeystead. (Five years ago to the day I took part in the two most exciting sporting days of my life. We shot two hundred and forty and two hundred and thirty-two brace of grouse in glorious sunshine.) We arrived at Bramdean at teatime having visited the Greenjackets' Museum in Winchester to see their new display of Robin Hastings' wartime medals, which Lucinda donated following her mother's death.

This morning before breakfast I took my five-year-old son Marcus down for a walk by the Itchen at Edward Grey's cottage. The low morning sun shone through the tops of the lime avenue giving the merest hint of the yellow autumnal colours to come. Aside from the woodpigeons cooing across the river at Avington, and the robins and wrens singing in the chalk pit, it is a relatively quiet time for birdsong.

Marcus and I stood on Grey's bridge transfixed by the long wavey waterweed wriggling in the clear current. A kingfisher shot past us at exactly the same moment that a dabchick whinnied a hundred yards upstream. Marcus looked at me as if to say what on earth was that? It was one of those charming moments you store away.

As we walked up the hill past the remains of the cottage, I told Marcus that exactly one hundred years ago the gentleman who lived here would have been in the prime of his life and embarking on another happy weekend break from the stress of his political career. From somewhere downstream the little kingfisher piped approvingly.

Wednesday, 13 September

Back in Derbyshire; a misty autumnal morning. Robins are busy performing their thin song on all sides, providing a constant background noise. The nuthatches are calling loudly and reeling again from the tops of the mature trees. Excitable flocks of twittering swallows are gathering on the telephone wires between us and Alsop signifying they are about to move off on their long migration to South Africa.

Friday, 15 September

Left Parwich Lees at 4.30 a.m. and drove to Exbury (Hampshire) via London. Nick de Rothschild and I set off from Lymington by ferry to the Isle of White. We had lobsters for lunch in Yarmouth and then went to view a house on Newtown Bay.

Before we left for the ferry Nick took me down to Lower Exbury to see if we could catch a glimpse of an osprey that had recently arrived on the Beaulieu Estuary. Interestingly enough the only time I have ever seen an osprey was in Newtown Bay about fifteen years ago. I was staying with Jeremy and Derek at Needs Ore for a September weekend and we took their small boat over to the Isle of White. Both birds would have been migrating to their winters quarters in West Africa. They arrive at their Scottish nesting grounds in April and depart in September. During their long journey south they are joined by Scandinavian birds and often stop off to spend a few days fishing *en route*. Nick's trout pond had presented an attractive proposition; his keeper pointed out a

large dead elm which the bird had been using as a perch. The ground below was covered with scales and fish heads.

The recolonisation of Britain by the osprey represents one of our most successful conservation stories and also a considerable public-relations coup for the RSPB. Egg collecters and trophy hunters brought the 'fish hawk' to the verge of extinction at the turn of the century, but the spectacular sight of an osprey diving into the water to catch a fish is once again a normal part of the Scottish scene. In 1959 (after an absence of over fifty years), a pair returned to nest at Loch Garten. They raised three young watched by fourteen thousand visitors. Since then the famous RSPB reserve at Loch Garten has attracted one and a half million people to view the ospreys in their pine-tree eyrie. The Scottish population is increasing annually, with seventy-two pairs found at nests in 1991 – although not all pairs lay eggs. On the south coast, September is the time to see them. They have long wings, which appear quite white from underneath, and a relatively short tail.

The south coast is a busy place generally for birds at this time of year. It is a season of hectic activity with warblers fuelling up for the long flight to Africa, passage migrants dropping in for a brief top-up and a few early arrivals among our normal winter visitors. As the ferry left the Lymington Estuary, we were lucky enough to see a single grey plover in its stunning summer plumage; mottled black and white on top with jet black underparts. Outside Jamie Chichester's office on Beaulieu Pond a common sandpiper bobbed daintily on the shoreline 'waiting for the off' and a willow warbler was frantically collecting insects on a nearby pine tree.

Saturday, 16 September

Stayed with my first cousin Alexander Muir at Fonthill (Wiltshire); I drove up from Lymington through the New Forest last night. A few years ago he converted the little Georgian 'cottage' in the walled garden at Fonthill into a charming country house. The walled garden was part of Fonthill House built by William Beckford in the middle of the eighteenth century.

I lay in bed reading Robert Massie's *Dreadnought*. His chapter on Sir Edward Grey and Liberal Foreign Policy begins:

> Sir Edward Grey was a countryman. He regarded the Foreign Office, where he spent eleven years as Foreign Secretary, as a dungeon from which he escaped on weekends to the sunlit glades of the New Forest or to the waters of a Hampshire trout stream. At his desk, he worked with devotion but without joy: he preferred talking about the majesty of Handel or the beauty of Wordsworth to talking about the balance of power or the Triple Alliance. He left Britain only once during this term of office, and spoke only a few phrases of primitive French, but he was the greatest British Foreign Secretary of the century.

Through my bedroom window came the fragile notes of a robin. Along with Hudson, Grey was also one of the greatest writers on birds this century. I keep jogging back to his vivid descriptions of the autumn song of the robin in *The Charm of Birds*. The robin is so important to a garden just now. Because of the relative silence, the thin gentle notes sound from all corners. Suddenly, a robin is looking down from some low leafy perch, baring its red breast while jealously proclaiming its territory. A little further up the bank a chiffchaff gave a hurried rendering of its song before moving on towards the coast.

A nuthatch and a great spotted woodpecker called from the browning beechwoods on the lip of the valley. The house martins are massing on the wires running across the garden.

In the morning I drove over to visit one of my closest friends, Greg Shenkman, who has bought a house on the River Avon near Amesbury. I followed the river up from Salisbury, through the Woodfords, to the little village of Wilsford. Edward Grey spent some of his latter years at Wilsford Manor when married to Pamela Glenconner, his second wife. Even she predeceased him, adding to a list of tragedies. Grey's first wife Dorothy was killed in a driving accident, he lost both his brothers big-game shooting in Africa and both Fallodon and the Cottage were burnt down. Wilsford Manor is now owned by a property developer who acquired it when Stephen Tennant died ten years ago. A poignant reminder of Grey's era is a touching memorial in the little village church to the Glenconners' other son, Edward Tennant, who was killed on the Somme aged nineteen.

Tuesday, 19 September

Drove up to Allenheads in Northumberland last night to shoot with my friend Robert Shields who takes a day here every year. Allenheads lies to the south of Hexham and is owned by the Beaumont family. It was once a thriving lead-mining community and now represents one of the most prolific grouse moors in Britain with six separate days driving. The fog conveniently lifted at 9.30 a.m. and it was decided that we should go to the Swinhope beat which had not as yet been shot. We ended the day with a particularly successful drive on Swinhope Head, producing over forty brace of grouse making a total bag for the day of a hundred and one and a half brace.

Allenheads has been disappointing this season bearing in mind how positive the signs were earlier in the year. When I met Robert Grainger,

the head keeper, at the blackcock lek in April he was hoping for a bumper year. However well you look after the heather you are always at the mercy of the weather.

Robert said that until 14 May everything was looking fine and the heather was greening up well. Then the north-east winds set in with a series of cold, wet, foggy days which did not let up until Wimbledon week. The keepers found a number of nests that had all hatched out and no tell-tale dead grouse that signify disease. Cold wet weather in late May means a lack of vital insect life for the newly hatched chicks and a resulting high mortality rate. There has not been a warm spring at Allenheads for three years now.

There was an unforgettable moment in the first drive. I was at the end of the line at the top of the hill in the number eight butt. I heard a familiar plaintive whistle somewhere out in front of me. A flock of ten golden plover catapulted low across the heather like racing pigeons. They then spiralled high over the middle of the line leaving the startled and unprepared guns no time for a shot. I, for one, gave a little sigh of relief and wished them well on their way.

Saturday, 23 September

A lovely autumnal Derbyshire day with the wind increasing towards evening. The chaffinches have flocked again and there were over twenty feeding under the copper beech. The males have lost their bright spring plumage. When Marcus and I returned from feeding the ducks a buzzard glided down the valley in front of the house into the freshening wind. This is the first buzzard I have seen at Parwich Lees and is further evidence of their widening geographical distribution. I knew one was around as it had been seen at Tissington where they have recently lost fifty young pheasants by decapitation. Someone suggested the crime might have been committed by the buzzard. Mindless killing in this fashion is the work of a fox.

Because of the number of foxes around, Richard FitzHerbert, Stan White and Tony Stone all came over from Tissington in the morning for a walk around our young plantations. The early morning is a good time to ambush a fox. When the sun is on the banks they tend to rest up in the undergrowth beneath a cosy hawthorn bush following a night's hunting. We saw three on my small eighty-acre patch and shot two dog foxes. One of them was an old dark creature that had a short stumpy tail and could well have been shot in the buttocks at some time in the past. The first fox calmly trotted away from the hawthorn bank before the forward guns moved into position. We stupidly drove the bank downwind and it had caught our scent.

A kestrel and a sparrowhawk flew out of the hawthorn bank. The kestrel is more often in evidence at Parwich Lees than the sparrowhawk, but both are fairly common. The sparrowhawk is the second most abundant raptor in Britain after the kestrel but it is much more secretive. It is a bird of the woods and its broad wings and long tail allow it to manoeuvre with great agility among the dense trees. The kestrel is more often than not seen in open countryside hovering above some grassy bank in search of voles. I always like to compare the sparrowhawk and its robust rounded wings with a Spitfire or a Hurricane, whereas the kestrel reminds me of the more delicate Lysander. The latter was used for reconnaissance and with its sharply pointed wings and fanned tail, spying is precisely what the kestrel is good at. A favourite hunting spot for the kestrel is the motorway verge where there is an abundance of voles. An enjoyable exercise to relieve the boredom of a long car journey is to count the kestrels. On 18 December 1988 I was driving back from shooting in Suffolk and between Bury St Edmunds and Grantham I counted eighteen. If you want to see a sparrowhawk you should keep your eye on your birdtable. The sparrowhawk relies on wheeling acrobatics and the surprise attack to obtain its meal of small song birds. It is often to be seen swooping low down over hedgerows or across the lawn to the birdtable in search of prey.

It is gratifying to report that both birds are now on the increase and getting back to their original numbers. They were unfairly persecuted by gamekeepers at the turn of the century and the sparrowhawk in particular was devastated by toxic agricultural chemicals in the 1950s and 1960s, as *The New Atlas of Breeding Birds* informs us:

> In the late 1950s the sparrowhawk population of Britain declined markedly following the introduction of organochlorine pesticides in agriculture. These are extremely persistent and highly fat-soluble – and so readily accumulated in the bodies of birds. The sparrowhawk, preying upon a wide range of other birds, accumulates concentrations of these chemicals large enough to depress reproduction and survival. The insecticide DDT came into wide use in 1947 and led to egg thinning and egg breakage with a consequent reduction in the breeding rate. The more toxic cyclodiene compounds, such as aldrin and dieldrin, were used from 1956 and poisoned many adult sparrowhawks.

In some of the arable districts of eastern and southern England the bird almost totally disappeared. With the voluntary and legal bans on the use of pesticides the situation improved dramatically. Kestrels were less affected by pesticides than other raptors and their numbers are currently estimated at seventy thousand pairs. They are welcome residents in our big cities where their diet switches from voles to sparrows. I often see them on the top of Manchester Cathedral or from the fifteenth floor of my office tower in the centre of Leeds. At Parwich Lees I have put up two nesting boxes for the kestrels but they have yet to take to them. I have never seen a sparrowhawk in a big city but apparently the population in Edinburgh alone numbers between thirty and thirty-five pairs! Kestrels will nest on window ledges but the sparrowhawk is less adventurous and sticks to parks and cemeteries.

Thursday, 29 September

Philip Snow and I set off from Parwich Lees before breakfast for Blenheim; Philip wanted to work on some sketches.

As we drove through the Triumphal Arch we turned sharp right down over the River Glyme towards Fisheries Cottage. This is a relatively undisturbed part of the lake and always a good spot for viewing the duck. We came looking for gadwell, but instead saw a small group of eight shoveler feeding behind the duck hides.

The shoveler is one of my favourite ducks. The drake is a distinctive and handsome specimen. It is white with a colourful chestnut belly and a bottle-green head. The enormous spoon-shaped beak, after which the bird has taken its name, gives it an almost comical look. I remember my first encounter with the shoveler. When I was an undergraduate at Cambridge, a group of us took a syndicate shoot at Heydon near Holt in Norfolk. One evening Michael Prideaux, Alexander Russell and I went flighting on a quiet lake at the edge of a wood. Instead of coming home with the statutory handful of mallard we bagged half a dozen strange looking ducks. A quick glance at a bird book when we got home told us they were shoveler. Although we did not know it at the time, the eastern counties represented the heartland of their territory in Britain.

I have always kept shoveler in my wildfowl collection. Not only are they attractive but they seem to do better than other ducks. I suspect this success stems from their specialised method of feeding. They like shallow muddy water that contains numerous organisms which they filter through their big broad bills. It is the most sophisticated bill of any

British duck. Water is pushed out through the sides and food particles are trapped on the serrated comb-like edges. Shoveler feed on plankton just below the surface but also seeds and insects that are stirred up by a feeding group. Hence today the little flock at Blenheim were feeding in a circle with their necks flat on the water. I kept one female bird at Parwich Lees for seven years and each season she would lay two clutches of eggs. The nest was always difficult to find, usually tucked away in a nettlebed about five yards from the water's edge. The tiny ducklings never seemed to survive more than a few days so it was essential to try and locate the nest and transfer the eggs to a bantam. Shovelers nest in marshland adjacent to shallow lakes and it is these very habitats that are vulnerable to drainage and changes in land use. Their numbers have recently declined in north-western Europe after a period of steady growth in the 1960s and 1970s. The birds we saw at Blenheim today were almost certainly British breeders of which there are around fifteen hundred pairs. These birds will migrate to places like the Coto Doñana in southern Europe for the winter, and be replaced by large numbers of continental shoveler from Scandinavia and Russia. November is the month when numbers peak in Britain. At this time around 10,000 birds will be present, as the continental duck have moved in and the British breeders have yet to move south.

As we drove past the Fisheries a group of a dozen snow geese were roosting in the shallow lagoon in front of the cottage. Although they were not present when we were living at the Lince they have been at Blenheim for well over five years now. I imagine they escaped from a wildfowl collection as they are very rare winter visitors. Anyway with their all-white plumage and black wing tips they make an attractive addition.

From the Fisheries we made our way to the Lince where we decided to park the car and undertake the usual two-hour walk to the Cascade and on up to the palace, via the boathouse. We stopped the car on William Chambers' New Bridge. It was a lovely sunny autumnal day with the wind buffeting the rather tired-looking leaves on the poplars and copper beeches. A kingfisher shot downstream from under the bridge, piping as he went. I was reminded of a paragraph in *Bird Watching* by E. W. Hendy (1928). He was mentioning the exceptional memory of W. H. Hudson and his ability to recall fifty images of the same species of bird. He then relates his own experiences of the kingfisher:

> When I think of a kingfisher two ideal images rise up in my mind: one is of him flying, on a windy summer day, over a field of young corn on whose emerald surface the impetuous gusts ploughed momentary troughs and gullies of paler light; imagine the joy of his metallic blue, flashed upon such a background! The other is of him darting headlong from beneath a bridge, like a green and cobalt scarab, across a smooth sheet of almost black water, on a still January day. The unexpectedness of this rare vision almost took my breath away and incidentally added another to the many beautiful bird memories I have gleaned from looking over a bridge.

During my forty months of living at the Lince, I only saw a kingfisher fourteen times in and around Blenheim Park. Today we saw three different birds. As we approached the Cascade another of those unforgettable moments unveiled itself. The air was full of scent so evocative of my childhood. The laurel, the cedar, the box bushes and a slightly pungent smell of brackish lakewater. There on the delicate Swiss Bridge in front of the Cascade sat another little kingfisher; from afar he looked like a tiny tangarine. Above him at the top of Capability Brown's waterfall, a grey wagtail skipped through the foaming spray. It was a juvenile bird as it displayed a distinctive peach chest. Later in the day as we drove home and crossed the River Dove between Burton and Derby a kingfisher flashed across the dual carriageway. When we arrived back and told my wife Lucinda she said she had recently seen a kingfisher by a roadside stream in the village of Fenny Bentley on the way to Ashbourne. A series of mild winters has obviously given the kingfisher a boost.

If today was 'a kingfisher day' it was also a 'wagtail day': we saw all three. A flock of around seventy pied wagtails were fuelling up on the vast lawns to the south of the palace. They were almost certainly on migration and in among this gathering was a solitary yellow wagtail that had decided to hitch a ride south. Again, like the grey wagtail, it was a juvenile bird as it sported only a limited flush of yellow on its underparts. A prominent eye stripe on its brown head (as opposed to grey) and shortish tail gave away its identity. This was the first yellow I have seen at Blenheim.

Philip decided to sketch Vanburgh's magnificent bridge from the site of Fair Rosamund's Well on the north bank. As we gazed across to the Victorian boathouse a raft of around thirty great crested grebes lolled on the water. They were escorted by seven cormorants like destroyers around a convoy. The presence of these skilled fishermen so far from the sea suggests an increasing lack of food in their traditional waters and bodes badly for our inland fish stocks.

As we left for home around lunchtime a chiffchaff was singing in Woodstock High Street and a few swallows flew over the church spire reminding us that the summer was not quite over. We drove north up the M40 and on to the M42 towards Lichfield when we enjoyed two separate sightings of a buzzard by the roadside; yet more evidence of their widening geographical spread.

OCTOBER

Sunday, 1 October

The leaves are nearly off the beech trees in the garden at Parwich Lees. The tops of the limes are turning yellow and the chestnut is full of orange. The browning hawthorn bushes are heavy with their red fruit, awaiting the arrival of the winter thrushes.

The tits are back in an argumentative mood and the chaffinches are pinking in the trees as they digest their beech mast. Little Jenny Wren is beginning to complement the robin's autumnal song.

Before breakfast I walked down the valley to fill the pheasant feeder. Our buzzard was present yet again, soaring high above the hawthorn bank, its peace shattered by six indignant carrion crows. A solitary grey wagtail took off from my duck ponds where it had doubtless been resting on its southward migration. They are noisy birds and utter a sharp metallic call as they fly off, similar to that of the pied wagtail.

There is a little more water in the ponds but they are still very low. The mallard drakes are now out of 'eclipse' and make a dazzling contribution to the ritual flypasts at feeding time.

Tuesday, 3 October

Had my first day of autumn hunting with the High Peak. We met at Flagg (where we have our point-to-point course) at 7.00 a.m. and finished by 9.00 a.m.; I then drove to our Leeds office. I don't know who was more unfit, Alfie or myself. The weather stayed fine and we jumped a good number of walls. It is some of our best country and no hunt jumps – large open fields on the 1,000-foot contour. I had a sticky start but went better towards the end.

I am not a hunting person in the strictest sense of the word. I am

simply not a good enough rider and do not have the nerve for what is undoubtedly a dangerous sport. If unfit and inexperienced it is important to proceed with the greatest caution! I only started hunting two seasons ago having experienced a handful of very tame days with the South Berks as a teenager. One might ask why I took it up again. The sport is in my blood. My father hunted with the High Peak Harriers as a boy and my grandfather Charles Waterhouse, better known as leader of the Suez rebels in the House of Commons, was master and hunted the harriers in the 1920s. In addition to all of which there is without doubt no finer way of enjoying our lovely countryside with its lush green rolling hills and network of limestone walls.

Edward Grey was first and foremost a fisherman but as a young man he also enjoyed both his shooting and hunting. His diary for 8 January 1885 states:

> Enjoyed my three days' shoot immensely: but all sport leaves a kind of dust and ashes taste to it. Political, literary and aesthetic pleasures never seem to leave off, but sport comes to an end each day.

Another entry reads:

> I was to have hunted at the Kennels, but frost stopped me; very provoking and I was much annoyed: perhaps in my heart of hearts more at the loss of the company I hoped to meet out hunting than of the sport itself.

He was of course referring to his future wife Dorothy.

The harriers put up at least half a dozen snipe which seemed strange as it is quite dry on these limestone tops. I suspect they were the advance guard of a large number of winter visitors or passage migrants that pass through the middle of the country at this time of the year. I saw the first of the year at the edge of my duckponds last weekend. I always look for the coming of the winter snipe around 1 October in the same way as I do the teal about a month earlier. Alan Richards writes in *Birds of the Tideline*:

> The bird's numbers are augmented by migrants from around the Baltic. Estimates of the total number that pass through north-western

Europe in late summer have been put at twenty to thirty million birds. In Britain and Ireland equally, numbers can be no more than approximations. However, about eighty-five thousand snipe are reckoned to be shot each year, so the wintering population in Britain must be well into the hundreds of thousands.

There are thought to be around thirty thousand breeding pairs in Britain. Most British and Irish birds make only local movements.

For several days now large numbers of my mallard have been waddling around the field under some hedgerow trees. They are supplementing my daily ration of barley with acorns.

Saturday, 7 October

Shot a hundred and four and a half brace of grouse staying with Gerald Westminster at Abbeystead. This was the last day of the season in which they have shot just over three thousand brace and left an excellent stock for next year. The mist came down at lunchtime and we would not have been able to shoot in the afternoon if a new road had not been put in last year which accesses two low-ground drives on Littledale. We were only seven guns with our host always on the flank. Two of the guns were Ralph Percy and Christopher Wills. If the former is one of the best shots of my generation, the latter is one of the most knowledgeable ornithologists. This is not entirely surprising as Christopher is the stepson of Henry Douglas-Home. Christopher grows over five hundred acres of spring corn on his Hampshire estate. He likes to keep the stubbles down. By doing this he provides winter feed for many different species of bird. In addition, spring-sown crops produce a less dense sward of vegetation in the breeding season which encourages the plovers to nest. He told me that in the past picking up plovers' eggs in a responsible fashion did little harm to the population. This they would allow in a two-week period up to 8 April before which the nests would be susceptible to frosts and rolling of the land.

There is no better example of country sports and conservation running hand in hand than at Abbeystead. When the protesters pile out of their cars in the second week of August and try to disrupt the day's sport, they should pause and ask the question, why has the number of grouse shot increased from five hundred brace a year to a high of over four thousand brace since the estate was acquired fifteen years ago. The main reason for this success story lies with a substantial increase in the area and quality of the heather moorland. This has been achieved by a combination of bracken spraying and a significant reduction in the number of sheep on the hill. A small number of sheep actually benefit the moor, the perfect ratio being around one animal to every three acres. They nibble the tops of the young heather and create the 'heather bed' so important to the success of the grouse.

New roads have been built across the hill accessing areas of moorland that were previously difficult to reach. This facilitates the burning of the old heather and means drives can be carried out in adverse weather conditions. There are now twice the number of keepers on the estate, both on the low and high ground, and the vermin is kept firmly in check. When Edward Grey was alive vermin included raptors, but not so today, when we saw five different species, a buzzard, a peregrine, a hen harrier, a merlin and a kestrel. Of course they are not all appreciated to the same degree and even the RSPB now admit that you cannot maintain a successful grouse moor with large numbers of hen harriers. In the current year significant numbers of young merlin were ringed on the Abbeystead moors and there is little doubt that the landlord is as proud of that fact as he is of his thriving grouse population.

Tuesday, 10 October

Hunted with the High Peak. We met at Monsal Head at 7.00 a.m. and were home by 9.30 a.m. It was a glorious morning with a spectacular sunrise. We saw a number of hares but didn't kill. I had an even worse start than last week but went a little better towards the end. This is lovely country overlooking Monsal Dale and the famous viaduct. It carried express trains from London to Manchester on a line which was opened in 1863 and closed just over a hundred years later. When the viaduct was built John Ruskin was so incensed he made the famous remark, 'Now every fool in Bakewell can be in Buxton in half an hour and every fool in Buxton in Bakewell.'

It has been very mild for the last few days, which might explain why the winter thrushes have not yet arrived. Philip Snow saw some swallows in Anglesey yesterday, although they would appear to have left us about ten days ago. The goldfinches have also gone south in the wake of the millions of warblers, although the former will stop and spend the winter on the continent rather than go on to Africa.

Friday, 13 October

A pair of pied wagtails are cavorting around the yard and calling loudly as if it was spring. Normally they would have gone south by now. No doubt it has something to do with the continuing mild weather. I got stuck in the London Underground on the District Line this week for a short time and nearly died of the heat. Despite this balmy spell our valley is a sea of colour and looking very autumnal.

The weather pattern obviously has not changed much since Grey's day:

> This year [1926] at Fallodon there were three days in October – the 2nd, 3rd and 4th – that were as hot by day and as warm by night as if it were midsummer. There are generally a few days in October that are very warm, but by the middle of the month we are left in no doubt that summer is over and that we are in another season. The woods, that for so many weeks have kept a steady sombre green, now reveal a riot of colour. Most beautiful of all are the common wild cherry trees, the geans, so wonderful and tender in colour that it would be almost indelicate to attempt to describe them. A few of our forest trees shed their leaves without any bright display: the ash and the sycamore do so; but most trees have an individual and distinct beauty of their own. Horse chestnuts turn early to pale gold; the 'English' elms do this also, but much later.

While working at home in the morning I heard a rather squeaky rendering from a chiffchaff in the walled-garden wood. This bird is very late in moving south – another result perhaps of the recent bout of mild weather. I was only yesterday thinking that this year I had not heard an autumnal finale from a departing chiffchaff.

Monday, 16 October

We arrived at Benbecula in the Outer Hebrides at midday having flown from Glasgow. We then drove up to our small hotel (Langass Lodge) on North Uist. Jamie Chichester organised the party with Henry Pembroke and Guy Rasch making up the other two guns. Henry lives at Wilton and Guy at Middle Woodford, both near Salisbury and only a few miles from the little village of Wilsford where Edward Grey married Pamela Glenconner in 1922.

October is the month to shoot snipe in the Outer Hebrides. It is the time of the main migration from the Baltic south to Ireland. We went out after lunch with the strong south-westerly wind having dropped to around force five. The keeper felt this was still too strong to drive snipe so we walked up for a couple of hours. You should always walk snipe downwind as they sit much tighter and take off into the wind. The most difficult part of shooting walked-up snipe is seeing the bird. As they rise into the wind you are offered a momentary flash of their white chests.

The machair was teeming with golden plover. They arrive from their breeding grounds in September to spend the winter in this relatively mild climate. They are a 'very bonny bird' but also immensely exciting to shoot. They rush at you over the fields like driven grouse, and twist, turn, wheel and climb in large flocks. They are confiding birds and can be walked up or even whistled in. When shot at they split like a covey of

English partridges except that they dive headlong to the ground. Your second barrel is one of the most difficult shots you will ever take.

In *The Birdman*, Henry Douglas-Home includes a delightful passage on the 'goldie':

> Golden plover are surprisingly approachable birds, despite their acrobatic flying, especially if you want to play tricks. One of the easiest ways to attract them is to walk through the field with a yellow dog, ideally a golden labrador. The resident flock of goldens will come running after you but not, for some strange reason, if you have a black dog. No less appealing is their reaction if you perform the grass pulling trick. When you come into the field you bend over and snatch a tag of long grass from the side of the dyke or fence and then purposely walk off in the opposite direction to the flock. But every now and then you pretend to pick more grass and each time you do it you adjust your course so that you slowly come full circle to the birds. Again for some reason they are transfixed by this behaviour, all looking wonderingly as if to say: 'Stupid old fool, what's he doing picking rushes for?' Until to their surprise you are not a distant figure but an awesome danger only twenty yards away.

Tuesday, 17 October

A morning flight for the geese is an unforgettable experience. The anticipation of waiting for the clattering call of the first skein of greylag pumps the adrenalin around the bloodstream. The geese start to come at first light.

We decided to go to some stubbles on the west coast of the island. Our hides were placed in a couple of stooks in the middle of the field and in between a ditch and one of those rickety Hebridean fences funded by the EEC. We were only five hundred yards from the sea. From over the dunes the distant roaring of surf hummed in our ears. The dark morning sky echoed with the harsh calls of unseen snipe as they flighted out from their night-time feeding grounds. Intermingled with this was the solitary whistle of a golden plover, the plaintive 'peewit' of the lapwing and the restful 'coor-lee' of the curlew. As the light came so did the croaking of a marauding raven and the evocative 'tulee' of a redshank. Suddenly the

sky was full of barking and clanging geese. The little barnacle came first; four settled in front of Jamie's decoys and grazed unconcerned for at least half an hour. A single bird played sentry while the others fed. The greylag were our quarry as the barnacle are protected. They were still flighting in as we left for a late breakfast.

During the pick-up I flushed a jack snipe from some rushes. It is quite easy to identify a jack, which is lucky, as they are also protected. It usually rises solitarily and always reluctantly and silently. The flight is much less erratic than a common snipe. It flits low across the rushes for a short distance and then drops in again. If you are unaware of the jack it is easy to confuse with a wounded common snipe. It is however two thirds the size of a common snipe and has a much smaller beak. It breeds in north-eastern Europe and western Siberia and along with the redwing, fieldfare and brambling is one of the few common birds that spend the winter with us and then leave to nest.

Grey thought it had great charm:

> It is a quiet little bird: I have never heard it utter; when disturbed it rises quietly without sound or fuss; there is something meek about its flight; even when shot at and missed it will settle again at no great distance, as if it could not believe that the shot was intended for anything so small as itself. It relies on concealment then on flight. I once found one crouching in the angle formed by the garden path and the edge of the turf. It sat still at my feet, and for a while I admired the purple feathers, not disarranged by shot or violent capture, on the back of a living and uninjured jack snipe. When a hand was put down it flitted easily and lightly away, with an appearance of airy unconcern, over a tall privet bush and the garden fence, to settle, no doubt, a few yards off up a little watercourse running into the pond, near which it had been sitting. It is a pity ever to shoot it, for its body is too small to give satisfaction when cooked, and all its ways and manners seem to deprecate violence or injury.

Wednesday, 18 October

I had a most exciting morning flight at Solas bog. It was one of those few sporting occasions which you file away and remember. The wind was force seven blowing from the south and the geese had been roosting out on the sands in the bay. My butt was beside a small dyke which ran from the bog in the direction of the sea. The geese came early, the first two while it was dark and, obligingly, in pairs or small skeins of seven to ten. They battled their way into the wind keeping to a good shootable height. I was using heavy shot (threes) and luckily did not wound any birds. This was an exceptional flight which would be difficult to repeat. Normally if you shoot a couple of geese on a morning flight you go home well pleased. The goose, like the woodcock at Parwich Lees, is a truly wild bird. They are very wary and a formidable quarry. The greylag population on North Uist is growing year by year. The current population is over 2,000 and around 250 will be shot from 1 September to the end of January. It has grown because the predators (mainly hooded crows) are kept under control and because the crofters are becoming more efficient farmers. Keeping a check on greylag numbers not only provides valuable income for the island but also good PR with the crofters. The geese that are shot are distributed among the crofters who are constantly complaining of the damage they do to the crops.

The dawn brought out the lapwing, golden plover and curlew; the stormy sky was full of their wild cries. The 'goldies' careered across the fields somehow managing to negotiate the maze of fences. Once over the dunes they twisted and turned in the distance like wisps of smoke. There was one delightful moment when a stag trotted down the fenceline towards my butt. It had been gorging itself overnight on the crofters' fields. I crouched down and it hopped the fence within twenty yards of me without catching my scent. I jumped up. The stag took off like a champion steeplechaser, clearing three fences in quick succession by at least four feet. I now understand the origin of the expression 'jumped like a stag!'

As I left my butt dreaming of well-earned kippers for breakfast, a family of whooper swans flew over the bog calling loudly. Listening to their trumpet-like call it is easy to see how they acquired their name. These wild swans are the most graceful creatures. They are much the same size as our mute swan and larger than the more goose-like Bewick swan. At a distance the best way to tell them from a mute is by the long erect neck. Close to they have a distinctive yellow-and-black bill and a flatter forehead than that of a Bewick. The whoopers arrive in the Uists in September having flown down from their nesting grounds in Iceland. Although the odd feral pair might now nest in Britain, they became extinct as a breeding bird in Orkney in the eighteenth century.

For the rest of the day we made a rather unsuccessful attempt to walk up snipe in a strong gale. They are extremely wild in this weather and rise too far in front of the guns. Driving them in such weather is hopeless as you lose them 'out the sides' and they gain height too quickly.

Thursday, 19 October

Morning flight at Baleshare; the wind had dropped slightly but was still very fresh. The golden plover carried out their usual pre-breakfast flight along the line of the dunes. They provided exciting sport as they swept over our butts on a broad front. Four whooper swans pitched in a field a hundred yards away from my butt.

The weather kept dry but it was too windy for successful snipe shooting. We saw four raptors, a kestrel, merlin, hen harrier and several buzzards.

Friday, 20 October

An uneventful morning flight at Bayhead (no geese) in an unattractive part of the island surrounded by houses and the usual barbed-wire fences. The boredom (we were out for two hours) was alleviated by a lovely sunrise, two particularly sporting 'goldies' and the sight of a lapwing mobbing a buzzard. I have heard that they will attack sheep and cattle that come too close to their nests; our keeper says 'they are as brave as lions'. How prophetic his words were to be. At the end of the day we witnessed a lapwing attacking a much more formidable adversary over the stubbles at Solas – a hen harrier.

After breakfast we started with a walk at Baleshare. For the first time this week the weather was calm. The sun shone and the skylarks were up and singing. It was not surprising that the snipe were much more settled. At one point I nearly trod on a short-eared owl that rose at my feet. There was no way of knowing whether this was a resident bird or a migrant. At this time of the year a large number of short-eared owls arrive from Norway, Finland, Germany and Iceland to winter on our shores. The short-eared owl has a good deal in common with the harrier. It shares the same moorland habitat and with its long wings and disciplined method of hunting it can easily be confused with the female hen harrier. As it quarters the hill it glides across the heather like a giant moth. Unlike the harrier the short-eared owl's diet consists almost entirely of voles and their lifestyle is totally dependent on their numbers. Some gamekeepers get excited at the presence of a 'moor-owl' on their patch. Historically, they have almost certainly been over persecuted. Later in the day we saw another bird settling on a fence post with a vole in its claws. If there is a plague of voles locally the owls will appear from nowhere. They will then lay up to ten eggs or even have two broods. In a poor vole year they may not breed at all or travel vast distances in search

of food. The short-eared owl leads a nomadic lifestyle and ringed British birds have been recovered as far away as Spain. Another safety mechanism when food is scarce is provided by the method of incubation. The female lays eggs at similar intervals and incubates from the start ensuring that the chicks hatch at two day intervals; in this way only the strongest will survive. This scenario is happily an unlikely one, on both North Uist and on many of our upland moorlands, as a result of a substantial increase in young forestry plantations. When the trees are small and the grass long, voles and owls thrive.

In the afternoon we did the most successful snipe drive of the week. The Balimore bog is only a hundred and fifty yards long by fity yards wide. It sits on the edge of the machair behind a row of residential houses. It is regarded as the best snipe bog on the island. It is difficult to put a finger on why it is so prolific. Maybe some sewage from the nearby houses seeps into it.

The drive couldn't have lasted more than ten minutes but it was another of those occasions one will remember indefinitely. As we took up our positions a buzzard inconveniently glided over the bog putting up a number of terrified snipe. The buzzard was followed by a heron. The snipe were by now pretty jumpy and the heron had much the same impact.

Once things had settled down the keeper entered the bog with three dogs. The sky exploded with snipe. We must have seen between two and three hundred. I shot my first 'right and left'.

Saturday, 21 October

I have visited South Uist on a number of occasions, staying at both Grogarry and Drimore. I prefer the morning flights on South Uist. Here the flight is always by a loch. This is invariably more interesting and of great beauty. This morning we set off for Loch Leodasay, renowned for its wigeon. We only shot seven head but the bag included three species, wigeon, tufted and golden eye. Dawn was alive with the bugling of whooper swans and the whistling of wigeon. As the flight was ending a lone cormorant glided down for breakfast on the loch. It was followed by a flock of acrobatic wigeon, which in turn were being tailed by a deadly peregrine falcon, like a Spitfire in the sun.

After breakfast we packed and left for the airport. Arrived back in Derbyshire in good time for dinner.

Sunday, 22 October

Put the tup in with the ewes and carried out what I hope will be the last mow. We are enjoying a slice of Indian summer and our grass is lush; quite a contrast to the barren lands of North Uist. Farmers are taking advantage and carrying out some very late silageing.

While I was bringing in the sheep a party of a dozen long-tailed tits flew past the barn roof like dainty little dragonflies. As usual they gave away their presence by the thin calls through which they keep in family contact when flitting down the hedgerows or moving high up in the canopy. When we lived at the Lince they were common in Blenheim Park. Until today I've never seen more than a pair at Parwich Lees. This is not surprising as they are a woodland bird.

Sunday, 29 October

A lovely sunny autumn day. The temperature has become more autumnal; we had our first real frost last night. I didn't hunt yesterday as I've pulled a muscle in my shoulder which is proving uncomfortable.

The two big beech trees beside my pond on the Tissington bank were lit up a deep orange by the morning sun. Grey had a love affair with the beech tree:

> No tree in autumn is more noble and honourable than the beech. Its dark leaves at first turn yellow; but the last stage before they fall is rich dark brown. As in spring there should be a Sunday set apart for seeing the young green beech leaves in their first beauty, so there should be a 'beech Sunday' for the colours in autumn. At Fallodon in an average year this is the last Sunday but one in October; in the South of England it is the first Sunday in November.

While driving into Ashbourne yesterday I saw my first flock of redwings. We did see a few birds in North Uist last week but you would expect to see them earlier than in the south. Because of the mild weather the winter thrushes have been very late in arriving from Scandinavia. Last year I noted seeing fieldfares at Parwich Lees on 7 October. Redwing are the smallest of our thrushes and identifiable by the white eyestripe and long thin calls. As they take off the red underwing is very obvious and quite unlike the yellowy buff of the song thrush. The birds in North Uist would almost certainly have come from Iceland whereas our Derbyshire birds probably originate from Scandinavia. The Icelandic birds are larger and darker: they have the longer wings necessary to carry them on a lengthy overseas migration. Grey tells us they are susceptible to harsh conditions:

> The redwing is a tender bird; it is one of the very first to suffer in hard weather; before any blackbird or a song thrush shows signs of distress, a redwing may be found hopping feebly at the foot of a house wall, pining and disconsolate. This little bird – it is the smallest of our thrushes – is less capable than our resident birds of feeding itself in snow and frost, yet, though it is almost too tender for our winter, it will not stay with us to nest, and disdains the softness of our summer.

Since Grey wrote *The Charm of Birds* nearly seventy years ago, the redwing has established itself as a breeding bird in Britain, albeit in very small numbers. *The New Atlas of Breeding Birds* states:

> Breeding redwings are currently confined mainly to ten kilometres square around and north of the Great Glen. It is worthy of note however that in recent years redwings have bred in a few English counties, particularly in Kent where at least five pairs bred between 1975 and 1991. The likely British breeding population size in any one year is in the region of forty to eighty pairs.

NOVEMBER

Wednesday, 1 November

A cloudy mild morning with still no sign of any serious rain.

I was unable to see them, but I could hear their cries – a distinctive 'chacking' high up in the sky. The tell-tale sign of an incoming flock of fieldfares. On 15 October 1994 I was stalking with Andrew Sebire at Glen Affric. We were out on the ridges at around three thousand feet and out of the mist appeared thousands of exhausted fieldfares. This was certainly their first landfall since taking off in Scandinavia. Like their close cousin, the redwing, they are gregarious birds and will shortly be gorging themselves on the berries in my hawthorn bank.

Grey tells us of their weakness for the hawthorn berry:

> Fieldfares and redwings are thrushes, and seem to be gregarious during their stay here. The 'chacking' note of the fieldfare announces its presence, and both it and the redwing frequent hedges and presumably feed on berries. I have seen fieldfares in enormous numbers in a large wood where the big trees were far apart and the space was filled with wild hawthorn. On one day of cover-shooting the fieldfares would not leave the wood, and were flying hither and thither in the air in such numbers as to be confusing to eyes that were on the watch for pheasants and other objects of a cover-shoot.

Since Grey wrote, the fieldfare, like the redwing, has colonised Britain as a breeding bird, but again in very small numbers. It first nested in the Shetlands in 1967. Recently there has been a shift southwards in the small breeding population with a pair successfully bringing off young in

Kent in 1991. *The New Atlas of Breeding Birds* suggests an annual breeding population of less than twenty-five pairs.

Returned home at dusk to feed the ducks. A bird I initially thought was a little owl jigged past me in the fading light. Only when it zigzagged down into the pond surroundings did I realise it was a woodcock flighting in for its night-time feed. I don't usually expect to see them this early in the year, particularly when it is so mild. Continental birds pass through on migration in good numbers later in November and December. Maybe we are lucky enough to have the odd resident.

The High Peak met at Tissington and Caroline FitzHerbert rode Alfie.

Friday, 3 November

On the way to work I passed two creatures that had been killed by the traffic. I have never seen a dead woodcock on the road; maybe there has been 'a fall' in the last few days after all. We have recently had some clear moonlit nights and it has become colder. Cars are taking an increasing toll of our wildlife and several thousand barn owls are killed each year while hunting on the roadside verges.

Sadly, a dead badger straddling the tarmac is becoming an increasingly common sight. They are nocturnal animals and are most likely seen at night in the car headlights. We have a flourishing population of badgers in our valley. In fact, they are much more common that people think. There are a number of ways of detecting their presence. The most obvious is by finding their conspicuous 'sets'. Contrary to popular belief, the badger, like the domestic pig, is a clean animal. If the set is occupied there is always evidence of 'dirty linen' outside the entrance. They even dig small pits some distance from their homes which they use as latrines. At Parwich Lees there are well-worn paths leading from the sets across the fields and up the banks. Every night badgers move off along these in search of food. In the vicinity of the set and these 'runs' the grass is likely to be ripped up and the topsoil disturbed by the badgers in the same fashion as a pig noses up his paddock. This points to a relatively harmless diet of roots, coarse grasses, bulbs and worms. However, if a badger were to come across the eggs of a game bird, they would be considered a delicacy, as would the incubating parent!

BADGER & WASPS' NEST

Badgers do not present a serious problem for gamekeepers. One of their favourite foods is wasps' nests. Signs of a completed meal are a sure indication of the presence of a badger. In a dry summer, the clay soil around my duck enclosure cracks where the chicken wire is dug into the ground. These holes present favoured nesting sites for wasps. Initially, I thought a fox had been responsible for the destructive excavations at the foot of the fence. Tell-tale pieces of honeycomb were strewn over the ground. I then read a paragraph in *A Scottish Naturalist* on the habits of the badger by Charles St John (1809–56).

> One of his most favourite repasts is the contents of the nest of the wasp or wild bee, great numbers of which he must destroy. However far under ground the hive may be, and in however strong and difficult a situation, he digs it up, and, depending on his rough coat and long hair as a protection from the stings, devours comb, larvae, honey and insects. Many a wasp's nest I have found dug up this way, and often far from the badger's usual abode; but the tracks of the animal always made it evident who had been the robber.

This summer a badger destroyed a wasps' nest at the foot of a large ash tree on our lawn within yards of the house. I wonder how many people realise that badgers render the human race this valuable little service!

Sunday, 5 November

Walked down the Bletch before breakfast. The prettiest time to go is always before the frost has burnt off and the sun is still low in the sky. The ponds have a thin covering of ice although the mallard have kept them open in places. A solitary mandarin took off from my duck enclosure. I saw a flock of eight at dusk one evening last week. They are very agile in flight, have a white belly and emit a short whistle; altogether not unlike the wigeon. It is no coincidence I put a pinioned pair of mandarin on the ponds last weekend.

A pair of snipe took off noisily from the little island on the Tissington pond. A few fieldfares have now joined the redwing in the hawthorn.

I drove over to Tissington in the morning to pick up some hay for my sheep. A fox decapitated Stan White's gander on Friday and came back for it last night. Although the Meynell Hunt killed six at Tissington a fortnight ago and we have shot four on our small patch in just two recent outings, we are still inundated with foxes.

Robin Page in *The Fox and the Orchid* tells us that hunting remains the most humane way of controlling foxes:

> The best and most sensible justification for foxhunting was put by a northern biology lecturer: 'The fact that fox damage can be serious, even with control as at present, can be confirmed by reports from various organisations that run reserves – RSPB, Nature Conservancy Council and local Naturalists' Trusts, etc. Of the various methods of control only hunting is biologically acceptable as it is as near to the natural process as possible: it cannot wound, doesn't kill or injure other species (as do traps, snares, poison, etc.) and tends to select out the old, sick, injured animals which are the very ones most likely to do damage.

Tuesday, 7 November

Left Parwich Lees at 5.45 a.m. for Anglesey. I picked up Philip Snow at Conway and we drove to the farm via the Cob Lake at Malltraeth. The Cob has been immortalised by Charles Tunnicliffe. He painted and watched birds there for over thirty years whilst living at Shorelands. The *Shorelands Summer Diary* is an account of his first season (1947) at Malltraeth and is as close as he got to writing an autobiography.

> The seawall is called locally 'the Cob' and it has its beginning very close to the village at a spot where a bridge spans the river and its two flood-water canals. River and canals are disciplined by high man-made banks for some miles inland, indeed as far as the river is tidal. The bridge marks the end of the village street and the beginning of the road over the marsh. After crossing the bridge the road swings slightly inland, the deviates shorewards again and touches the Cob at its far end. Thus, between Cob and road, there is an area of blackish pool and swamp which is beloved of the birds and both road and Cob make ideal vantage points for their study. Many are the happy hours I have spent there. The pool in this diary is called 'Cob Lake'. On the other side of the road are fields which are often flooded and, even in summer, are rarely without water. Here too the birds love to congregate and there have been occasions when I have not known which way to turn, Cob Lake or field pools, because of the richness of birdlife on them.

We arrived at the Cob just before 9.00 a.m. – a good time, as it had been undisturbed by walkers on the seawall. The sky above the Cefni Estuary was alive with frenzied flocks of golden plover, suggesting the presence of a peregrine. The Cob pool, on the other hand, presented a tranquil scene. A flock of lapwing were roosting in the ankle-deep water with a few 'goldies' and four black-tailed godwits for company, the latter in pale comparison to the russet-coloured birds I saw last May in their breeding plumage at Needs Ore. Philip said this was the latest he had seen them on the island. They winter in numbers on the Dee Estuary.

While viewing this peaceful scene, I was quite unexpectedly confronted by my first bittern. A brown bird with rounded wings, which I initially took for an owl, flapped lazily across the Cob. This bittern could not have been more obliging. It flew the short distance from a hidden corner of the pool to a reed bed opposite us under the seawall. They are secretive birds that seldom venture into the open and rarely take to the air. We could not believe our good fortune. Philip said there was normally no more than one sighting a year at the Cob. It was too early to be a wintering bird from the continent. They tend to arrive in December and January. In all probability it was a young bird that had been dispersed from the RSPB reserve at Leighton Moss in Lancashire. The RSPB, funded by the National Rivers Authority, have a current policy of acquiring marshland on Anglesey and planting reed beds. Their primary aim is to attract the bitterns and marsh harriers as nesting species. We are hoping that the Plas bog on our farm at Valley will shortly become part of the overall plan.

The bittern is a master of camouflage. Its golden-buff plumage streaked in dark brown blends perfectly with the patterns created by dry reed beds. When surprised it adopts a sky pointing posture that exposes stripes on its head and breast. These resemble the reeds in which it lives. Our bird did just about everything except 'boom'. It stalked along the edge of the reed bed carrying its erect neck in a weird angular fashion.

Although as a young man Edward Grey spent time wildfowling on the Norfolk Broads, he would not have been over familiar with the bittern. Drainage and persecution drove the bittern to extinction as a breeding bird by 1900. There are records of it breeding again in 1911 and thereafter its fortunes improved – in the early 1950s about eighty booming males were recorded. This strange springtime call of the male bittern can be heard as far as three miles away. Today there are fewer than twenty pairs breeding in Britain, almost all on RSPB reserves. Their more recent decline has resulted from an increase in drainage, reed cutting and recreational activities. With new reserves being developed on Anglesey, together with the strategic planting of reed beds, their future looks much brighter.

After all the excitement on the Cob we made a brief visit to the farm. There were good numbers of ruddy ducks on both the Valley lakes, suggesting the Wildfowl and Wetlands Trust's cull last year was not very successful. On the way back to Conway we visited the Tunnicliffe exhibition at Llangefni.

Saturday, 11 November

It was wet, grey and misty all day; the first significant rain since September. The leaves are now falling fast from the trees. Those of the ash cover the country lanes with a green carpet, making driving quite hazardous. I had an invigorating walk down the Bletch in the rain after breakfast. Three teal sprang off my ponds and two snipe flew into the edge of the Tissington pond as I walked around it. I drove over to Middleton before lunch and took some of our roses to my mother's grave. It is her birthday tomorrow. Birdsong continues to be provided by the wrens and robins. There is also the occasional whistle from a nuthatch high up in the canopy or a thin cry from a dunnock as it calls out to an unseen friend. I took the back road home to Parwich. As I came through the little village of Elton I counted nearly fifty collared doves on the telephone wires. I think this ornithological phenomenon would have surprised Edward Grey above all others. The collared dove was only seen in Britain for the first time in 1952.

The tawny owls have been very noisy in the garden of late. This evening they were hooting up and down the valley and screeching around the house. It is in the autumn that they establish their territories and much calling and hooting can be heard. They are our most common and widespread owls but unlike the little owl and the short-eared owl they are nocturnal. Their eerie chorus begins at dusk. Two popular misconceptions surround the tawny owl's song, and for one Shakespeare is responsible. He described the owl's call as 'tu-whit, tu-who – a merry note'. In fact these notes belong to a pair of owls. The song most well known is the tremulous hoot but the more common call is a sharp 'kewick'. Unwittingly Shakespeare refers to one bird calling (probably a female) and another (male) returning with an offering of song. He should have written it the other way round – 'tu-who, tu-whit', with the male singing and the female answering.

Some say that both sexes hoot and both call 'kewick' but the sounds are never uttered together by the same bird. Grey suggests that the hooting emanates from an amorous male and that the rather inviting 'kewick' call is given by the young birds.

> The normal hoot consists of one fine, smooth long note; then a pause of about four seconds; then a long note, quavering at first and ending smooth and full. Sometimes the bird will give the first long note without following it up by the quavering note, but this is a broken and imperfect performance. I have occasionally, when standing unperceived near an owl, heard it go on for some time uttering one plain but fine-toned hoot with very little pause. The hoot of the

> brown owl enriches our woodlands, and without it they would be seriously impoverished. If the owls have a period of silence when they may be expected to hoot, I become restless and anxious lest they should have left the place. The hoot is, I suppose, the note peculiar to the male bird when he is in vigour; it is often answered by another bird at some distance, and appears to be, like some birdsongs, a proclamation of territory. A note which seems to be simply a call note sounds like 'ke-wick'; in the time when young owls are about it is sometimes repeated in a single tree with such frequency as to be tiresome if near the house.

I know what Grey means. When putting the dogs out last thing at night, I am often caught unaware by a blood-curdling shriek from the chestnut tree by the ha-ha which then continues at intervals. Quite a contrast to the gentle reassuring 'hoot' we are always used to hearing. I understand Grey's concern over a temporary absence of song. They are very local birds and become a treasured part of the surroundings. Their reticence to move far from their place of birth is evidenced by their absence from the Isle of White and the Isle of Man as a breeding species. They dislike long journeys, especially across water.

The tawny owl or brown owl hunts by night and roosts by day. A roosting owl can often be located by following up noisy groups of smaller birds – as I discovered when shooting at Exbury as back-gun in an oakwood. Grey describes a similar experience in *The Charm of Birds*:

> The mobbing of an owl by small birds raises one question that has always puzzled me. The animosity of little birds against the brown owl is intelligible enough: it is well known for them to be in safe roosting places before the owl comes around; and whatever the hoot may convey to human ears, there is reason enough for it to suggest beak and talons and to be full of foreboding to small birds. But why, if they mob the owl at all, do they do it so seldom? The occurrence is well known. We are in the woods and are arrested by an excited chatter of small birds of different species, drawn by common interest towards one thick fir tree. If we approach the tree, or if we watch till

> the annoyance becomes intolerable to the owl, we see it fly from the tree; the small birds then pursue it with cries that express hatred and disgust. The brown owl and the small birds are in these woods every day, but we only see this mobbing very occasionally, a few times in the whole year; it is not reasonable to suppose that it is only on these few occasions that the other birds become aware of the presence of the owl. Why is it so seldom that they take any notice of it? Possibly the fuss begins as some small bird comes upon the owl unaware, and finds itself so close to it as to get a fright. The scared note of the small bird would draw the attention of other birds who would assume that the owl had done something menacing contrary to its habits in daylight. This would be a breach of the custom of the woods which enables small birds and brown owls to exist together in the same wood in peace during daylight. The birds would resent it and combine to shift the owl, knowing that it is not formidable to them by day.

During Grey's lifetime tawnies suffered unmerited persecution from gamekeepers. Small birds are not an important part of a brown owl's diet. Although, when perched on one of my duck enclosure posts, they find the ducklings hard to resist, it is mice, voles and shrews which constitute everyday delicacies.

Wednesday, 15 November

The beech, lime, sycamore and chestnut have mostly shed their leaves but the oaks are still full of colour. Pride of place must go to the wild cherry. They look like they are on fire. The leaves at the top of the tree are a dark red while the heart is a cocktail of orange, bronze and yellow.

I went into Stockport for a meeting and then returned home to work in my office. Outside in the yard a pair of noisy pied wagtails were playing on the barn roofs. Unusual for this time of year; they are probably on their way south.

I walked down to feed the ducks at lunchtime. We have had more rain and the ponds are filling up again. The only sign of life in the hawthorn bank was the piping of a bullfinch hidden in the undergrowth. Owls generally are enthusiastic contributors to the limited birdsong. A little owl gave a plaintive cry across on the Tissington bank, only to set off a chain reaction from colleagues up and down the Alsop valley. And then, at dusk, the tawny owls commence their repetoire of hoots and shrieks. W. H. Hudson writes in *Hampshire Days*:

> I heard only that nightly music of the tawny owl, fluting and hallooing far and near, bird answering bird in the oak woods all along the swollen stream from Brockenhurst to Boldre.

Friday, 17 November

Motored down from Derbyshire to Woodstock to pick Robin up from Summerfields, arriving at Blenheim at 8.30 a.m. A beautiful sunny morning but very cold with a heavy frost overnight. I drove through High Park towards the Lince. The ancient forest floor was covered in a brown carpet of dead bracken. Together with the medieval oaks and Capability Brown's beeches they presented a panorama of autumnal colour.

I walked from the Lince along Bladon Water to the Cascade. There can be few places further from the sea than Woodstock, yet this morning around forty cormorants were gathered on the lake just above the Cascade. When I was living at the Lince ten years ago we saw one or two of these seabirds a year. A raft of over thirty great crested grebes drifted serenely on the water in their usual place opposite the boathouse. I wonder if they will be here in such numbers in another ten years' time.

The cormorants must be playing havoc with Blenheim's fish stocks.

The only sign of winter ducks on the lake was a group of fifteen drake pochard sheltering behind the island. They are handsome birds with a chestnut head, grey back and steel-blue bill. I have often wondered why the sexes segregate into separate flocks over the winter months. The males leave the breeding sites well before the females and arrive at their wintering grounds much earlier. By the time the females arrive the more northerly wintering grounds may already be full of males. The males will feed in deeper water further from the shore and being larger they can dive deeper and stay submerged for longer thereby exploiting a different food source. Only around four hundred pairs nest in Britain. In October they are joined by continental birds that have nested in Russia and Eastern Europe, swelling the winter population to well over fifty thousand.

Although there were no tufted on the main lake, they will arrive in December or January and happily co-exist with the pochard. Both species form common rafts as they are not in direct competition having different food preferences: the 'tuftie' is carnivorous and the pochard herbivorous. Pochard are less common nesters than the tufted because of their breeding habits. They are much more restricted in their choice of nesting sites. Pochard build their nests close to or on the water whereas the tufted is much less discerning and will build on almost any patch of land. The pochard's natural habitat is marshland and tens of thousands of acres have been drained since the war. Gravel pits present the largest surface area of new habitat in southern Britain. These are not favoured by the pochard as they often have steep sides which deter the establishment of reed beds.

TUFTED DUCK & POCHARD - BOATHOUSE, BLENHEIM -

The best place to see 'wild duck' is on the stretch of Bladon Water from the Lince to Bladon Gate. It is peaceful, the water is shallow, there is a good reed growth and there is thick cover along the banks. In the slightly deeper water opposite the Lince there was the usual gathering of eight or nine tufties accompanied by a few pochard, this time containing the odd female in their midst. Down at the other end of the lake where the water is more shallow, I saw a solitary drake shoveler and thirty teal. The beautiful colours of the male shoveler were not well defined, suggesting it was either immature or still at the tail end of its annual moult.

It was encouraging to see teal. When at the Lince I rarely saw them in any quantity. Maybe they are on their way back. It is interesting to note how duck populations fluctuate as habitat changes. In the 1950s the silted Queens Pool (the Woodstock side of the Grand Bridge) was dredged creating a new habitat. Immediately the wintering teal and wigeon disappeared, to be replaced by diving ducks like the tufted and pochard together with the great crested grebe. In 1977 the glyceria bed by the Fisheries was flooded creating a shallow water area where teal can now be found. Parts of Bladon Water are now quite badly silted up which makes an increasingly attractive habitat for the teal.

The duck I wanted to see was the gadwall. Much to my delight two pairs lifted off the water with the teal. They are relatively easy to identify in flight as both sexes have a distinctive white patch on the back of their wings. The female can be confused with a mallard except that she sports conspicuous orange sides to her bill. The drake is one of my favourite birds. At a distance he appears a dull grey but close to he has a most attractive plumage. The gadwall has an interesting history and for me it occupies as important a part of life on the Blenheim Lake as does the great crested grebe.

Edward Grey was almost certainly as unfamiliar with the gadwall as he was with the bittern. In Appendix I ('Fallodon Green Book') of Trevelyan's biography of Grey there is a list of the duck that bred in his collection during 1903. Although the shoveler, pintail, wigeon and red-crested pochard are all mentioned, the gadwall is missing. It is of course possible he came across it on one of his visits to the Norfolk Broads. A pair of migrant birds were caught at the Dersingham Decoy and introduced on to the Breckland Meres in the middle of the last century. These birds probably represent the ancestors of today's small breeding population. For over one hundred years their advance was slow but in the last twenty years there has been a dramatic expansion of their range. The first breeding record at Blenheim was in 1975 and before then they were merely rare winter visitors. When we were living at the Lince in the mid-1980s Blenheim was thought to be the only breeding site in Oxfordshire. I counted six pairs when walking around the lake on 5 May 1989, so possibly between five and ten pairs now nest annually. The gadwall frequents inland freshwater lakes and is essentially vegetarian. Even the ducklings are dependent on a diet of green material and are not insectivorous. They therefore do not compete with the mallard and generally mix well with other ducks.

Gadwall migrate to warm temperate zones in winter and are sensitive to cold, wet conditions which would explain their limited occurrence. A combination of warmer weather in recent years and an increase in suitable habitat such as gravel pits, reservoirs and wetland reserves have no doubt assisted their expansion. There are currently around seven hundred and fifty nesting pairs and their numbers increase to around five thousand birds over the winter months. Their main breeding areas are in eastern Europe, southern Scandinavia and Iceland. We do not really know whether any of these winter visitors stop over and breed with our feral birds; in all likelihood some do.

One thing is for sure. It is highly unlikely that one hundred years ago Grey would have seen any gadwell around his cottage. Now, not only do I see them on the flooded water meadows in the winter months, but feral birds are also to be seen in April and May by Grey's bridge on the Itchen. Perhaps they are breeding on nearby Avington Lake.

Tuesday, 21 November

Last week Lucinda saw a fox sitting out in the open in a field on the edge of the village. Just before lunch today our builder, Fred Knight, came up to the house and told her he saw a fox taking a cockerel in a garden in the centre of Parwich. They are such successful animals and, it appears, becoming increasingly bold. You do not expect to see them operating in the daytime.

Spent the day in our Leeds office and then took the train to London to attend to the RSPB/Sotheby's private viewing of the Tunnicliffe sale.

Friday, 24 November

I stayed overnight with the Chichesters at Exbury in Hampshire before driving up to Bramdean to check on the house in the afternoon; we complete the sale on 4 January. There are few better places to enjoy winter ducks than on the Beaulieu Estuary, and today conditions were perfect. We drove over to a stormy Needs Ore on the other side of the river. There was a full spring tide and a strong south-westerly blowing. The water was lapping at the foot of the cottages; I have rarely seen the tide so high. The creek was totally submerged and Storm Beach only a small strip of shingle that provided a temporary refuge for huge flocks of waders. Behind the spit, hundreds of sheltering teal, wigeon and

brent geese huddled together out of the wind and spray. When the tide is high and the wind strong, the duck are unable to hide in the saltmarsh creeks and they move inshore to find shelter from the elements. The brent geese are back in force and there were several hundred sheltering behind Gull Island. The waders seemed to be enjoying the rough weather. An enormous flock of mixed waders lifted off into the wind from Storm Beach. They turned, twisted and spiralled playfully upwards like a swirling thundercloud before settling back down again on the shingle. At a distance it was only possible to identify good numbers of grey plover by the conspicuous black spot under the 'armpit'. Others in the congregation would have included dunlin, ringed plover, turnstones and redshank.

When wild duck are mentioned it is always the wigeon that first come to mind. I love to hear their desolate call – maybe emanating from a wintery moonlit sky as they flight into the fields, or maybe from a raft far out on the choppy sea. There is something about that evocative whistle that brings me out in goose pimples.

The drake wigeon is our most beautiful common duck. There is a small piece of saltmarsh that backs on to the road between Lower Exbury and Inchmary. Today, by staying in the car, we got within a cricket pitch's length of around thirty wigeon feeding in a creek. Among them were a handful of teal. There are three aspects of the drake wigeon's plumage that I find particularly pleasing. At the one end there is a light brown head with bright yellow crown and at the other a pointed black tail that contrasts with a snow white rump and wing flashes. Sandwiched in between is a soft mushroom-brown chest. The little drake teal does not let the side down. He has a handsome green-brown head divided by the thinnest of yellow streaks.

While only around five hundred pairs of wigeon nest in Britain, one half of the total population of north-western Europe winters in Britain and Ireland. Upwards of two hundred and fifty thousand wigeon winter with us at coastal sites where they are often found in the same company as brent geese, thanks to a similar diet of eel grass and salting grass. These birds nest in northern Europe, Russia and Iceland. Our nesting birds are predominantly found in Scotland, particularly in the far north.

Although wigeon have always proved successful breeders in captivity as part of my wildfowl collection, I have only once seen a brood in the wild. In June 1993 I went up to Sutherland to stay at Ledmore. We spent a day fishing for brown trout on Loch Urigill where the black-throated divers were nesting and the greenshank still displaying on the adjacent flats. A female wigeon and her tiny brood were foraging on a small reedy lochan beside the burn that feeds Urigill. *The New Atlas of Breeding Birds* states:

> The 1988 survey of Caithness and Sutherland flows yielded eighteen broods. The emerging midges are the most important food of adults and young during brood rearing. In Caithness and Sutherland broods of wigeon, especially broods with well-grown young, were most commonly found along streams at their convergence with lochs. At this stage adults and young probably graze marginal vegetation and browse underwater plants as well as feeding on insects.

We drove back to Beaulieu via Sowley Pond where around fifty drake pochard had begun their winter holiday. On Beaulieu Pond itself there was the nowadays rather common sight of a little egret stalking its prey, but in addition the unusual occurrence of female gooseander fishing in the deeper water. The clearly demarcated red brown head and neck differentiated her from the merganser. Normally the gooseander haunts inland fresh water habitats but Beaulieu Pond consists of brackish water and is only a mile or so from the sea. Unlike the more coastal merganser, the gooseander is fairly sedentary and only hard weather will bring influxes in from Europe.

Saturday, 25 November

I stayed with my cousin Alexander Muir at Fonthill. We went for a walk down to the lake before breakfast. There was heavy rain overnight but the weather has turned very mild. The song thrushes have started singing again. They were busy in the woods up and down the valley as if to remind us what we had to look forward to in the New Year. I have yet to hear them recommence their song in Derbyshire. In *The Charm of Birds*, Grey points out a significant difference between the south of England and Fallodon. He observed that in the south the thrushes started singing again in October whilst in the north he had to wait until January before hearing them.

> At Fallodon there is a great difference in habit: after the summer the thrushes leave the garden and the woods.

He goes on to suggest that large numbers gather in the root fields and on the links to feed. Maybe the same exodus takes place with us in the Derbyshire hills.

The thrushes were not the only participants in this select autumnal choir. A multitude of starlings were whistling and chattering away in a wood at the end of the walled garden. Across the valley a woodpigeon was singing in the now bare beechwoods. Grey was grateful for its staying power.

> It is hard to say when the woodpigeon and stock dove do not coo: they begin early in the year; in the mild winter of 1924–25 they were

heard at Fallodon in December and January. The cooing of the wood-pigeon is exceedingly soothing. It does indeed speak comfortable words. For a poetic description of it I would refer to the whole passage in Wordworth's lines to a nightingale.

Down on the Fonthill lake yet another small flock of drake pochard sat sleepily on the water, this time with a few females in their midst. In the winter months most inland freshwater lakes seem to play host to a group of visiting pochard.

Wednesday, 29 November

A grey, damp and overcast Derbyshire day. The first big flock of fieldfares have appeared in the park. They have arrived very late this year. I put the nuts out on the birdtable a couple of weeks ago and the tits are only just beginning to take them.

A nuthatch visited the birdtable in the afternoon. They are such attractive, noisy, acrobatic birds that I am surprised Grey failed to write about them in *The Charm of Birds*. He does, however, include reference to a pair in the party of regulars that took food outside the cottage. The nuthatch has only recently increased its range northwards and it would not have been present at Fallodon one hundred years ago. In *A Year with the Birds*, Warde Fowler confirms how much these birds like a ready-made meal:

> We have another much smaller bird in the village which can hold large objects between its mandibles – objects almost as large, and sometimes more bulky than the egg of the cuckoo. This is the nuthatch which will carry away from a window any number of hard desert nuts, and store them up in all sorts of holes and corners, where they are sometimes found still unbroken. These plump and neat little birds, whose bills and heads and necks seem all of a piece, while their bodies and tails are not of much account, have been for years accustomed to come for their dinners to my neighbour's windows.

Interestingly enough the 'pair of nuthatches' fetched top price in the Tunnicliffe sale at Sotherby's last week. I've always wanted to own a Tunnicliffe, and I was lucky enough to buy the 'pair of drake shoveler'.

DECEMBER

Saturday, 1 December

Winter birdsong is dependent on the weather. A still, mild day is what is needed to trigger off the thrushes. Unfortunately at this time of the year in the Derbyshire hills such conditions invariably lead to dense damp mists. Today it was difficult to see the end of my nose. The hounds were going to meet at Parwich but were cancelled. Wenty Beaumont and Ian Beith were staying to shoot at Okeover which is a few hundred feet lower than Parwich Lees. We managed to get out and make the most of a pretty hopeless day.

While I was feeding the bantams in the morning, the song of both a song thrush and a mistle thrush wafted through the mist from behind the Swiss cottages – their first performance at Parwich Lees since the summer break. The song of the mistle thrush gives a special thrill as it reminds us that the blackbird will be performing in a few months' time. In his book *Birdwatching*, E. W. Hendy alludes to the similarity between the two songs:

> The songs of the various members of the thrush clan, though they vary far more than do their respective call notes, show an obvious cousinship. If the throstle is the most brilliant performer of this group – his art is that of a virtuoso – the blackbird, to many ears, tunes a sweeter, simpler melody; one might call him a naïve folk-singer. The storm cock's rather monotonous strains are a connecting link between the two.

In a sycamore high above the bantam enclosure a starling was whistling away contentedly and an expectant carrion crow was cawing loudly awaiting the rich pickings below. The only leaves that are now still on the trees are found in a small hornbeam hedge that I planted on the edge of the old drive in the hope of attracting an elusive hawfinch.

Tuesday, 5 December

I walked down to feed the ducks at teatime having spent the day in our Manchester office. We are on the receiving end of our first spell of Siberian weather. The valley is covered with a thin carpet of fresh snow. In these conditions the stillness can be quite eerie.

On the way back I stopped for a few minutes below the hawthorn bank to enjoy the dusk and its special music.

A cock pheasant went noisily up to roost and further up the valley a brown owl hooted reassuringly. Two night-time feeders strirred in the fading light. A yard or so behind me a woodcock rose from its slumbers under a cosy hawthorn bush, with a sharp crack of its wings. A snipe called harshly as it flighted into my ponds.

Thursday, 7 December

Two inches of snow overnight. Some inconsiderate gentleman stole my Discovery from the yard in the middle of the night. The police think it was used as the getaway car for a raid on a local post office. It meant that I couldn't get to work in Leeds and Marcus missed school.

At dusk we walked down the valley and I stood with my gun in the little field between the hawthorn bank and my ponds. I suspected the woodcock might 'be in' on account of the cold weather. The woodcock is a woodland wader and is a solitary bird that is never far from boggy ground for feeding. In the daytime the birds roost quietly in warm hardwood cover, perhaps of oak, hazel, laurel and bracken and only at night do they venture out to feed.

Few people seem to have experienced a woodcock flight. You can enjoy the special sounds of dusk in addition to the challenge of 'bagging' a woodcock as its flies into its feeding grounds like some exotic tropical bat. I was first introduced to this unusual ritual by Jamie Chichester in December 1980 when staying at Tarbert Lodge on Jura with a group of Cambridge friends. Along the east coast of the island, from Lagg to Tarbert, there is a dense Forestry Commission plantation. It is here that

the woodcock roost by day before making the short journey at dusk to feed on worms in the damp grasslands of Tarbert Bay. If the cock 'are in' for five minutes or so before dark the sky explodes with determined woodcock making for their night-time feed.

Saturday, 9 December

We set off for Bramdean after breakfast for our final weekend at the Malt House; Lucinda is understandably very sad. Marcus and I drove down to lunch with Jeremy and Derek at Needs Ore. It was a lovely crisp cold clear day with a full covering of snow still lying on the downs.

In the afternoon we walked down the creek towards Gull Island. We came across two kingfishers within one hundred yards of leaving the cottages; proof that the cold weather drives these delicate birds down to the saltings. A streak of orange over the furze bushes gave the first bird away. Its friend was fishing at the far end of the creek. You could have been forgiven for believing you were watching a little tern in midsummer as the tiny kingfisher hovered above the outgoing tide. Its irresistible iridescent turquoise plumage flashed in the low watery sun. Behind this exotic fisherman an old Thames barge complete with claret sails made a dignified entry into the mouth of the estuary.

There is a point at the end of the creek, just past the Beaulieu River Sailing Club, where you can stand surrounded by water on all sides. If you look due east to Spithead directly opposite across a small channel lies Gull Island. The Solent lies to the south and to the north the river meanders past Lower Exbury. It is a wonderful vantage point. Today the estuary was as busy as Oxford Street in Christmas week. There was a constant traffic of teal, wigeon and brent geese whilst white clouds of small waders corkscrewed across the saltmarsh. The Exbury side of the river was patrolled by colourful shelduck and behind us a solitary greenshank called mournfully from the creek which was policed at intervals by motionless grey plover. Across Storm Beach in the Solent a small group of divers and great crested grebes rode out the swell.

On the way home we stopped on the heath above Beaulieu in the hope of seeing a Dartford warbler, but we were disappointed. These rare birds, which until recently were our only resident warblers (since joined by the Cettis), are now confined to a few small areas of low heathland in Hampshire and Dorset. They are entirely insectivorous and the key to their survival in winter lies with the depth of cover provided by the heather and gorse, where they search for spiders and beetles protected from the weather. In the severe winter of 1962–3 the population was cut to ten pairs from around five hundred. The current count is approximately double the latter figure as a result of a series of mild winters.

Dartford warblers occupy large territories, and on account of a propensity to skulk in the gorse, always prove elusive. I have not seen one since my first outing. In March 1988 I was staying with Jamie Chichester and no sooner had we arrived at a suitable thicket on the Brockenhurst Road than we came across a single bird. It had a slate grey back with rich chestnut underparts; most striking of all was the piercing red eye. For a moment it was perched on some gorse with a characteristically erect tail and in a flash it had dived into a thicket. It was a much smaller bird than I expected and had a very long tail in relation to its body. We saw five to six birds in a matter of minutes, and it was hard to believe that Eric Simms wrote in his *Natural History of Birds*:

> Accidental fires and mistakes in programmes of cutting and burning heath have destroyed large tracts of the rarest wildlife habitat in Britain and have led to a decrease in the population of Dartford warblers to a 1979 figure of about seventy pairs.

I am amazed that Grey omitted to write about the Dartford warbler in the *The Charm of Birds*. Not only did he spend a good deal of his recreational time walking in the New Forest after Dorothy died, but he also seemed to have a particular affection for the whitethroat which is close cousin to the Dartford warbler. It resembles the whitethroat both in song and display flight. The song, which is emitted through a puffy throat, is very similar to the chatter of the whitethroat. Its call note is a harsh rasping churr and a fleeting glimpse of the Dartford can be caught as it makes a low darting crossing from one gorse bush to another. The display flight has many of the characteristics of the whitethroat. It ascends vertically in song above a bush and then dives back down into the undergrowth.

The Dartford warbler began to decline in numbers with the general retreat of heathland in southern Britain well before Grey wrote the *The Charm of Birds*, as evidenced by Kelsall and Munn in their *Birds of Hampshire and the Isle of Wight* (1905).

> Mr Meade Waldo writes that it is probably the only small bird, with the exception of the goldfinch, that has decreased in numbers during the last half century, the restricted area of furze cover in which it alone will live and the greed of the collector having contributed to circumstances.

E. M. Nicholson writing *Birds in England* in 1926 goes even further:

> Unlike its neighbours on the heath, the stonechat, whitethroat and nightjar, it is totally dependent on a mixture of heather and gorse for its survival. Gorse is the main feeding place as it is richer in invertebrates than heather. Unless a state of emergency is declared and vigorous action taken the furze wren will soon be extinct.

Over the past decade or so conservation has achieved some notable successes in protecting our heaths from the ravages of housebuilding, roadbuilding, fires and the quest for more productive agriculture. Around this area of Hampshire no doubt the New Forest Foxhounds have played their small part.

Sunday, 10 December

Philip Snow came down from London and spent the night with us at Bramdean. A very cold foggy morning with snow still lying in the garden; it froze heavily overnight. When I woke I thought my mother-in-law's parakeet was back in its cage but in fact it was a song thrush performing on the coldest of mornings. There were also a few woodpigeons singing in the lane; I suspect the birds are put off more by the wind than the cold.

After breakfast we took off for the Itchen. This was Philip's first visit to the cottage site. It is important he experiences the atmosphere as it is here that *The Charm of Birds* was conceived. We stopped at the cress beds on the road from Alresford to Itchen Stoke. We sat in the car and watched a wintering green sandpiper bob contentedly in the shallow water. We managed to approach within a few yards with the aid of the swirling mist.

The view from the cottage was obscured by the mist. A solitary mistle thrush tried a few half-hearted notes across the meadows at Avington and a dabchick whinnied downstream. Otherwise all was quiet. A family of mute swans glided gracefully on the river in front of the cottage. The cygnets were just beginning to shed their drab grey plumage and take on the snow white dress of their parents. Grey would have been pleased to see the family of long-tailed tits that skipped through the canopy of the lime avenue. I wondered if they were the distant relatives of his very own. On Grey's bridge we enjoyed a pair of grey wagtails flycatching from the river bank. A flash of yellow does wonders for the spirits at this cold drab time of year.

From the bridge we made our way across the fields to Avington Park, once the home of Grey's cousin, Lord Northbrooke. Its ornamental lake is badly silted and a favourite haunt for dabbling duck. Today it played host to over a hundred teal and a flock of thirty gadwall. The latter took off into the mist with their white wing flashes clearly visible. You need to be close to the drake to appreciate his subtle plumage. He challenges the drake shoveler as my favourite waterfowl. The gadwall then circled the lake uttering a stream of curious nasal croaking calls. The drake teal can also be a noisy little duck. His distinctive musical whistle emanated from every reedy corner of the lake. It is not a shrill call and is reminiscent of one of those old-fashioned whistles policemen used to carry.

I drove out of the yard of the Malt House at Bramdean for Derbyshire at 2.00 p.m. A happy twelve-year Hampshire chapter of my life was closed.

Wednesday, 13 December

The three birds that I most enjoy visiting the birdtable are the nuthatch, the great spotted woodpecker and, rarest of all, the sparrowhawk. As I returned from feeding the ducks just before dusk a cock sparrowhawk careered past the conservatory and over the birdtable in a desperate bid to secure its evening meal of an unsuspecting bluetit. In his commentary on the sparrowhawk in *Tunnicliffe's Birds*, Noel Cusa writes:

> It is shy of human company but can be very bold and dashing in pursuit of its prey. Recently at our Norfolk home a pair have taken to snatching tits from the birdtable notwithstanding that it is situated just outside the kitchen window. They very occasionally perch on the birdtable but the slightest movement disturbs them and they are off, far away over the fields. The practice of taking birds from birdtables is comparatively unusual in Britain but it is a well-known habit of the very similar sharp-shinned hawk in North America.

The short broad rounded wings and long tail are well designed to give the bird great manoeuvrability when in pursuit of prey. Sparrowhawks are such secretive birds that it is easy to forget that in some parts of the country they are more common than the kestrel. The winter months represent the best time to see them as the birdtable lures them into the garden and they are often flushed from a pheasant covert on a shooting day. During the late 1950s the population collapsed in Derbyshire as a result of poisoning by pesticides. So much so that in 1966–7 only one nest was reported in the county. Now that the use of pesticides is subject to much stricter controls numbers are flourishing again as they were before the war. Only this time the gamekeeper is taking a more enlightened attitude to their presence.

Saturday, 16 December

My brother-in-law, Rick Beckett, was staying to shoot at Okeover. There was a sharp east wind but otherwise the weather was kind and we shot two hundred and fifty very testing pheasants.

If shooting high birds, with good friends, in beautiful surroundings are the three prerequisites for a successful pheasant shoot then we have all three at Okeover. Robert Shields and Peter Walker Okeover are in the process of developing a most exciting shoot. We shoot over several thousand acres centred along a picturesque two-mile stretch of the Dove valley. The southern end of the estate borders on the pretty market town of Ashbourne while at the northern end you gaze from the ancient Caldwall Bridge into the jaws of Dovedale, immortalised by Isaac Walton.

The woods along the valley were planted in the 1950s by Peter's father, Sir Ian Walker, renowned as one of the best shots in the country. Today, as part of improving the shoot, Peter is planting five to seven acres of 'infill' a year. The pheasant thrives in these small patches of 'rough' that are planted to provide cover, as indeed do countless other species of wildlife. The parts of England where pheasants are scarce tend to be the intensively farmed areas in the east of the country where hedgerows and spinneys have been 'grubbed out' to form arable prairie lands.

It is easy to overlook the benefits that shooting and hunting bring to conservation in Britain. Small woodlands are under threat from modern farming because they are uneconomic. Patches of thorn and furze in particular are liable to be ploughed up. Copses, spinneys and rough areas of thorn that we take for granted are needed by sportsmen. Most of our small woodlands were planted for hunting or shooting and that is how the majority are still used. I quote from an article in the November 1995 *Field*:

> Peake's Covert near Burrough on the Hill in the Cottesmore country, is a small mixed wood of about eight acres. Its history is typical of the majority of small woodlands in Britain. Planted by Colonel Peake of Burrough Hall on his return from India, it was intended as a fox covert. Hunting coverts all over the British Isles bear the names of those who have owned or worked the land, commemorate famous local events and great national ones or remind us of types of local land use that have long since disappeared. Yet it is the recent history of Peake's Covert that is perhaps the most interesting. It has now been bought by the Badminton Trust for Conservation of the Countryside. The Trust was set up in 1986 specifically to protect small woods and spinneys and to ensure that they remain part of our landscape. The Trust encourages the propagation of wildlife and consequently field sports.

The same article asks the all important question of what would happen if hunting was ever banned. The Warwickshire Hunt manages two hundred and twenty-five coverts in its country. The master is quoted as saying:

> The habitat needs of foxes are similar to those of small mammals and butterflies. Last year we planted three new coverts, each of about two and a half acres, bought one four-acre covert and spent £4,000 on hedgerowing.

We are told that there are 99,000 acres of coppice in Britain and 96,000 acres are currently in private hands. The Forestry Commission own just 3,000 acres of coppice as opposed to 2,040,000 acres of forest.

The countryside is man-made and not natural. Many features are fashioned and preserved by the pattern of country sports. On my ninety acres of limestone grassland at Parwich Lees I have planted eight small copses, totalling ten per cent of the ground, with a combination of trees and shrubs like hawthorn, holly and blackthorn. I have put in seven ponds and created a small area of water meadow. All because I wanted both to enjoy the wildlife and have the ability to walk round with my boys and bag the odd pheasant. Owls and kestrels hunt the long grass in the fenced plantations, which in turn provide a home for hares and pheasants. The wetlands are visited by wild duck and provide a fertile feeding ground for snipe and woodcock. The ponds provide a stopping-off point for sandpipers on migration: the common going north in April and the green moving south in August. In the summer the water meadow becomes a tapestry of cuckoo flowers attended by hundreds of dancing butterflies.

An argument used against pheasant shooting is that is is 'destructive to wildlife'. Although gamekeepers have to keep on top of certain predators

like foxes, stoats, magpies and crows, it is just not true that they indiscriminately kill owls and hawks. This was probably once the case in Edward Grey's lifetime, but today at Okeover we saw kestrels, sparrowhawks and, most telling of all, a buzzard.

In his chapter on pheasant shooting in *The Fox and the Orchid*, Robin Page concludes by writing:

> Because of the pheasant, many thousands of acres have been spared from the plough, the chemical spray, the chain saw and flail mower. Through the pheasant we have an unexpected link with our historical past, and it is through the pheasant that we can help save what is left of our traditional countryside for the future.

Tuesday, 19 December

I had a meeting scheduled in Banbury for mid-afternoon so I made a brief visit to Blenheim in the morning. Aside from a pair of gadwall and a few teal on Queen Pool, the Lake was uncharacteristically deserted. When I arrived at the Lince I was soon to find out why. There was a flock of well over a hundred pochard – mostly drakes – on the water in front of the house. I have never seen so many pochard before, let alone on Bladon Water. The largest flock so far recorded at Blenheim was two hundred and forty-three in December 1977.

The pochard is nearly always found in the company of the tufted duck and today there were about a dozen in their midst. The tufties are much more relaxed than the pochard. As I approached the peaceful little valley was turned into a scene akin to the morning break at the school swimming pool as the pochard flock prepared for take-off. They scampered and splashed along the water in a comical fashion using a particularly long runway, as described by Noel Cusa in his commentary to *Tunnicliffe's Birds*:

> It is a diving duck and feeds largely under water. It thus has a different body shape from other ducks that feed on the surface, rounder and flatter, and with the legs more to the rear and with the feet relatively larger. In consequence, along with most other diving ducks, it does not rise from the water with the instant vertical leap

> that characterises say mallard and teal, but needs a long surface-pattering run before take-off. Moreover it is reluctant to move on to land, where it walks in ungainly fashion in a near vertical posture.

This explains why they are the only duck to build beside or actually on the water. There has been no proof of breeding at Blenheim since 1974, although a maximum of thirteen pairs nested in 1939. No doubt the Lake had a denser fringe of reedbed in those days.

Saturday, 23 December

Arrived at Rievaulx (on the edge of the North Yorkshire moors) late last night to spend Christmas with the Becketts.

My sister Libby and two of her daughters went hunting with the Sinnington while the rest of us went shooting. The hanging woods in the valley make for a thoroughly enjoyable small shoot. There was little wind but we finished up with just under two hundred high pheasants. Although it tried to snow the weather remained kind for most of the day.

Unusually enough, we failed to see any woodcock but the presence of two sparrowhawks in the morning was further welcome proof of their continuing rehabilitation. The piping of nuthatches and the piercing calls of numerous marsh tits echoed through the woods. We ended up the day on the Rievaulx Terraces, landscaped in the late eighteenth century and now owned by the National Trust. A huge flock of mixed tits moved through the beech trees in front of the beaters. In winter these roving flocks of tits operate from ground level to the top of the tree canopy. Great tits prefer the ground, marsh tits operate in the shrub layer up to about twenty feet, blue tits and coal tits feed on the slimmer twigs, using their extra agility to the full, and long-tailed tits feed above the marsh tits. In this way the trees are exploited for food on every level. An important advantage of mixed flocking is that a large group of birds has many eyes to watch for predators.

Sunday, 24 December

Woke up to a 'white-out'; there were ten degrees of frost overnight. Before breakfast I went for my usual walk through Greencliffe Hagg and down to the river. Hundreds of cawing jackdaws provided a gentle background chorus. Somewhere below me a jay gave a raucous screetch and a solitary woodpigeon sang far down the valley. The latter must rank with the robin and wren as our most prolific songster. Otherwise there was silence. Just the rustle of hidden pheasants as they scurried across the frosty leaves and the distant music of the river.

When I reached the river there was no sign of a dipper. I wondered if they moved downstream during the cold weather to enjoy a more clement climate. As I turned the last bend in the river before Bow Bridge, which carries the old drove road across the Rye, a pair of dippers bobbed on the icy rocks and then whirred upstream calling loudly – the surest proof that they stay in their desolate territories even in the harshest weather. I was hoping to hear that liquid warble as beautifully described by Grey in *The Charm of Birds*:

> The dipper is the most certain January singer, for even the hardest weather does not silence him. When the woods are hushed and white

with snow, and the burn is pinched with frost so that only a narrow dark channel of running water shows between the ice and snow at the side of it, there on some stone in the burn the dipper will stand and sing. It is water rippling over a stony bed that he frequents; the soft luxuriance of the chalk stream has no attraction for him. His song seems part of the sound of the rippling water from which he is never away. 'I hear thee where the waters run,' may be said of the dipper. His song is very sweet and lively; it has no marked beginning or close, but goes on indefinitely. It is as if 'beauty born of murmuring sound' had passed into the bird who was giving it back as song to the stream whence it had come.

Monday, 25 December

A white Christmas – a thin covering of snow with a bitingly cold north wind. Rick and I went for a walk on the 'tops' before church. Big flocks of fieldfares and redwings feeding on the berries in the woods.

Tuesday, 26 December

Arrived back at Parwich Lees for lunch. It has been very cold in Derbyshire but there is surprisingly little snow. The ground is frozen hard and both the Boxing Day meets the – Sinnington in Kirbymoorside market square and the High Peak in Bakewell – were cancelled. The hounds turned out anyway and the Sinnington went on foot. On Boxing Day, approximately one million people turn out to see hunts – twice the size of the crowds that watch football league matches on that day. The hunt is an important part of the local community.

We have been feeding the birds continuously as they must suffer terribly in this harsh weather. There are numerous great and blue tits on the nuts and the dunnocks, robins and blackbirds shuffle around the base of our stone birdtable. As I shut the chickens up at dusk I watched a dozen or so wrens creep up the barn wall and snuggle under the wooden eves. This practice of communal roosting must save the lives of thousands of these tiny birds. They are well known to huddle together in nest boxes or 'cock-nests' built the previous spring.

A grey wagtail on the terrace in front of the house presented an unusual yet most welcome sight, its yellow plumage adding a touch of the exotic to our British winter. They are quite common on Derbyshire's fast-flowing limestone rivers but I rarely see them at Parwich Lees. With all my ponds frozen over it seems a strange time for a visit. Down on the neighbouring River Dove would be happier ground. The Revd C. A. Johns writes in his *British Birds in their Haunts* (1885):

> The grey wagtail is among the most elegant and graceful of British birds and in delicacy of colouring is surpassed by few. Its habits are much the same as those of the pied wagtail, but it is even lighter and more active in its movements. It is less fequently observed away from water than that species, and though, like it, not altogether a permanent resident in England, it visits us in the opposite season, coming in autumn and retiring northwards in spring.

Friday, 29 December

A glorious winter's day. The valley is covered in a heavy frost. Clear blue sky with bright sunshine but extremely cold. The only pond which is not entirely iced up is a small one that supplies the duck enclosure. I am presently feeding up to fifty mallard on it – this morning there was a solitary teal in their midst. I walked on down to the Tissington pond where I disturbed a fox. It lolloped back towards Parwich Lees; they never seem to be in a hurry. My brother David was staying and as we walked back through the hawthorn bank his labrador Archie put up a dozen pheasants. It is very rewarding to build up a flourishing local population on the back of a few eggs under a broody and a single pheasant feeder. There are now large numbers of fieldfares working and roosting in the hawthorn.

JANUARY 1996

Monday, 1 January 1996

We spent New Year with the Beaverbrooks at Denchworth in Oxfordshire. The house sits in rather flat, wet country several miles north of the Ridgeway. Max has built up a small estate of three hundred and fifty acres around the house and has taken advantage of the woodland set-aside scheme, planting over fifty acres of mixed deciduous trees and shrubs. There is no economic advantage to this type of land use, it has all been completed for conservation purposes and in order that the boys can walk around for a pheasant. In the morning we did exactly that for a couple of hours, shooting half a dozen pheasants and two woodcock. In the process I dispelled the old adage that if you flush a woodcock and it drops back in you rarely put it up again. Three woodcock emerged from the main covert and one broke back to settle under a hedge four hundred yards away. I marked it down and flushed it an hour later. On the far side of the same field a small flock of golden plover announced their presence by their plaintive piping calls. Although the golden plover is a relatively common bird in winter you do not expect to bump into it within yards of the Great Western Railway.

A big thaw is in process which gave rise to a damp, grey foggy day only relieved by a flash of turquoise as a kingfisher set off across the moat. The Revd C. A. Johns, in his *British Birds and their Haunts*, writes:

> Its flight is rapid, and the colour of the plumage so brilliant that I can compare it to nothing less dazzlingly bright than the richest feathers of the peacock or a newly dug specimen of copper ore.

Aside from the planting programme, there are two other interesting examples of conservation at Denchworth. The sluices on the garden stream have been rebuilt and kept in good working order. This has the dual effect of ensuring the moat is full and of raising the water level in the stream. It is little wonder that kingfishers find Denchworth an attractive home. A few hundred yards upstream an area of rough has been fenced off to provide the perfect hunting ground for the local barn owls. They have even been provided with an architecturally imposing home on stilts. A tap with my stick raised the elegant white owl from its slumbers. As it glided silently from its box and circled its palatial home with slow deliberate flight I was reminded of another passage from Johns:

> Returning from our summer evening's walk at the pleasant time when twilight is deepening into night, when the thrush has piped its last roundelay, and the nightingale is gathering strength for a fresh flood of melody, a sudden exclamation from our companion, 'What was that?' compels us to look in the direction pointed at just in time to catch a glimpse of a phantom-like body disappearing behind the hedgerow. But that the air is still, we might have imagined it to be a sheet of silver paper wafted along by the wind, so lightly and noiselessly did it pass on. We know, however, that a pair of barn owls have appropriated these hunting grounds, and that this is their time of sallying forth; we are aware, too, how stealthily they fly along the lakes, dipping behind the trees, searching round the haystacks, skimming over the stubble and all with an absence of sound that scarcely belongs to moving life. Yet, though by no means slow of flight, the barn owl can scarcely be said to cleave the air; rather it fans its way onwards with its down-fringed wings, and the air, thus safely treated, quietly yields to the gentle force, and retires without murmur to allow it a passage. Not without meaning is this silence preserved. The nimble little animals that constitute the chase are quick sighted and sharp of hearing, but the pursuer gives no notice of his approach and they know not their doom till they feel the inevitable talons in their sides. The victim secured, silence is no longer necessary. The successful hunter

THE DENCHWORTH BARN-OWL LOFT

lifts up his voice in a sound of triumph, repairs to the nearest tree to regale himself on his prize, and, for a few minutes – that is, until the chase is resumed – utters his loud weird shriek again and again. In the morning, the owl will retire to his private cell and will spend the day perched on end, dozing and digesting as long as the sunlight is too powerful for his large sensitive eyes.

Friday, 5 January

Shot with Johnny Manners at Haddon near Bakewell. It is always a joy to visit Haddon. It is the ultimate fairytale medieval castle, never more so than on a summer's evening, when the roses are out on the terraces which overlook the River Wye. The shoot is in the high limestone country and the birds can be very testing.

As I stood on the bank of the Lathkill – only a few yards from where I caught my first trout thirty-five years ago – waiting for the pheasants to appear out of the mist, a mistle thrush sang up towards Youlgreave. Behind me in the willows the great tits had recommenced their spring song. Grey reminds us: 'The contribution of the great tit to the bird sounds of this month [January] is no mean one. The notes ring out loud, vigorous and clear.'

The great tit probably has the most extensive vocabulary of any British bird; today it was ringing its little bell. Warde Fowler tells us: 'The ringing note of the great tit is the first to be heard in the garden in winter time and is always welcome.'

At the end of a foggy yet enjoyable day, when we saw yet another Derbyshire sparrowhawk, Pev Manners and I went down to the Wye to flight a duck. The ponds were still frozen over but at dusk there was plenty of activity up and down the river. We were greeted on arrival by a flock of twenty mandarin. They have become successful breeders in the wild, spreading across most of the country. With their white bellies they are quite distinctive in flight but can sometimes be confused with the wigeon.

Saturday, 6 January

A damp foggy day. I was going to hunt but the meet at Moynash was cancelled due to the weather. I nearly trod on a snipe at the point where the little stream enters the Bletch pond. There is often a bird sitting in this spot and it never takes off with any great fuss – maybe it was a jack?

Wednesday, 10 January

Lucinda and I went down to London for the Astors' twentieth wedding anniversary party. We arrived back at Billing Road at 2.45 a.m. where a robin was in full song. Robins are often reported as nightingales in built-up areas as they will sing close to street lamps for much of the night.

Thursday, 11 January

Arrived at Knockdolian in Ayrshire mid-morning to stay with Richard and Joanna Wellesley on my way to Jura. Richard is a true countryman and a fisherman in the mould of Edward Grey. Knockdolian is situated a mile or so from the coast between Girvan and Stranraer which is one of the most isolated yet beautiful parts of Britain. It is a good two-hour drive from Carlisle via Dumfries and then Newton Stewart in the heart of the Galloway region. If I have any claim at all to Scottish ancestry it must lie here as two of my great grandfathers married daughters of the Earls of Galloway. In her book on the Fifth Duke of Marlborough (*The Profligate Duke*), Mary Soames writes:

> For over six hundred years Stewarts have inhabited that broad and gently undulating peninsula in south-west Scotland which lies between Wigtown Bay to the east and Luce Bay to the west. Today to the traveller from the crowded south it seems remote – two hundred years ago it must have been a world apart.

If there was one weekend in the sporting calendar we specially looked forward to it was going to stay at Knockdolian. We nearly always visited late in December or January when the weather was hard and the woodcock were in. I used to love climbing on to the sleeper with my Birley's sandwiches and a bottle of wine knowing I would wake up next morning on Stranraer Pier. One year the points were frozen south of Girvan and I jumped the train at Pinwhirry so as not to miss the first drive. The train conveniently ground to a halt on the Stinchar Bridge offering a fine view of Knockdolian Hill in the distance. The house sits on a bend in the river looking down on a pretty wrought-iron footbridge. It is dominated to the west by Knockdolian Hill, an ancient volcanic plug, and the twin peak of Ailsa Craig, which rises out of the sea in splendid isolation some miles to the north west.

Knockdolian has so much to offer to the sportsman. I have many happy memories going back nearly thirty years, having shot seventy brace of grouse on the moors, caught a brace of salmon in as many minutes in the Lynn Paeth pool, walked up snipe in the hills and flighted teal into the ponds and wigeon and greylag geese on to the floodwater. I have shot some of the best pheasants of my life at Knockdolian and ended a day with nine woodcock to my own gun.

Shortly after my arrival I went for a short walk up to Mellemon Loch above the house. This was constructed in the sixties by Richard's father at much the same time that he planted so many of the woods – all to enhance the sporting potential of the estate. The benefits to conservation are plain to see. A small mixed flock of pochard and tufted duck rode out the gentle waves in the middle of the loch quite unconcerned by my presence. Four nervous goldeneye immediately took off, easily identifiable by their white wing bars. In addition their rapidly beating wings make a loud shrill whistling noise in flight.

Mellemon Loch always seems to attract goldeneye in winter. At this time our tiny breeding population is augmented by upwards of fifteen thousand birds from Scandinavia which overwinter on our freshwater lochs and reservoirs. The recent emergence of a native breeding population has been a triumph for conservation – they were first proved to have bred in 1970; the project has been run by the RSPB in conjunction with local landowners. Goldeneye take readily to nest boxes and their provision in Scotland led to forty-four nests in 1986 and ninety-five in 1990. The provision of boxes has been carried out for over two hundred years in Scandinavia where there are now over seventy-five thousand available.

In the afternoon I participated in two drives on the 'keeper's shoot'. The weather was wet and there was a wild south-easterly blowing. We drove Finnart's bank above the Stinchar which contains a young plantation of larch and I counted ten woodcock come forward. Their preference is for cover bushy enough to provide a safe roost yet young enough to ensure access. A scarcity of pheasants in a particular covert will often attract numbers of visiting woodcock as they dislike daytime disturbance. If the woodcock 'are in' there is little doubt that they greatly enhance the enjoyment of a day's pheasant shooting.

The same anticipation seems to have prevailed two hundred years ago. Mary Soames quotes a letter in her book from the Earl of Galloway to his brother-in-law in 1797 enticing him to come and stay at Galloway House:

> I much regret you could not visit us this autumn and stay thro' the winter, this is an admirable winter residence, altho' the waves roar and break into our garden, we are perfectly sheltered notwithstanding and always dry, and bathing in a machine on sands or diving off the rocks every day. My children are not the same since their residence here, being so improved in health. Now what have you to do so material that need prevent you coming Bag and Baggage here for the winter, and before which sets in we will if you please take a trip to Inverary; afterwards growl and find fault over a good sea coal fire with the newspapers at all parties, a grand privilege I conceive and applicable to Britain alone. I have a billiard table, an old library, a little game of all sorts, and much wild scenery to employ both time and imagination and nobody to interrupt us or to annoy; and woodcocks are coming.

The sleeper no longer runs to Stranraer. The Stinchar now rises and falls faster than when I first visited owing to drainage high up in the hills which restricts the fisherman's options. The floodwater has recently been drained by a local farmer. The grouse have all but vanished, not least because of overplanting by the Forestry Commission. The woodcock may not visit in the numbers they once did as a result of disturbance by the increased pheasant population. Change is inevitable and it is often not for the good, but for me Knockdolian – and the Galloway region as a whole – will always retain its special charm.

In the chapter 'Retrospect', which Grey wrote for the 1930 edition of *Fly Fishing*, he tells us about the changes that had taken place around his cottage on the Itchen and takes a more optimistic view.

> The cottage that I put up by the Itchen in 1890 was intended only as a fishing cottage; a place in which to get food, sleep and shelter when I was not fishing. It became a sanctuary. The peace and beauty of the spot made it a sacred place. The cottage belongs to angling memories, but the fishing became a small part of the happiness that was associated with it. For thirty-three years the chosen spot remained a place of refuge and delight, not in the fishing season only. For the last four years, indeed, I had been unable to fish with a dry fly, and the original purpose for which the cottage had been put there had ceased to be. Great changes, however, had been taking place that were inseparable from a new epoch. For the first fifteen years there was little change and had been little change for many years before

this time. I had seen the old mill in the village not far away replaced by a new building, and the dull, monotonous sound of a turbine had replaced the lively splashing of the waterwheel; but otherwise things remained as they were. The cottage was invisible from any road; it was approached by an old lime avenue, long disused, and the track down this was not suited for any wheels but those of a farm cart. There was a little wayside station on a single railway line close by; but the quickest route from London was to go by a fast train to Winchester and thence drive a distance of four or five miles to the nearest point to the cottage that was accessible by wheels. This was a drive of at least half an hour in a one-horse fly. Presently taxicabs took the place of the horse conveyance and reduced the time of the drive to a quarter of an hour. Was this an advantage? On balance it was not. For escape from London meant that hurry, noise and bustle had been left behind: I had entered into leisure, where saving of time was no object, and often I would walk from Winchester to enjoy the country. There was a footpath on each side of the river. By one of these one entered the cottage without, except for the momentary crossing of one road and of three secluded lanes, having had touch or sight of a road. There were thirty-three stiles on this path. It happened not infrequently that I could not get to Winchester till the latest train, arriving there some time after eleven o clock. The walk then lasted well into the midnight hour. In the dusk or dark it was easier to walk by the road than by the path. There was much charm in this midnight walk. Traffic had ceased, cottage lights had been put out, the inmates were all at rest or asleep. Now and then one heard in passing the song of a nightingale or a sedge warbler, but in the main there was silence. It was pleasant after the hardness of London streets and pavements to feel the soft dust about my feet. On a still summer night there were sweet and delicate scents in the air, breathed forth from leaves and herbs and grass and from the earth itself. It was as if one's own very being was soothed and in some way refined by the stillness, the gentleness and the sweetness of it all.

Then came the age of the motors and tarred roads. Few people, I imagine, seek the smell of tar for its own sake. To me there is nothing unclean or nauseous in it, but it is a coarse, rough smell. The sweet and delicate scents of the night were obliterated by it, as if, overpowered and repelled, they had sunk back into the leaves and earth from which they had ventured into air. The strong smell of the tar seemed to disturb even the stillness of the night: the soft dust was no more, and the road was hard as a paved street. Not all, but much of the charm of the night walk was gone. There were other changes too; small houses of the villa type were built along the road that was nearest to the cottage; doubtless there are more of them now, for the cottage was accidentally destroyed by fire in January 1923, and I have not seen the place for some years. The sense of change was in the air. It may be that change is for the good:

> The old order changeth, yielding place to new,
> And God fulfils himself in many ways
> Lest one good custom should corrupt the world.

Saturday, 13 January

Arrived on Jura by helicopter from Glasgow yesterday morning to spend a couple of days with William Astor at Tarbert. He makes an annual visit at this time of the year which combines an opportunity to check on the stock and the forestry with some woodcock shooting.

The wind is in the south east and the weather stays mild. Not the ideal conditions for woodcock but they are still on the island in good numbers as part of their migratory progress from continental Europe. Yesterday we walked the birch scrub around the shore and cliffs on the crofts of Knockcrome and Ardfernal. Today we shot around the house at Tarbert. As we set off up the park a pair of golden eagles soared in the sky towards Ardlussa in the north. I was glad they were there to greet us as I failed to see any on our summer visit when they would have been well out in the forest. There were a surprising number of snipe in the damp rough pastures of the park. This is where the cattle are fed in winter and the snipe are no doubt attracted by the relative abundance of earthworms which you would not normally expect in the acidic soils of Jura. Over the two days we shot forty-five pheasants, two snipe and twenty woodcock. I am at my happiest when participating in this type of rough shooting.

Nobody forgets their first woodcock. I shot mine in a long belt between the A34 and Bladon Wood on the Blenheim Estate. Few sportsmen forget last season's woodcock and indeed memorable encounters of winters past. What gives woodcock their charisma? I believe it lies with their unpredictability. In many parts of Britain they are rare and only occasionally chanced upon. The woodcock's ranking by sportsmen is demonstrated by the exalted achievement of the 'left and right' or the desire to collect 'pin feathers'. At his Derbyshire home, Peter Walker Okeover has a superb Victorian fan made entirely out of woodcock pin feathers. There are three occasions when a countryman will chance upon a woodcock (I say chance because they are secretive birds that quietly roost during the day). The first is when they flight out to feed at dusk, the second is when they are disturbed at roost probably during a pheasant shoot and the third is during the mating season when they undertake their fascinating roding flights.

The latter is one of two interesting characteristics that stand the woodcock apart from other waders. The slow steady owl-like roding flight over certain carefully selected areas is characterised by a grunting call interspersed with a high pitched 'tswick'. My best memories of this nuptial roding are while fishing the Spey in the long evenings of late May. The perfect time to watch them is at dusk just before the sea trout come on. Each evening without fail the same birds follow their predetermined paths, criss-crossing the river.

Colin McKelvie in his *Book of the Woodcock* puts forward a now generally agreed theory. The woodcock is not monogomous. One male will mate with a number of females. McKelvie states that roding is not territorial (as is a snipe's drumming) but a method by which dominant males advertise themselves to females. Research in Germany has shown that the spring shooting of males did not result in fewer birds roding as they were quickly replaced by non-roding males. Spring shooting in continental Europe sounds barbaric, but there is an interesting argument in its defence. The woodcock leaves central Europe during the normal shooting season for the frost-free zones of Atlantic Europe and only returns in the spring to nest. If only roding birds are shot then it is the male bird that will be taken. As the woodcock is polygamous there should be no decline in the nesting population.

I quote one of the most interesting paragraphs in McKelvie's book:

> Hermann Goering was probably as grossly selfish in his framing of the Third Reich's hunting laws as he was in every aspect of his public life, but he left his mark with some very enlightened, if self-interested, policies and decisions. While he did not stop spring woodcock shooting altogether, he made it illegal to hunt woodcock over pointing dogs in spring, or to beat them out of coverts. An important study of the woodcock in Germany published in 1867 has shown that walked-up and driven woodcock shoots in spring combined with the shooting of roding birds could produce up to thirty-eight per cent of females in the bag. The thinking behind Goering's law was that the *Jaeger* should take up a static position, usually in a clearing or along a woodland edge, and shoot only at those roding birds which passed within range overhead. This is the European purist's style of spring woodcock shooting and various studies have shown that this results in a bag consisting almost exclusively of males, especially if only those birds which give both the 'quorr' and 'twsick' calls are shot.

Although large quantities of woodcock migrate to Britain and move through to south-west Ireland in late autumn there are considerable numbers of indigenous birds that breed locally. Ringing studies in Alnwick Park in Northumberland in the late 1890s proved that many birds stayed within a few miles of where they were originally hatched. East Anglia, Northumberland and the great river valleys of the Scottish Highlands are all famous for their indigenous woodcock. However, it is on a full moon in late October or early November that our local birds are joined by substantial numbers of migrants from their breeding grounds in Scandinavia and northern Europe. Woodcock 'wrecks' have been sighted in the North Sea where migrating birds have dropped from exhaustion into its icy waters. On migration they hit the east coast first and then follow the milder weather down the west coat of Scotland to

Cornwall and south-west Ireland. The famous woodcock shoots of the last century were located in the latter area and coverts were managed especially for this purpose.

The other endearing characteristic that stands the woodcock apart is its tendency to carry its young. I have never witnessed it but undoubtedly many countrymen have enjoyed this enchanting experience. It seems it usually takes place when a female is unexpectedly disturbed and feels a compulsion to move her brood to a place of safety. The chicks are picked up singly and securely wedged between the thighs of the parent bird. A friend, Alistair Campbell, claims to have enjoyed this mysterious event. While out rabbit shooting one summer evening in the mid-1970s at his home in Kent he noticed a strange looking bird flying towards him. At the end of a woodland ride, the bird was flying slowly and methodically – as if roding – when it turned and crossed the setting sun. The silhouette clearly showed it was carrying a large object beneath its body. The bird flew very close, having failed to see the intruder.

Wednesday, 17 January

A damp foggy day characteristic of the Derbyshire Peak District at this time of the year, especially if the weather is mild. A song thrush is back in the walled garden singing continuously, reminding one that spring is now just around the corner. It was complemented by the soothing song of a woodpigeon that I suspect is quite capable of performing in every month of the year. The tits have become noisy and argumentative. When I fed the ducks a solitary female wigeon took off from the ponds.

Thursday, 18 January

Motored over to Anglesey to spend a few hours at the farm. I arrived at Conway around 8.30 a.m. to pick up Philip Snow. The mild weather over the last few days has also started the song thrushes and greenfinches singing in his garden.

We drove on via the Cob at Malltraeth in the hope of seeing some pintail. The Cob is always worth a visit as the brackish water of the roadside pool is a favoured spot for both duck and assorted waders. Today they were all congregated just over the seawall in the Cefni Estuary. A flock of around five hundred knot were roosting on a single spit by the bridge. Aside from bumping into a small migrating group at Glenbatrick on Jura in late summer I've never before come across a large gathering of knot. While stationary they seem grey but when a packed flock wheels in unison over the water exposing their paler underparts and rumps they appear a brilliant white. Knots are remarkable migrants. They undertake vast journeys leaving their breeding grounds on the Arctic Circle and flying as far south as Patagonia and Australasia. Most of ours originate from Canada and Greenland. The birds I saw on Jura in August would have been passage migrants, moving along on their exhausting journey from Siberia to the southern hemisphere.

There was an interesting contrast between the duck population at Lake Traffwll and that on the shallow water of the Cefni Estuary. When we arrived at the farm the deeper water of the lake contained a good number of 'tufties', ruddy duck and a few goldeneye – all divers. The margin of the Cob on the shore of the Cefni Estuary presented a canvas of dazzling colour. Hundreds of dabbling duck, teal, wigeon, shelduck and pintail were feeding on the edge of the saltmarsh.

As many as three hundred wintering pintail will feed on the seaward side of the Cob. The drake pintail is our most chic duck. With its chocolate head, white bib and long pointed tail, set off by black rump and lemon underparts, the bird exudes class and elegance. I have kept up to three pairs in my wildfowl collection and always found them successful breeders. Only about fifty wild pairs breed in Britain. They form scattered groups that are widely distributed over both England and Scotland. Favoured are Kent and East Anglia where they build under tussocks in wet pastures. I have also seen wintering pintail off Gull Island at Needs Ore. They arrive in Britain from Iceland, Scandinavia and northern Russia in the autumn and numbers peak in December at around thirty thousand. Seventy-five per cent of our wintering population use the Dee and Mersey Estuaries, where they take snails and other invertebrates from the mudflats.

I arrived back home in Derbyshire at teatime and walked down to feed the ducks. There are over forty on the main pond in the enclosure. Half a dozen mallard took off in the company of yesterday's wigeon and a solitary teal to give me a personal fly past.

Friday, 19 January

Spent the morning in our Leeds office and then drove down to Exbury in Hampshire with Marcus and Lucinda to stay with the Rothschilds. A pair of magpies were chattering excitedly from a small tree outside Boots in a pedestrian precinct in the centre of the city. They were busy constructing the base of a nest. Members of the crow family are early nesters and a series of mild winters seems to have thrown everything further forward. It is easy to see why magpies are so successful – they adapt to any environment.

Saturday, 20 January

Lower Exbury is the only house for which I would consider leaving Parwich Lees. It sits on a bend in the Beaulieu River overlooking Needs Ore and, in the distance, the Isle of Wight. On a mild January morning the sky is full of the distant growling of brent geese, the flutey calls of redshank and, if you are lucky, a few bubbling spring notes of the curlew.

We spent most of the day shooting the scrubby maritime oakwoods in the heart of the estate. Their thick ground cover provides a warm refuge from the biting winds of the Solent for many different species of bird. One of the most enjoyable aspects of covert shooting is the variety of wildlife you are likely to see as you wait. Three buzzards glided over Moors Wood opposite Inchmery House. From the wood appeared five roe deer, a barn owl, a female sparrowhawk and a seemingly endless caravan of long-tailed tits. I heard a green woodpecker 'laugh' for the first time this year and a cock pheasant chucked and whirred as if he knew spring was in the air. Robins sang in the wood throughout the drive.

At dusk Jamie Chichester and I made our way across the little creek below Lower Exbury and on to the seawall which cuts across the saltmarsh. Every winter thousands of migrating teal and wigeon visit the Beaulieu Estuary. It is the ultimate in wild natural shooting. It is a tidal flight. The best time to shoot is on the high spring tides which push the duck off the saltmarsh. About an hour before high tide the duck start moving. A few hours later they will begin to flight back into the muddy channels.

A cold south-easterly blew in across the marshes. A yacht ghosted home up the river, identifiable by its navigation lights. Across the estuary the snug little cottages of Needs Ore were a hive of weekend activity. The peewits came first, corkscrewing across the seawall. Then hundreds of barking brent geese rose from the Blackwater meadows making for their nightly roost. Small groups of teal catapulted downwind following the contours of the creek like radar-guided exocets. Finally it was the turn of the wigeon, whistling high in the dark sky, as they flighted out to feed on the eel grass.

Sunday, 21 January

In the morning I drove over to Needs Ore with Nick and Jamie. It has turned very cold and there was a strong east wind blowing down the Solent. One of the highest spring tides of the year meant that Storm Beach had been reduced to a shingle spit. The creek had disappeared and water was lapping at the foot of the cottages.

As we approached Needs Ore hundreds of waders were flighting into a muddy pasture to the west of Blackwater. It was an extraordinary sight and matched anything seen in the Coto Doñana. We stopped by the roadside and watched them feed within yards of the car. The exceptionally high tide coupled with the stormy conditions were combining to push waders and duck alike off the saltmarsh. It seemed that most of the local wintering population of black-tailed godwits (two hundred) flighted in, displaying their attractive white rumps and wing bars. They proceeded busily to probe the damp grass with their long bills. They were in the company of curlew, redshank, oystercatchers, lapwing and golden plover, all oblivious of our presence. A stream of beautifully marked snipe dropped in to feast on the earthworms that had been forced to the surface on this flooded grassland. Most interesting of all was the presence of five wintering ruffs, identifiable by their shortish bills, reddish legs and a plumage similar to that of a hen pheasant. I have only seen ruffs on two occasions before in Britain: a single bird in May on the Blackwater meadows, probably on its way north; later in the same year a small returning group which dropped into Martin Mere while I was lunching with Dr Janet Kear of the Wildfowl and Wetlands Trust.

Back at the seafront a large flock of roosting dunlin and grey plover had turned the thin shingle strip of Storm Beach into a carpet of grey. In front of the cottages a solitary greenshank with its well-defined white rump settled on a tiny island of vegetation which was all that remained of the saltmarsh.

After lunch we set off back for Derbyshire, arriving home at 6.30 p.m.

Wednesday, 24 January

Our second cold spell of the winter has bought the tits back to the birdtable. The great tits aggressively drive away their more delicate cousins, the blue tits, from the nuts. They are not quite as sweet and innocent as they look. The stout beak represents a formidable weapon and one of my bird books records a great tit killing a goldcrest and then carrying it away in its feet like a miniature hawk. Grey tells us of a similar tragedy:

> To one who knows the ways of the great tit the sharpness of his notes suggests the sharpness of his beak. Among others of his own size he is a strong, bold bird, capable of tragedy, as the following story will show. There were traps kept in the garden for rats and other small nuisances. Some of these traps were cages so constructed that it was easy from outside to find a way in, but difficult from the inside to find the exit. Into one of these there had entered a dunnock and a great tit. Presumably the dunnock had entered first, and the tit had come later, attracted by seeing the cage occupied. Whether the tit entered with full design, or whether having entered he was roused by what Shakespeare calls 'vile opportunity', we cannot tell, but the design is known. When in due course I visited the trap the dunnock was a pitiful sight: it lay dead; the skull was broken into and the brain had been eaten. The great tit alone was alive, a patient and thriving murderer.

Thursday, 25 January

Bitingly cold north-east winds with snow expected. In the morning I drove over to Nottingham for a meeting. Just south of Ashbourne, two large rookeries were bubbling with activity as the occupants were busily engaged in the refurbishment of their nests. It is very early to start building, particularly in light of the recent spell of Siberian weather. They are obviously stimulated to a degree by the longer hours of daylight but I can't help feeling that global warming is playing its part.

Friday, 26 January

It is milder now that the east wind has dropped. Snow flurries all day. A solitary coal tit visited the birdtable late in the afternoon to join a boisterous swarm of blue and great tits. The coal tit is the smallest of our breeding tits and my own favourite. It has a distinctive white spot on its nape and rather pretty buff underparts. In the summer it is largely invisible but draws attention to itself by its distinctive high-pitched song. In the winter it is a regular visitor to the birdtable where it seems to hold its own even though bullied by the larger blue tits. Like the nuthatch, the coal tit carries off small particles of food left by its larger cousins and stores them away for a rainy day. This compensates for its inability to carry large fat reserves. Coal tits have a preference for coniferous trees and with the rapid expansion of commercial forestry since the war they have increased both in numbers and range. Their fine bills and acrobatic skills make them well suited to feed among the pine needles. I have yet to find a coal tit in one of our nest boxes. Their nest is normally in a hole and often low down, in the ground or among tree roots.

FEBRUARY

Saturday, 3 February 1995

I was up at 7.30 a.m. and walked in the walled garden; a lovely still mild morning with patches of blue sky and a fiery sunrise. It is one month into the New Year and the birds are finding their voices again.

The first song of the chaffinch is one of the great events of the bird calendar. Edward Grey had 5 February down as a possible date for hearing the first chaffinch at Fallodon. There was plenty of 'pinking' going on in the valley but no sign of that well-known song, 'a rollicking cadence ending with a flourish'. I heard the first performance from a high beech tree next to my duck enclosure. Again it was a disappointment, suggesting lack of practice – in the same way as the yellowhammer fails to complete 'a little bit of bread and no cheese' early in the season, so the chaffinch fails to produce his flourish. Grey alludes to this in *The Charm of Birds*:

> Warde Fowler gives a very apt description of it in one of his books. He compares the manner of it to a bowler running with quick steps up to the wicket and then with an overhead turn of the arm delivering the ball; and he notes that when the chaffinch first begins to sing it cannot for some days deliver the ball; it gets to the wicket and stops. To those who know the song this illustration will surely commend itself. I have known people complain of the persistent iteration of the chaffinch's song and I must admit that it does suggest a happiness that is a little trivial and commonplace. If the chaffinch were human one can imagine that he would say 'cheerio' as a greeting to a friend.

CHAFFINCH.

While watching my chaffinch perform, I heard the soft, high-pitched song of a treecreeper – Grey calls it 'a very sweet little wisp of sound'. I often confuse its song with that of the goldcrest. Although I failed to locate the bird, what makes the treecreeper's song so distinctive is the fact that it ends with a lovely flourish.

Later in the morning I hunted with the High Peak. The meet was at Brassington, famous in the past for its local lead mining. As you would expect, the country was pock marked and dangerous. Not much jumping and the rain descended after lunch. Still, home in one piece to watch England give the French a good beating at Twickenham.

Sunday, 4 February

One of those thick Derbyshire fogs that fill me with gloom covered the valley. There is nothing worse than a dense, damp, still mist, as it obliterates our beautiful view and inerrably appears at a weekend. It suddenly lifted mid-morning to reveal a characteristically grey February day.

The chaffinches were in good voice, 'pinking' boisterously from every corner of the garden. I often confuse this call with that of the great tit, as did Grey:

> One trick of the great tit must be mentioned before passing on: I have heard and watched at close quarters a great tit keep up for some time a perfect imitation of the 'pink-pink' of a chaffinch. The imitation was so perfect that, had I not been so close that the tit could be seen to be making the sound, I should have considered the performance by any bird but a chaffinch to be incredible.

The great tit is one of our earliest songsters starting in January. He has a remarkably varied repertoire of calls. Grey thought that the rhythm of one of the most common spring notes suggested sawing, while another sounded like a little bell being rung.

> The rhythm of the notes suggests sawing, but they are evidently intended by the bird to be a song as much as that of any other bird

that sings. I have known them to be mistaken early in the year for those of the chiffchaff, before the latter has arrived.

Outside our kitchen window we have a pretty stone birdtable under the canopy of a glorious copper beech. In the winter months, this little area becomes the centre of the great tits' universe. They are the bullies of the birdtable, aggressively asserting their dominance over the more delicate blue tits. The only bird that seems capable of dislodging the great tit from the nuts is a nuthatch. He lowers himself acrobatically upside down into the feeder and makes off with a single nut, probably to hoard in some secret hideaway.

Away from the birdtable, the best way to locate a nuthatch is by his distinctive call notes. This morning, I heard his piping dual note, 'chwit-chwit', from the other side of the house. Just over the ha-ha there is a sycamore which is rapidly going back, and, as a result, presents a favoured kitchen for nuthatches. The first year I placed a nestbox on the trunk it was occupied by a family who succeeded in rearing eight young. They are very sedentary and will not wander far from home so they become part of everyday life. You can always tell if they have taken up residence as they have a habit of encasing the nestbox hole with a layer of mud, presumably to make it smaller. They are an attractive busy little bird with slate-grey upperparts and orange-buff underparts.

A pied wagtail announced its arrival back with us by uttering its high pitched 'tschizzik' call from one of the yard roofs. Maybe this was the male advance guard as they normally return to nest in early March. In the spring and summer they become an important part of the yard, nesting on the flat roof above the back door and sunning themselves on the barn roofs. The pied wagtail demonstrates an interesting halfway stage between migration and all-year-round residence. They are one of the few insect feeders to stay in Britain over the winter, for which, this being the case, there is a definite migration to the milder south. They leave us at Parwich Lees in early November. Any birds seen in the north of England in winter are most likely immigrants from Scotland and Norway. It always amazes me how many pied wagtails summer on Jura in the Inner Hebrides. Maybe as we normally go there in August they are moving southwards from the far north. I had an interesting experience on the ferry from Islay to the mainland in early September 1987. I was watching gannets from the deck when suddenly a pair of pieds came bouncing into view of my binoculars – miles out in the Sound of Jura – no doubt commencing their journey south.

While we were having lunch, a great spotted woodpecker alighted on the birdtable nuts and we watched him feed through the window no more than five yards away. As he hung on the feeder he rather rudely presented us with his bottom – a beautiful bright scarlet patch beneath the tail. I say 'he' because the bird had a scarlet patch on the nape of his black crown which is only evident in a male. The great spotted is our most widespread and numerous woodpecker, with around thirty thousand breeding pairs in the UK. The species feeds mainly on invertebrates extracted from dead and dying timber and we don't see so many at Parwich Lees now that I've taken all the dead elms down.

Tuesday, 6 February

Outside our back door at Parwich Lees, we have two small holly trees planted in Versailles tubs. Practically touching one is a lantern which we keep on at nights. As I let the dogs out before going to bed, I discovered a dunnock snugly roosting in the holly bush beside the lamp – presumably attracted by the heat. I've always wondered where and how the millions of our little garden birds roost. The dunnock was tucked up like a tiny fluffy ball with his head under his wing and was quite unmoved by my presence.

Over the years ornithologists have lamented the fact that this delightful and unobtrusive little bird has been referred to as 'a hedge sparrow', and how right they are. Apart from the physical differences, their personalities are poles apart. The sparrow is a noisy and boisterous bully whereas the dunnock is gentle, modest and self-effacing. Undoubtedly history has labelled it 'sparrow' because it seems at first sight to be an 'ordinary brown bird'. In fact the only sense in which one could call it ordinary lies with the statistic that there are two million pairs in Britain. On close observation the dunnock has a pretty blue-grey throat and breast with a spotted head. The house sparrow, which is probably my least favourite British bird, has a finch's beak equipped for seed eating. The dunnock should really be classified as a warbler, not only on account of its long thin insect-feeder's beak, but also because of its musical song.

The dunnock is not, however, a true warbler as it is not entirely dependent on insects for its diet – but then neither is the blackcap. It is, of course, a resident; in winter it survives chiefly on seeds and is a regular underneath the birdtable. Its crowning glory is its beautiful blue egg. I still remember to this day the first dunnock's nest I found as a child. It was in a low box hedge by the orchard at our home, Kidmore End House in Oxfordshire. The nest presented itself like a delicate Easter present.

It was thirty-five years before I discovered another – this time outside our dining-room window at Parwich Lees, as before in a box bush. They are difficult to locate as the dunnock shuffles through the vegetation and along the ground rather than flying direct to its nest. With the lovely blue egg lies one of the mysteries of nature. In most cases, the colours and patterns of birds' eggs have a clear purpose – that of camouflage. This can hardly be said of the dunnock's egg, which is laid in a shallow nest and more often than not in an accessible position. It is normally hole-nesting birds, like owls, woodpeckers, starlings or redstarts, that lay white or blue eggs. Bright colours help birds to locate their eggs in the dark.

Perhaps the dunnock's beautifully conspicuous egg is the reason why it is one of the cuckoo's main victims? Anyway, that egg and his gentle personality make the dunnock one of the most endearing of British birds.

Thursday, 8 February

The wind is now in the east. It is much colder and keeps threatening to snow. I drove over to Humberside for lunch; the visitors' car park of a multinational chemical company is not exactly the most likely spot to hear the song of a marsh tit. I failed to locate it, but I clearly heard its distinctive call – a soft 'pitchew'. There are no two British birds more difficult to tell apart than the marsh tit and the willow tit (with the possible exception of the chiffchaff and the willow warbler). In fact it wasn't until 1897 that the willow tit was classified as a separate species of tit in Britain. They are pretty well impossible to distinguish at a distance, so it is only by song one can be sure of their identity. The problem even defeated Edward Grey:

> . . . the willow tit I have not yet distinguished from the marsh tit, and with impaired sight I could not now discover it for myself.

He did not have the advantages that I have had – many long lonely hours on the M1 going to my Leeds office and listening over and over again to *British Bird Songs and Calls* on tape! The call of the marsh tit ranges from a distinctive 'pitchew' to a scolding 'chickabee-bee-bee'. The willow tit has a loud nasal 'tchay' and a high-pitched 'zee-zee-zee'.

At close quarters the marsh tit has a glossy black cap as against the willow tit's sooty cap. The crown cap on the latter is more extensive and the neck broader and more bull-like. The marsh tit has a smaller, rounder head and sits up straighter. The willow tit also has a conspicuous white panel on its wing feathers.

The two species tend to live subtly different lives. One mustn't be misled by the name, as the marsh tit prefers dry deciduous woodland whereas the willow tit will frequent damper woods (where it can more easily excavate its own nest site) and conifer plantations. A black-capped tit in the garden or on the birdtable will invariably be a marsh tit. I have yet to detect a marsh tit on our birdtable at Parwich Lees, although they were regular visitors to the nuts at the Lince in Blenheim Park.

Saturday, 10 February

Arrived at Bywell in Northumberland to stay with the Beaumonts last night. Long train journey from Chesterfield, via Leeds, York and Newcastle, to Stocksfield.

Two species of diving duck could be seen on the Tyne from the drawing-room window. People always make the mistake of referring to

goosanders under the generic name 'merganser'. In fact, if you see a large sawbill over ten to fifteen miles from the sea and on freshwater it is almost certain to be a goosander. A pair of goldeneye were busy diving in the pool in front of the house. These birds were females as they had a brown head and grey buff on the flanks.

A coal tit, a mistle thrush and a nuthatch were all singing in the garden before breakfast. They always used to say that the Peak District was the northernmost range of the nuthatch in Britain. They must have spread rapidly north over the past twenty years or so as they've sung at Bywell early in the year for as long as I can remember.

After lunch, together with my cousin David Bowes-Lyon, we drove up towards Allenheads to go for a short walk on the moor. There were seven goosanders on the Tyne near Riding Mill, including three drakes. The male is a particularly attractive bird with a dark bottlegreen head and with a subtle pink wash to the flanks and underparts. Wenty told me he once shot one on the North Tyne which had ten salmon parr inside it. Together with the dramatically more numerous inland cormorant, they must take quite a toll of the fish stocks. You now need to obtain a licence to control the goosander.

We arrived at Harwood Shield in light rain around 3.45 p.m. Harwood lies to the north east of the Allenheads Moor, marching with Westmanhope and Blanchland. Wenty only owns the shooting rights and the moor is sadly overgrazed, with a herd of cattle currently assisting the demise of the heather. If someone took them off and cut back on the numbers of sheep, the heather would be back in two years in places. Overgrazing is the major enemy of our upland moors. The grouse are paired up and very tame, jealously guarding their territories. The cockbirds are sporting their splendid crimson 'eyelids'. There is an excellent stock on each Allenheads beat and if the grouse are given a good spring, it looks like being a bumper year. This truly wild bird would be in danger of extiction if it were not shot. This may seem ironic but without proper habitat management the grouse will surely disappear. Heather is vanishing across the country at an alarming rate as it is.

Monday, 12 February

Arrived home to make the tail-end of Marcus's sixth birthday party. While both boys are developing their skills in bird recognition, I think it is Marcus who will turn out to be the real countryman of the two. He has already developed a keen interest in the countryside while Robin prefers his sport.

Walked down the valley to feed the duck enclosure; there must have been around fifty mallard on the ponds. At least half took off and circled the valley while I was feeding, then they quickly dropped back in – a glorious sight.

A dunnock was singing in the hawthorn bank and being aroused by another in the Lees hedge. The first I've heard this year. It is a thin jingling song, which Grey found attractive if not memorable.

> The dunnock's song has spirit and uplift and is quite adequate in loudness and is pleasant, but there is little shape or feature by which to remember it.

Wednesday, 14 February

Down in the South on business and spent a few hours at Needs Ore before it got dark.

It was a wild evening and, although the tide was low, few birds were feeding in the creek. There were, however, a large number of shelduck present, all of which seemed to have paired up. The male is markedly larger than the female and has a distinctive red swan-like knob at the base of the bill. Aside from their vividly pretty white, black and chestnut colouring, I think they are a characterless duck. They are quite shy and often emit an unattractive growling sound when taking off. Interestingly (unlike all other ducks), both male and female have the same bright plumage – maybe demonstrating they are a halfway house between duck and goose. In late summer they begin to disappear from Needs Ore as they embark on a lengthy moult migration that for reasons unknown takes them to the Heligoland Bight or Bridgwater Bay. They breed over most of our coastline, usually taking to rabbit burrows. They are moving further and further inland to nest and I will never forget my surprise at seeing a pair in the field immediately in front of Alastair Campbell's house near Sevenoaks in April 1988.

The only wader present in the creek was one characteristically sad-looking grey plover. They are often alone like this, which only adds to their general air of misery. They tend to adopt a hunchbacked and dejected posture. In summer, when breeding in the Arctic, they thoroughly dispel these impressions. They then develop a very handsome plumage – spangled grey upperparts and black underparts. I was staying in Sandwich Bay during August 1988 when I met with three recent arrivals from the north on the beach, looking devastating in their black breeding plumage.

I remember identifying my first grey plover with Jeremy Norman at Needs Ore in February 1987. Why I at first got it mixed up with a sanderling I have no idea. The latter is much smaller and frequents the waveline on sandy beaches, whereas the grey plover is more likely to be seen on mudbanks. The grey plover is the shore-feeding counterpart of the golden plover and has a highly conspicuous black armpit, easily seen in flight.

During the winter months at Needs Ore, the grey plover is the one wader you can always be sure of seeing. Invariably it seems to be contemplating the misery of a damp cold English winter with its joyful colourful summer lifestyle no more than a twinkle in the eye.

Saturday, 17 February

Incredibly wet underfoot and a nippy north-westerly wind. There is no doubt now that a fox got into the enclosure during the cold spell last month. All four pinioned duck have vanished and I've found the remains of a wing and a carcass in the fields. He probably jumped over the new wooden gate. They are such cunning animals. There was a grey squirrel on the birdtable this morning. They are a real pest and in the predator league-table I place them runner-up to the fox. They cause damage to young trees, eat the nuts put out for the birds in winter and in the spring and summer think nothing of destroying the eggs and nestlings of our garden birds. The magpie comes next, closely followed by the carrion crow – both will devastate the duck nests in the enclosure given half the chance. Finally, when the ducklings hatch they have to face an assault by the stoats and weasels. Nature is cruel to a degree.

A mistle thrush sang his heart out around the house for an hour before breakfast. He moved from the top of one mature park tree to another. The Revd F. O. Morris, in his *History of British Birds*, writes: 'The supposition that the bird loves the berry of the mistletoe is not borne out by fact.' Although the mistle thrush, the largest of our songbirds, probably does supplement its diet of mountain ash, hawthorn, yew and holly berries with berries of the mistletoe, it is nevertheless more apt to refer to this domineering bird by its lesser known name of ' storm cock'.

Christmas 1987 was a mild one but with a blustering south-westerly that blew up late on Boxing Day and stayed with us over the weekend. A few days before Christmas I thought I heard a blackbird singing down the Lees valley and put it down to the very mild spell. The Monday after Christmas the wind was still blowing and once again I heard this 'spring-like song'. This time I could hardly fail to notice the performer as he sat at the very top of a dead elm, braving the elements and repeating his song every thirty seconds or so. Although so evocative of a warm April day, the quality of the song was inferior to that of the blackbird.

... THE FOX & THE TEAL

Grey's wintery description of its bold song is most evocative.

> The Mistle Thrush is best appreciated in January and February. Not that he sings better then than later on; indeed his song is more perfect in April, but it is very good in the first two months of the year and it stands out clear in the comparatively silent air. There is boldness and wildness as well as sweetness in the tone. It has not the rich and moving quality of the blackbird and yet it stirs us. For on a windy day in January when the blackbirds seek the shelter of the laurels and thickets and have not a note of song in them, the mistle thrush sings, aloft and conspicuous. There is, it has been said, 'weather in his song'. Birds as a rule seem to dislike wind more than any other sort of weather, but the mistle thrush is less discomforted by it than any other songbird. On a windy day early in the year, the 'storm cock' will mount his tree and there in full exposure proclaim by song that he is vigorous and glad.

The call most frequently associated with the mistle thrush is a sharp churring which resembles a football rattle or the grating sound produced by running a finger nail down the edge of a comb. This call is either given in alarm or more generally during its undulating woodpecker-like flight. The mistle thrush is a very aggressive domineering bird which defiantly defends its territory, reputedly driving away bigger birds and even attacking cats. I remember two years ago watching a pair of mistle thrushes from our kitchen window attacking a carrion crow. The crow had stolen one of the young from their nest which was lodged conspicuously in the fork of a sycamore tree in the park. There was little they could do but time and time again they dive-bombed the offending thief, crying out loudly in their furious indignation and distress.

Wednesday, 21 February

4.30 p.m. and snowing quite hard – just got out of a long hot bath after a day's hunting with the High Peak at Tissington. The Tissington Estate lies just to the south of Parwich Lees. It has one of the prettiest estate villages in the country and is owned by my friend, Richard FitzHerbert. We had the lawn meet at Parwich Lees and Humphrey Wakefield came down from Northumberland to hunt. Grey would have approved of Humphrey's visit. He has recently undertaken the considerable task of restoring Chillingham Castle. In his biography of Grey, Trevelyan writes:

> And on the other side of Fallodon, to the west, rise the heather moors, crowned by Ros Castle Camp, Grey's favourite point of view, closely overlooking Chillingham Park with its white cattle and castle where his family had borne rule in the old border times. Beyond Chillingham, the green, rounded Cheviot range hides Scotland and shelters this outpost strip of England between hills and sea. All North Northumberland is visible from Ros Camp, now dedicated as a memorial to Edward Grey.

The weather stayed fine in the morning but blew a strong south-westerly. We saw plenty of hares but I don't think the harriers came anywhere near catching one. The thought of a kill simply doesn't cross my mind – I love seeing them dashing away with their ears flat back. My main interest is negotiating the next wall without breaking my neck. We had a lovely first hour on the high ground jumping lots of walls. It was too wet underfoot lower down in the hedge country and we shouldn't really have been there. I got into lots of trouble with the post and rails, hedges and ditches – they scare me to death!

I heard and saw my first skylark of the year; I don't know what it had to sing about in that wind. We just surprised it and up it went. Also present were a small group of meadow pipits; again the first I've come across this year. They are semi-migratory and move south in the late autumn with a good number crossing to France and Spain.

As we moved off a grey heron took off lazily from the little pond in the hawthorn bank. With their enormous wings they are able to gain height very quickly, often calling harshly as they ascend. Herons will think nothing of travelling over ten miles for food; when, in the late 1980s, we put some trout and goldfish in the Lees ponds, they appeared overnight from nowhere. They still visit us in smaller numbers, I imagine to feed on the large quantity of frogs that frequent our wetlands, particularly in springtime. They are ambitious and fearless hunters and will seek out goldfish from the smallest garden pond. They have even decimated Jeremy Norman's goldfish in his tiny Pimlico garden at Moreton Terrace. My overriding memory of herons will always be of the thin, ghostly sentinels sitting motionless on the rocks around the narrows of Loch Tarbert on Jura. The key to their hunting success is their statuesque patience. They are proving successful breeders and after the very hard winter of 1962–3 their numbers in Britain have increased to over ten thousand pairs. This can be put down to a combination of warmer winters, less persecution and cleaner feeding grounds.

Thursday, 22 February

Took the 7.00 a.m. train to London. As we approached Kettering I noticed that the rooks had started building – maybe a week or so earlier than up in the Derbyshire hills. The first sign of spring must be the 'cawing' emanating from the refurbishment of the local rookery.

The use of pesticides and seed dressings as part of the intensification of post-war farming led to a significant decrease in numbers until the 1980s. From the 1940s to 1975 there was an overall forty-per-cent decrease in breeding numbers. Rooks are beneficial birds and are often wrongly accused of damaging crops – they mainly eat worms and leatherjackets.

We have a small rookery at Parwich Lees that I guard most jealously. There is an old superstition that when the rooks go – the owner of the house goes. Our rookery used to have over twenty nests but with one of the four main trees being hit by lightning, we had half the number last year. I become nervous around this time of year.

Saturday, 24 February

There were no more than a dozen mallard in the enclosure which I suppose is not surprising as they are dispersing and looking for nesting sites. Together with the rook they are one of our earliest nesters. Unlike the rook, the mallard's early broods always seem prone to disaster. This is because the young ducklings are dependent on insect life in their early days for survival.

Looking at the weather there's not much chance of that materialising for a few months. No sooner had I reached the valley bottom than down it came again – albeit a soft summer rain. It didn't seem to stop the chaffinches; the valley was ringing with the strong descending notes of their song; it won't be long before its the willow warblers' turn.

I heard a wren singing for the first time this year. The lusty song of the tiny wren gave Grey great pleasure, not least because it is such a regular performer.

> It may be said of the wren that in a not unfavourable year its song may be heard in every month, but not as certainly as that of the robin'.
>
> The wren's song is a succession of rapid notes, forming a long musical sentence, that is repeated again and again at intervals. The full sentence is a long one, but the bird very often begins it and leaves off in the middle or even after the first few notes: a good example of what we were taught at school to call 'aposiopesis'; like the woman who, after speaking for a time at a public meeting, began a sentence with the words, 'But still . . . ', then stopped and sat down. But when a wren is in good form he sings as it was said the young Queen Victoria danced at a court function in Paris, 'with decision, and right through to the end'.

In relation to its tiny body, the wren has an immensely strong voice. If it wasn't so obsessively vocal the wren would easily be overlooked. Indeed who would have thought it was our most numerous breeding bird, with around eight million breeding pairs.

When I drive to our Leeds office, I leave the house around 6.15 a.m.; it is a drive of seventy-five miles but the early start means missing the traffic. Practically every morning at the height of last summer a wren sang his heart out from a branch outside my bathroom window. The little bird would open its wings and flutter them at the climax with its throat wide open. Sometimes if it saw me it would fly off singing, which would always remind me of yet another engaging passage from *The Charm of Birds*.

> In front, some ten yards away, was a poplar tree, and from it a wren sprang into the air, and singing in an ecstasy as he flew, passed straight over me and over the cottage roof to some other place of bliss on the farther side: 'like a blessing', said one [Dorothy] who was with me.

Grey had just arrived down at the Cottage after a week in London – 'I was indeed standing on the top of the golden hours.' I had exactly the same feeling on Friday summer evenings in the early 1980s when I walked from Long Handborough station through the Evenlode water meadows to our house, the Lince, in Blenheim Park.

As I write, a tiny wren is lustily singing outside the drawing-room window.

The High Peak met at Long Rake above Middleton so I took the boys over mid-morning. I called in at The Hall to see my father who

has just returned from Florida. I couldn't hunt as I broke my little finger when my horse refused one of those horrible Tissington hedges on Wednesday. After the meet, the boys and I took the dogs down Bradford dale for a short walk.

There was plenty of water and we saw two out of the three 'regulars' that I enjoy watching so much when walking in the dale – the grey wagtail and little grebe – but no dipper.

The grey wagtail loves the rush and tumble of a limestone river like the Bradford. They perch on boulders, looking splendid in their grey coats with yellow underparts, flicking their long tails and then darting off to catch a passing insect. W. H. Hudson, writing in his *A Foot in England*, thinks: 'that the delicately coloured grey-and-yellow bird is the most attractive wagtail, it has the longest tail and can use it more prettily'.

> Her tail is as much to her, both as ornament and to express emotions, as a fan to any flirtatious Spanish señora. One always thinks of these dainty feathered creatures as females. It would seem quite natural to call the wagtail 'ladybird' if that name had not been registered by a diminutive podgy tortoise-shaped black-and-red beetle.

The little grebe (or dabchick) is a shy bird and when I visit the Itchen the surest way of detecting its presence is by its long trilling cry. It reminds me of a high-pitched horse whinny; when I first arrived at the Lince, I found the sound most eerie, not knowing what it was. The Bradford dabchicks have become quite used to the many walkers who enjoy the dale and are therefore easy to observe. They look like dumpy little puffballs on the surface and it's easy to understand why they acquired their nickname 'Tom Pudding'. When submerged, they have a delightful habit of 'raising a periscope' if they feel they are being watched. Suddenly, from the middle of a cressbed a tiny head appears with rich burgundy cheeks and a small yellow spot at the base of the bill.

This afternoon was bright and sunny but with a cold westerly wind. I walked down the valley again and the mallard were back in numbers, no doubt to feast on the barley I brought them this morning. I watched two

hares barely ten yards away in the big meadow. At first they crouched low with their ears flat but then lollopped around playfully with little concern for my presence.

Sunday, 25 February

The most glorious sunny morning with the air full of birdsong. The sun is quickly burning off a thin covering of white frost on the northern-facing bank.

A cock pheasant crowed and beat his wings in the hawthorn bank – a sure sign that spring is on the way.

I broke the ice and fed the ducks. Pair after pair of mallard flew in to feed, the bright colours of their plumage enhanced by the low sun. I was immediately reminded of the concluding paragraph in *The Charm of Birds*, when Grey was describing a scene at his waterfowl enclosure:

> It was Christmas morning, many years ago when my sight was less impaired; the sun does not rise until half-past eight in Northumberland at this season. I went out after breakfast; the waterfowl had been fed rather later than usual: they were still finishing their meal under the big larch tree or were assembled at this end of the pond, which, being much shut in by trees and shrubs, was still in dark shadow. I went to the other pond some two hundred yards away and sat on the garden seat on the farther side. This pond is more open: there are no tall trees on the east side and all the water was full of sunlight. There was not a bird on it; there was not stir in the air; the surface of the water was smooth and without motion. Presently pintail, wigeon, tufted ducks, pochards and one or two other kinds began to come flying over the intervening shrubs and trees from the pond where they had been fed. They come, some singly, some two or three together. None of them had yet seen the sun that morning, and each and all, as in greeting to it, began to sport and play. They threw the water over their bodies, they raised themselves up on it and flapped their wings; they swam rapidly about in all directions, low in the water with quick and eager forward dartings of the head and neck. They sprang from the water into the air and took headers from the air into the water; they made short flights in one direction, hit on the water for a moment and made another flight back in the direction whence they came; they dived unexpectedly, travelled under water, came up in some new place, and then, as if surprised at what they saw, dived again with exceeding suddenness. They splashed for the sake of splashing: there was not a square foot of water that was not in constant agitation. For some time the scene was one of motions of delight and exhilaration. At length first one bird and then another flew up on to the bank that faced the sun, or on to the south end of a little island; they then stood and sat, many of them side by side in pairs, and rested motionless or slept. Some half-dozen birds only remained on the water, and each of these was still, the head turned round and the bill resting in the feathers of the back. All was quiet; there was no sound or stir; the water was again smooth, the reflections in it were composed once more; the sun still shone: on the water and the birds; on the scarlet-barked willows and the delicate

bareness of winter trees on the opposite side. Anyone who had come upon it now might have thought the place was under some spell. He would have seen the man on the seat sit motionless, too, for a long time; entranced rather than asleep: the scene had indeed sunk down into his heart and 'held it like a dream'. There are times when man's consciousness seems laid to rest in some great whole of which he has become a part. There are hours of which it can be said 'thought was not: in enjoyment it expired'. So it was now, and if anything stirred in the mind at all, it was an echo of the words 'and God saw that it was good'.

MARCH

Friday, 1 March

Arrived home at lunchtime after visiting a business near Lichfield. It's very wet underfoot – also windy with snow showers. I had a short walk down the Bletch having fed the ducks. I saw four hares in all, two of which sat quietly within yards of me under a hawthorn bush. I later drove over to Tissington to pick up some hay for the sheep and saw three more grazing in the fields. It's pleasing to see them in such numbers.

I dislike shooting hares and in any case find them too rich when it comes to the pot. I have placed a pheasant feeder just out of sight of the house at the end of the lawn. I love seeing pheasants strutting about in the garden. They seem to have found it as I watched three hens scratching around over the ha-ha from the kitchen window. I must be getting old as I increasingly dislike the idea of shooting any of my resident ducks, pheasants and hares.

Saturday, 2 March

The pied wagtails are back in force and I heard a treecreeper in the park while walking back to the house. That high-pitched flourish now makes it very easy to recognise.

Hunting was cancelled as there was a heavy frost overnight and there is still a good covering of snow following the fall on Wednesday night. What a sadness, as Sheldon represents our best country, with plenty of open grassland and stone walls.

While walking in the hawthorn bank I heard the tell-tale piping call of a bullfinch. This single note is by far the most effective way of detecting the presence of bullfinches. They are very shy birds and although well distributed (two hundred thousand pairs) they are seldom seen. A

typically sighting would be on a small country road when for a split second a flash of white rump is glimpsed as a bullfinch bounds into a protective hedgerow – as described by W. H. Hudson in *Hampshire Days*:

> On that hot day in the silent time of the year it was strangely still, and gave one the feeling of being in a country long deserted by man. Its only inhabitants now appeared to be the bullfinches. In these deep shaded lanes one constantly hears the faint plaintive little piping sound, the almost inaudible alarm note of the concealed bird; and at intervals following the sound he suddenly dashes out, showing his sharp-winged shape and clear grey-and-black upper plumage marked with white for a moment or two, before vanishing once more in the overhanging foliage.

It is both a modest and anti-social bird. Unlike other finches it never flocks in winter, despises colonial nesting and is very inconspicuous in the nesting season, never undertaking display flights. Although anti-social by nature, the bullfinch is an affectionate bird and is supposed to mate for life, pairs often being seen together in the winter.

It will always be the sheer beauty of this unobtrusive finch which stands it apart from other garden birds. This was nowhere as well demonstrated as one July day at Bramdean in Hampshire when I was staying with my parents-in-law. I heard a loud and continuous screeching from the garden. An adult green woodpecker was halfway up a telegraph pole using its tail as a prop and on top of the pole was a young bird. They were being mobbed by magpies. Quite unconcerned on the wire sat a cock and hen bullfinch. The rose-red and pinkie-browns of the bullfinches contrasted quite beautifully with the greens, yellow rump and crimson crown of the woodpecker. I always associate Bramdean with bullfinches; they would sit sedately in pairs in a Philadelphus bush outside the kitchen window. Bramdean is the only place I have heard their song. Flegg, in his *Birds of the British Isles*, describes the song:

> Bullfinches sing most often in the breeding season. Not many people have heard the song because it is very quiet. A soft pleasant mixture of short clear piping notes and hoarse wheezes which the cock seems to reserve for its mate.

The latter sounds like a door opening on rusty hinges.

A pair of hares stand out huddled together in the snow. They remind me of the days when there were partridges in the countryside. It is now nearly thirty years since I used to take the London train from Cambridge as an undergraduate and count the pairs of partridges in the snow-covered fields around Royston.

Sunday, 3 March

A bitingly cold westerly wind. The only sign of spring was a pair of courting rooks. They faced each other like sparring gamecocks, their heads bobbing up and down. When walking to feed the ducks at mid-morning, I flushed a woodcock out of the hawthorn bank, its russet tail conspicuous for a moment before it dropped back in a hundred yards or so ahead. I wondered if it might be a resident bird which would stay and nest or just the tail-end of the winter migration.

GREEN WOODPECKER : THE LIMEKILN

Even though there was a strong wind, somewhere across the valley I heard the distinct cry of a green woodpecker. He was laughing in flight as only a green woodpecker can with the sheer joy of life and the sound echoed all down the valley. It is from this laughter that the bird obtains the name of 'yaffle'. Edward Grey stated that he had never heard it drum and some people think that, unlike their spotted cousins, green woodpeckers never indulge in this curious habit. However, most reference books suggest they do drum but it is rare. W. H. Hudson is unlikely to be wrong and in *Hampshire Days* he describes 'the favourite drumming tree of a green woodpecker', and speculates that 'it may be that the two big woodpeckers, who play equally well on the same instrument, are intolerant of one another's presence, and that in his case, the spotted bird had driven the larger yaffle from his territory'.

Monday, 4 March

Drove into our Manchester office at 6.15 a.m.; a pair of magpies were busy building a nest near the centre of the city. It amazes me how well they have adapted to urban life in the last twenty years or so. Magpies and foxes have a good deal in common. They are both scavengers that have been able efficiently to utilise a wide range of food resources. Man has made his environment more conducive to these predators and artificially raised their populations. They happily forage in urban rubbish tips and dustbins in built-up suburbs.

They are becoming an increasing problem and their numbers need to be controlled.

While driving through south Manchester I stopped at a set of lights and watched, entranced, as my first blackbird of the year performed from a roadside tree. The blackbird may not be charismatic, it certainly doesn't lay an aesthetically pleasing egg or construct a very creative nest, yet its song is quite beautiful. We only have around four months of the year to enjoy it and Grey ranks it alongside the nightingale, blackcap and curlew in terms of excellence:

> It is not possible to explain why the blackbird's notes excel and why they mean so much to us. To me there is something in them that I can best describe as intimacy. The songs of other birds please or delight us, but that of the blackbird seems to make a direct appeal to us and stirs some inward emotion. The song is a linked phrase, repeated again and again at intervals.

The blackbirds are not singing with us yet – maybe it's just that little bit warmer in the centre of a huge conurbation like Greater Manchester. Grey hoped that this longer season of song gave a little compensation to people unable to leave town.

Wednesday, 6 March

Sleet and snow showers all day. It's still very cold – apparently the coldest start to March for ten years but after a very mild winter.

A pair of Canada geese have arrived on my ponds and are no doubt prospecting for a nesting site. They arrive every year about this time and try and occupy one of the small islands. I let them nest for three years but now encourage them to leave! They are noisy and aggressive; in addition, they shatter the peace of my poor ducks and make a terrible mess of the surrounding grass.

The Canada goose was introduced into Britain during the eighteenth century by wealthy landowners in order to grace their parks and lakes. At the time of the first census in the 1950s there were thought to be three thousand pairs in the country. The 1991 census threw up a figure of well over fifty thousand. The British population is growing at the staggering rate of nearly ten per cent a year. They have benefited in much the same way as the tufted duck from the recent increase in gravel pits and reservoirs. They tend to flock up again in the winter and our birds probably come from the nearby lakes at Kedleston or Osmaston. In fact, the Canada goose is rapidly acquiring the status of a pest. It eats huge quantities of grass, then puddles and fouls large areas with its droppings. A fast throughput of food leads this goose to produce droppings every four minutes or so while it feeds, so one can easily imagine what a flock of one thousand can do. These birds are not good fliers and therefore produce poor sport for wildfowlers, so all in all they are becoming very difficult to control.

Whenever I visit Grey's cottage at Itchen Abbas, Canada geese are either grazing in the water meadows on the other side of the river or calling loudly from Avington Lake. In early spring Titchbourne Brook and the Itchen valley are alive with the sound of noisy nesting pairs. Kelsall and Munn, writing in their *Birds of Hampshire and the Isle of Wight* in 1905, only make one mention of the Canada goose:

> Up to about the year 1890 a pair belonging to the Earl of Portsmouth nested for many seasons on an island in the river at Hurstbourne and frequently reared their young.

It seems likely that Hudson and Grey would today be amazed at this invasion by a bird they would only occasionally have seen on waters such as Avington Lake or Alresford Pond. Or perhaps in Grey's case, St James's Park, as he strolled from his home in Queen Anne's Gate to the Foreign Office, dreaming of happy days spent on the Itchen.

Saturday, 9 March

Overcast but still, so plenty of birdsong after the wet and windy spell. A hen pheasant was sitting on the east wall in the walled garden and a cock crowed in the wood behind. I had a great deal of trouble in deciphering whether a rather monotonous nasal wheezing call was coming from a greenfinch or a starling. Maybe the latter was up to his old tricks. Starlings are very effective mimics and I have heard them take off both curlews and woodpeckers at Parwich Lees in the past. There was definitely a greenfinch in the walled garden as I heard its characteristic flight call ('chi-chi-chi-chit') and it has recently been on the birdtable.

Left for Blenheim after breakfast and arrived in the Park at around 10.30 a.m., having decided to leave my car at the Lince.

The Lince is dwarfed by three enormous cedar trees. In fact Blenheim Park must contain some of the finest cedars in the country. We used to love to burn cedar wood on our sitting-room fire because it smelt so delicious. There was always a good supply as the snow had a nasty habit of bringing down some of the bigger fan-like branches. From underneath the canopy of these giant trees, I listened to the spring song of numerous invisible goldcrests. The goldcrest is our smallest bird and Grey reminds us that consequently it is easily overlooked.

> It is only when we know the song of the goldcrest that we realise how common the bird is.

There are, in fact, over five hundred thousand pairs in Britain. It is one of the miracles of nature that this little bumble-bee of a bird migrates across the North Sea from Scandinavia. There is an old wives' tale in East Anglia that they hitch a ride on the back of short-eared owls.

The song is a high-pitched double note that ends in a flourish, described below by Grey. There is also a fine single note used for keeping in contact with family and friends in that fir jungle.

> Its voice, as we should expect, is very high pitched; the little call notes are needle points of sound. The song has little volume, but on a still day can be heard from some distance. It suggests to me a tiny stream trickling and rippling over a small pebbly channel, and at the end going over a miniature cascade.

I decided to take my normal circuit up to the palace via Spring Lock Lodge, the Cascade and the boathouse and then back across the lawn, down the sheepwalk and along the far side of Bladon Water. A pair of great spotted woodpeckers were drumming either side of the Lince drive and I watched them for a good ten minutes. Particularly interesting was the fact that both sexes were drumming. It seemed as if they were communicating, as no sooner had one stopped than the other started. For some time I just couldn't make up my mind whether they were perhaps of the lesser spotted variety, as they appeared on the small side. I was quite excited as I've never seen a lesser spotted woodpecker, but a quick glance at a reference book at the end of my walk confirmed my disappointment. Both birds had the red rump characteristic only of the bigger bird and they also had conspicuous white flashes on their backs. The lesser spotted has white bars across its back. Nothing is more

GT. CRESTED GREBES THE BOATHOUSE, BLENHEIM.

evocative of early morning in an English spring than the drumming of this delightful bird from a high beech tree. Each drum consists of about sixteen blows delivered by the beak in less than a second.

I walked over the wooden bridges and along to the Cascade. It was in full spate and the roar and spray from the water was spectacular. I crossed the stepping stones above the Cascade and walked through the rather spooky remains of Gladys Deacon's rock garden. I was able to cross back over the bridge as my uncle had ordered all the gates to be unlocked because the Heythrop were meeting in the Park. From there I wandered up to the Victorian boathouse built by my great-great-grandfather and his American wife Lillian. It is my favourite vantage point for watching the great crested grebes. I counted around ten from the boathouse, all quite unconcerned by the presence of a number of flat-bottomed fishing boats.

I will always associate the great crested grebe with Blenheim. The magnificent lake created in the latter half of the eighteenth century by Capability Brown is one of the largest tracts of water in Oxfordshire and has probably always provided a haven for this lovely bird, even when it was so seriously threatened in the middle of the last century. The fortunes of the great crested grebe have improved dramatically over the past fifty years or so with the explosion of the sand and gravel industries. In the 1860s there were only about thirty pairs left in Britain due to their wanton destruction for use in the clothing industry. Grebe furs were high fashion in Victorian England and their colourful feathers were used to decorate dress and hat alike. The species became perilously close to extinction and it wasn't until protective laws were introduced in the 1870s that numbers began to pick up – reaching an impressive four thousand breeding pairs today. Unlike its near relative, the dabchick, the great crested grebe needs deeper and larger expanses of water in which to fish and rear its young. It is an expert fisherman and I have always been fascinated by the length of time it remains submerged and the speed at which it travels underwater. An excellent vantage point for enjoying the latter is from the top of Vandburgh's Grand Bridge where one can gaze many feet downwards and see the grebes propelling themselves underwater like torpedoes and scattering shoals of tiny silvery fish before them. The stage is set here to observe the many peculiarities of this decorative bird. On a still warm June evening the whole lake will reverberate with the croaks of the parent birds as they deliver small fish to their squealing offspring. The average family is probably two and each parent will take care of one member of the family and become responsible for its feeding. Broods should be bigger as they lay five or six eggs but many young grebes are taken by the pike during the first week or so of hatching. One of the most charming sights to witness is a fluffy zebra-coloured chick being carried on its parent's back. Just occasionally the latter will pluck a feather from its body and offer it to its offspring as an aid to digestion.

The great crested grebe is best known for its courtship display. Sadly I didn't witness any mating activity on this occasion, although I have often seen it in progress on Blenheim lake in the past. It commences with raised crests and fanned frills and a frenzy of shaking heads. The two birds dive and play a game of hide-and-seek, swimming towards each other and then turning and rushing away. The ritual culminates with the reed-dance where they emerge with waterweed in their beaks and then rise high out of the water facing one another and splashing furiously.

As I walked back to the Lince past the Chambers Bridge on Bladon Water, a very early nesting grebe sat on its exposed nest with its head tucked under its wing. The nest consisted of a nasty platform of rotting vegetation cleverly anchored to reed stems so it can rise and fall with changing water levels. When I finally returned to the Lince, there was a colourful throng of diving ducks on the water below the house. Nine tufted drakes with one female and a single pochard drake with two wives. The beauty of the snow-white flanks and black drooping crest of the tufted drakes and the chestnut head and grey back of the pochard was very striking.

I picked a few early daffodils and took them to my grandparents' graves in Bladon churchyard and then set out to visit William Astor at Ginge, near Wantage. In mid-afternoon Will and I went for a nostalgic walk on the Ridgeway and reminisced about the wonderful days shooting we had at Ginge in the 1970s and early 1980s. There are no partridges here now as the local farmer has turned the once beautiful landscape into a prairie, with a good bit of help from Dutch elm disease.

Thursday, 14 March

Left for London at 6.30 a.m. – a beautifully clear snowy morning (about two inches of snow having fallen overnight) with a glorious sunrise. I lunched with Tom Sackville in the Commons; he is currently a junior minister at the Home Office. I walked to Westminster through St James's Park. It is lovingly cared for, with the wallflowers and crocuses joining the daffodils in bloom. They maintain an impressive collection of wildfowl, all needless to say looking very overweight. The tufted duck are the most numerous (after the mallard, of course) and are seemingly the greediest; they are followed closely by the red-crested pochard. I have only once seen these duck in the wild and that was at the Medina de Laguna, just south of Jerez in Spain. Whenever we stay in Sotogrande, we invariably visit this exciting lakeland reserve.

As I walked through the park I remembered how much it meant to Edward Grey when he was 'imprisoned' in London. A delightful passage in the *The Charm of Birds* immediately came to mind:

> One pretty way that the dabchick has with its young was shown to me on the water in St James's Park. When I was first in office and kept in London from 1892–5, I made the acquaintance of the man who then looked after the waterfowl, and who lived across the isthmus that is opposite the windows of the Foreign Office. At his cottage I used to call in the season to hear the news of the breeding waterfowl, and he would show me various nests. One morning as he was taking me round the island he pointed out a dabchick's nest attached to some willow branches that hung into the water. When we came near he exclaimed that the eggs must have hatched since he had seen the nest earlier in the morning, for the nest was now empty. We heard a curious little noise on the water, and looking out beyond the branches saw the parent dabchick and her lately hatched young ones. Being suspicious

of us, she had warned the young and now presented her body to them as they sat in the water. Instinct told them what was required: each bird got on to the back of the old one and was there covered by her folded wings. When all the young had mounted, the parent swam away with her whole family, compact, concealed and safe.

The black-headed gulls are developing their mating plumage and reverting to name; their cries are most evocative of the Needs Ore saltmarsh.

Saturday, 16 March

A sunny morning but with an uncomfortably cold wind. I walked down the valley after breakfast to look at the new plantations. The yellow gorse is coming out on the Tissington bank and the dogwood in the duck enclosure is turning a deep red.

A little owl called from across the valley. When we first arrived at Parwich Lees, I was mystified by the loud clear cry ('kieu') that came from the wooded areas on the Tissington bank. On a still day these cries would be repeated by other birds right along the valley. Initially I thought they came from a bird of prey; however, it soon became obvious we were living among a healthy local population of little owls. They prosper in open limestone grassland and tend to steer clear of woodland areas where they are attacked by the larger tawny owls. They are the most diurnal of all owls and can often be seen in daytime sitting on the telephone wires on the road to Alsop. When walking I often flush them out of a small tree; they have an unmistakable bouncing flight like that of a woodpecker or mistle thrush. The little owl has been one of our most successful birds. They were only released in Northamptonshire in the late 1880s and they have now colonised most parts of the country, reaching some ten thousand pairs. They particularly like nesting in hollow trees so when I cut down all the dead elms in 1987, I restricted their nesting sites; but since then we have put up a number of nest boxes and there are plenty of alternative sites in walls, old barns and rabbit burrows.

The loss of nesting sites like hedgerow trees together with the effects of pesticides caused numbers to decline slightly from the 1960s onwards. There was a time when these small owls were badly persecuted by

gamekeepers as well as other birds, as described by E. W. Hendy, in his book *Bird Watching*.

> A little owl, flitting with quick, spasmodic wing beats from hedgerow to hedgerow, awoke from the chaffinches, thrushes and blackbirds a chorus of protest which betrayed his evil reputation.

In recent years the little owl's diet has been well studied, and although birds are an important food source in the breeding season, they predominantly feed on insects, frogs and small rodents. Little owls are now actively encouraged by farmers.

Sunday, 17 March

One of the most evocative sounds of an early spring morning by my duck enclosure is the sharp 'kruuk' cry of the moorhen. They are shy birds but this morning I watched three bathing themselves in the early morning sun before they detected my presence. Although in many ways a clumsy looking bird, like its cousin the coot, it is a pretty creature with a distinctive red comb and base to its yellow bill. It has an attractive habit of flicking its white tail feathers as it swims along. Its presence enlivens the life of any small pond. There is, however, another reason for being grateful for having moorhen on your water. The moorhen has become an important part of the diet of the feral mink. The latter has developed into one of the countryside's most ruthless predators and has become a thorn in the side of riverkeepers and gamekeepers alike. It is said that if your moorhen vanish you can be pretty sure you have mink. Luckily mink are quite easy to trap in wire cages with any sort of smelly bait. I thought at first that it could have been a mink that took my pinioned duck. However, the fact that there were no remains in the enclosure and in addition that there are plenty of moorhen about, points to a fox.

We have now had six lambs, two of them born dead. An old shepherd once said 'there is a lot of death with sheep'. I currently have eleven breeding ewes but I'm going to cut the numbers back next year. I sat a clutch of ten bantam eggs under the first broody of the year. Looking at the number of mallard I will be hatching off I think I'd better get the bantams out of the way early on! Pinioned duck are bad mothers and one

has far more success if the eggs are lifted and placed under a bantam; particularly with the numbers of crows and stoats we have about.

Wednesday, 20 March

I took the train from Manchester back to Buxton at the end of a lovely spring day – the hills around Chapel-en-le-Frith looked quite beautiful in the evening sun.

Three curlew were feeding in a field between Whaley Bridge and Chapel; the first I've seen with us this year. They arrive in Derbyshire from their coastal winter quarters around Cheltenham Week, although I've yet to hear one at Parwich Lees this year. I always associate their glorious bubbling song with wild open places – maybe on a sunny May evening high on the hill at Allenheads which the curlew shares with the grouse and golden plover, or perhaps sitting inside at Needs Ore on a winter's day when the now mournful call echoes across the Beaulieu Estuary.

Unimproved habitats such as extensive areas of moorland and rough grazing are their favoured breeding grounds. Hence the migration to us from the estuaries around the middle of March. This would tie in with my only sighting of a curlew at Blenheim, which was on the Evenlode water meadows on 9 March 1986, during our last few months at the Lince. The bird was obviously on its way north.

There is nowhere in *The Charm of Birds* that Edward Grey better describes the joy of birdsong than where he tackles the curlew:

> Of all birdsongs or sounds known to me there is none that I would prefer to the spring notes of the curlew. I have seen the bird finish its notes on the ground after alighting, but I have not observed if it ever gives them without any flight. As a rule the wonderful notes are uttered on the wing and are the accompaniment of a graceful flight that has motions of evident pleasure. The notes do not sound passionate: they suggest peace, rest, healing, joy, an assurance of happiness past, present and to come. To listen to curlews on a bright,

· DERBYSHIRE CURLEW

> clear April day, with the fullness of spring still in anticipation, is one of the best experiences that a lover of birds can have. On a still day one can almost feel the air vibrating with the blessed sound. There is no rarity about it where curlews breed: it is to be heard through long days in April, May and far into June. In autumn and winter curlews resort to estuaries and the seashore and the call note is melancholy; but even at this season on a mild day one may be surprised to hear a single bird give a few of the joy-notes, just enough to revive memory of the past spring and to stir anticipation of the next one.

I had this very experience one mild Boxing Day in the late 1980s. I was staying with my father-in-law, Robin Hastings, at Bramdean for Christmas and I drove down to the sea at Needs Ore for a walk. Jeremy and Derek were away spending Christmas at their house in Key West. When I heard those intoxicating spring notes calling across the saltmarsh, in my excitement I immediately penned a postcard to Florida containing those immortal lines from Edward Grey.

Thursday, 21 March

Another lovely sunny start to the morning. Ducks seem to appear from everywhere for their breakfast. Our valley is full of chaffinch song intermingled with the jingling of the dunnock and the wheezing of the greenfinch. I never knew there were so many of the latter around until they started singing. A cock pheasant chucked and whirred deep within the hawthorn bank and three hares lolloped lazily around the outsides. There is still a chill in the air and there was a slight frost overnight but not enough to freeze the ponds. I think the cold is deterring the blackbird from really letting rip. I listened to one rather low-key performance from an alder tree in the duck enclosure.

Arrived at Beaulieu early evening. Jamie Chichester and I then went up to see his nursery via the Natonal Motor Museum. As we drove over the river bridge, a kingfisher shot downstream. It is a shy bird and is usually only seen as a flash of sky blue darting low and fast away across the water. It is more often than not first located by its shrill whistle

KINGFISHER · BEAULIEU

which is repeated in a series of 'chees' as it tears away. I've only once seen one at Parwich Lees and that was in the duck enclosure which is located beside the tiny Bletch Brook. Because it is such an exotic bird, individual sightings are often clearly remembered. There was one such encounter that is vividly etched on my memory. I was walking back to the Lince on the south side of Bladon Water at a part of the lake where the banks are planted with a dense cover of yew and box. I stopped to listen to the local aquatic choir – coot, reed warblers and whinneying dabchick – when I heard a 'plop' as if a large pebble had been dropped into the water. There was a distinctive whirr of wings and it happened again. I then noticed the kingfisher sitting on a branch of dead elm protruding from the water. It momentarily hovered like a tiny humming bird, proceeded to dive again and this time emerged with a small fish which it beat against the branch. I have many times seen kingfishers on the saltmarshes of the Beaulieu Estuary; in winter young birds disperse to the coast to find food. Kingfisher numbers should have picked up strongly over the last decade. Their main enemy is severe winter and we've had a series of mild ones in the 1990s. It was estimated that in the 1980–1 winter the kingfisher population declined by over sixty per cent in England. God knows what happened in 1962. Nature's remedy provides for the kingfisher to have up to three broods a year.

Friday, 22 March

I spent the night with the Chichesters at Gatewood on the Exbury Estate. Woke up to a chilly but sunny spring morning. A green woodpecker was laughing and a great spotted gently drumming in the distant Exbury woods. The garden at Gatewood is alive with French partridges that can't be doing the flowerbeds any good.

The Exbury Estate lies on the south-east edge of the New Forest with the Beaulieu River at its western boundary. Edward Grey loved the New Forest – it was one of his 'places'. When he was in office and time was too short to make the long journey north to Fallodon, he would spend weekends at a hotel near Brockenhurst. From there he would venture forth on to the heath and into the woods to enjoy the birds.

This morning a sight presented itself which would have been totally foreign to Edward Grey. A pair of mandarin duck glided lazily across the lawn, possibly prospecting for nest sites in the ancient New Forest oaks. This duck has always been popular as a captive bird and kept in waterfowl collections. There is now a substantial feral population in Britain with perhaps around a thousand nesting pairs. It is not known when they started breeding freely in England; however, a small number were released in the south of England in the 1930s. They are a fun bird to keep in your collection as they will attract their wild colleagues. Last year a group of a dozen wild birds spent a day or so with us at my Derbyshire duck enclosure – slap in the middle of the country. The drake is very over-dressed and most unlikely to be confused with anything else.

After breakfast I drove the short distance to Lower Exbury and picked up Nick de Rothschild. Lower Exbury is one of the most attractive houses I know. It sits just above the saltmarsh on a bend of the River Beaulieu and looks south west to Needs Ore and the Isle of Wight. At Lower Exbury one lives alongside the wild cry of the redshank and the evocative clanking of the rigging of yachts moored in the river. Nick is an old Cambridge friend and, along with his father, is the current custodian of what he calls 'the most colourful place on earth in summer'. Exbury Gardens are almost certainly the finest example of a woodland garden in Britain. They were created in 1919 by Nick's grandfather and consist of two hundred and fifty acres of trees and shrubs with twenty-two miles of interconnecting paths. The gardens retain the atmosphere of the old forest while underneath the canopy thousands of rhododendrons and azaleas generate an exotic flavour. He has inherited the passionate pride and interest of his forebears and is busy designing new pond systems. Today the magnolias and camellias were looking glorious and the Red Admiral rhododendron was a blaze of crimson – what Nick calls 'the herald of spring'.

High up in the canopy of ancient oaks and Scots pine a very different herald of spring trumpeted its presence: the chiffchaff had arrived. For a countryman the first song of the migratory chiffchaff is the most eagerly awaited event of the bird calendar. It excites him more than the song of the resident chaffinch a good month earlier as it signals the arrival of spring. Along with the wheatear, he is the forerunner of a number of migrants which make the long journey from Africa to spend the summer with us in England. Chiffchaffs begin to arrive in numbers around the middle of March. The earlier songster is one of the small number that, like the blackcap, overwinter with us in the south.

Aside from the willow tit and marsh tit, the chiffchaff and willow warbler are the two most difficult British birds to tell apart. Grey tells us that, on the one hand, they have enough characteristics in common to be part of the same family but, on the other, the chiffchaff's song procludes its classification as a warbler.

> In appearance, habits, food, habitat and the manner of nest, the two birds have a very close resemblence to each other; so close as to make the difference of song remarkable.

Grey is not entirely correct. The chiffchaff tends to prefer taller more mature trees whilst the willow warbler is happier in low scrub. Nowhere was the contrast more marked than when we left Blenheim for Derbyshire. At Parwich Lees the dales echo with the song of willow warblers from the ancient hedgerows and hawthorn scrub. But not a chiffchaff can be heard. In Blenheim Park, with its mature oaks and beeches, the opposite is true and chiffchaffs predominate. In addition, the nests of the two birds are of a similar dome-like construction but are subtly different in location. The chiffchaff's nest is built just off the ground and the willow warbler's actually on the ground. Apparently they have both, in the past, been known as 'oven-birds' owing to their specialised building technique. One of the earliest bird recollections I have is of trying to find a chiffchaff's nest at Blenheim. I can't have been more than eight years old when my grandfather announced that a nest had been found near the Victorian Rose Garden on the way to the Cascade. I remember setting off on my own at a trot from the palace in a state of great excitement, only to burst into tears halfway there as my young legs had underestimated the distance. The spoilt boy was then taken by Land Rover.

Grey writes in *The Charm of Birds*: 'There is a spirit in the two notes of the chiffchaff that suggests the same motive as song . . . The sound also suggests industry, as of the passage of a shuttle to and fro.'

I well remember my surprise at hearing a chiffchaff singing on the last day of September at Eaton in Cheshire when out shooting with my friend, Edward Hay. It was a rather lack-lustre performance with none of the spirit and sharpness of its spring rendering, mirroring Grey's comment in *The Charm of Birds*:

> Then comes the moult, and the bird falls silent till September, when energy is restored and expresses itself in a saddened repetition of the 'song' – a sort of quiet farewell before the chiffchaff leaves us on its long journey southwards.

After an hour or so at Exbury, Nick and I drove the short distance around the estuary to Needs Ore. Six black-tailed godwits were feeding in the creek at low tide in front of the cottages. One or two of the birds were just beginning to develop their colourful summer plumage – a rich chestnut with russet head, neck and upper belly. A good way of recognising a godwit is by comparing it to a curlew. If a largish grey wader is seen (but not as large as a curlew), with a straight rather than a curved beak, it is very likely to be a godwit. The black-tailed godwit is more elegant than the bar-tailed godwit, it has longer legs and a more pronounced neck and is usually seen feeding in muddy channels of the inner estuary. Hence they are often to be seen in the creek at Needs Ore. It is one of my favourite birds and I have come to associate it with Needs Ore in the same way as I associate the great crested grebe with Blenheim.

One of the most exciting success stories for conservationists in post-war Britain is the recolonisation of the black-tailed godwit as a breeding species. Until the early nineteenth century breeding was quite widespread, especially over parts of Yorkshire and much of East Anglia. This elegant wader nests in small colonies among damp vegetation and tussocky grassland in flooded meadows. More intensive agriculture meant that huge tracts of the country were drained in order to allow pasture to be put to the plough. Three hundred years of land drainage have reduced the fens of East Anglia by a fifth. As if the destruction of their nesting habitat was not enough, the black-tailed godwit was also ravaged by egg collectors and shooting. Morris, in his *British Birds*, states: 'They are highly esteemed for the table and are both shot and taken in snares.' Yarrell, in his *British Birds*, tells us that Sir Thomas Browne, writing his natural-history notes three hundred years ago, states: 'Godwits are taken chiefly in marshland, though other parts are not without them: they are accounted the daintiest dish in England.'

In the early 1950s a few black-tailed godwits nested successfully in the Ouse Washes on the Cambridgeshire/Norfolk border. This was probably the first time they had bred in England for over fifty years. By the time the news was announced some ten years later the land was safely in the hands of three conservation organisations – the RSPB, the Wildfowl Trust and the Cambridge and Isle of Ely Naturalists' Trust. This area held over ninety per cent of the population until the mid-1970s when there were over sixty pairs. In the 1980s, however, extensive spring floods seriously disrupted breeding, causing a fifty-per-cent decline in the numbers of breeding pairs.

Small numbers of black-tailed godwits have bred on other coastal grazing marshes although I'm not sure if these now include the Blackwater Reserve at Needs Ore. It would be difficult to determine the identity of the birds I saw in the creek today at Needs Ore. Early April is probably the time that the largest number of black-tailed godwits are in Britain. These birds spend the winter, and in increasing numbers the summer, with us; however they are almost certainly of two different races. The Icelandic race breed in Iceland and winter in Ireland and Britain – the small number of breeding birds in Orkney and Caithness are probably representatives of this clan. The European race breed from Russia across to Britain in the west and winter as far and wide as India to Africa. As at today's date the Icelandic birds have yet to leave Britain and the European birds are arriving to breed. Godwits return to their breeding grounds as early as March.

As we moved closer to the birds they took off and displayed their most distinctive recognition features – an attractive white wing bar and long legs that project beyond the tail. We walked eastwards down the creek towards Gull Island. The black-headed gulls had arrived in their hundreds and their sharp cries filled the air. We met three 'twitchers' at the end of the creek with regulation woolly hats and telescopes. They were in a state of excitement about the presence of three Mediterranean gulls. They are bigger than the black-headed gull and their black cap descends further down the neck. In fact the black-headed gull is wrongly named as its cap is really dark brown.

Tuesday, 26 March

A heavy fall of snow overnight which continued until lunchtime. I managed to get Marcus to school but then spent the day at home. I walked down through a blizzard to feed the ducks. We are definitely missing one of the wigeon drakes and I found the tell-tale sign of a white wing feather that had been severed right though. I don't know what to do about these wretched foxes. Grey was experiencing the same problems over eighty years ago. On a spring day in April 1914 Grey visited his neighbour Walter Runciman's house in Northumberland to fish his lake. He writes to Runciman on holiday in Greece:

> There was a sort of bright spring happiness that makes me feel not only the prospect of summer, but the possibility of heaven in some

> other planet not so very unlike earth, but with no cities and no influenza and where the foxes are not carnivorous (for my collection of waterfowl that I began thirty years ago is being destroyed and broken up by a fox).

Last night my neighbour, Stan White, failed to lock up his bantams and lost a couple to a fox. One was found tucked into a stone wall for the fox to return to. The best deterrent would be an electric wire around the base of my duck enclosure but it is too far away from the mains and a battery is not very practical for so large an area. Poison is illegal and in any case I wouldn't want to use it. Snaring would be the most effective way of dealing with them but I would probably catch the odd badger, so that is a non-starter. Shooting foxes with a lamp at the dead of night is also not very practical. The hunt doesn't come up to us very often and the days of estates and gamekeepers are long gone. The fact is that hunting is by far the most humane way of control. Nature can be violent, as those bantams and ducks found out. At least they would have been dispatched with one bite of the fox's jaws, in the same way as the much larger foxhound dispatches the fox.

Thursday, 28 March

Had two meetings in Mansfield in the morning and then drove back through Bakewell. As I crossed the Lathkill and climbed up on to the 'tops', I watched a pair of lapwing courting above a rare field of spring corn. They weaved, tumbled and corkscrewed happily as they wheeled around the small field, uttering their evocative shrill cry as they went. The female settled in the field, followed by the male who alighted a hundred yards or so away. The latter then proceeded to scrape out a nest site with his chest thereby displaying his chestnut feathers under his tail. This action is a means of attracting the female to a potential nest site.

Grey enjoyed the spring notes of the lapwing as much as those of the curlew:

> A yet more common and widely distributed pleasure [than the curlew] is the spring flight and note of the peewit. It is a real joy flight accompanied by cries of joy: the seeing and hearing of it for the first time in the early months of the year are something longed for and welcomed, as is the first song of the blackbird. Someone in the wholesale trade in birds for food explained 'that peewits are of no use after they have begun to lap'. I suppose therefore that the name lapwing is suggested by the joy flight in spring. At other times the peewit gives an impression of plaintiveness.

The lapwing has had an up-and-down history since the prime of Edward Grey. In 1926 the Lapwing Protection Act ended the ancient practice of netting the adult birds and harvesting their eggs. In the 1880s early eggs were fetching up to fifteen shillings each. Specially trained dogs working throughout the two-month season were used to find nests for their handlers. E. M. Nicholson in his *Birds in England* (1926), writing just before the Protection Act, feels genuinely sorry for the lapwing:

> The lapwings live on the land; they are wholly useful and, compared with all their competitors, limited in diet. If there are floods they are

COURTING LAPWINGS

> washed out, while the tree-top or cliff-ledge nests of their rivals escape, being in a different world; if rolling takes place their eggs are crushed, unless the farmhand sees them and takes them home; they suffer all the perils and discomforts of the fields, while powerful intruders in large flocks sweep down to take the lion's share of the rewards and often devour their eggs into the bargain. If food fails they are destitute while their competitors simply change their diet for the time being. A great number of lapwings are shot for the poulters each year and a great number of their eggs taken. A growing body of people aim at having this prohibited; if they succeed, and the lapwing begins to increase again, they will certainly say 'there you are, we told you so; the scarcity of the lapwing has nothing whatever to do with rolling or rooks and gulls or anything except human persecution'.

Edward Grey also hinted at their demise in *The Charm of Birds*:

> The peewit or lapwing is a beautiful bird, much praised by farmers for consuming pests in their fields, but it has the misfortune to lay eggs that are an unrivalled delicacy and these are taken in vast numbers for the English market, not only in this country but in breeding grounds abroad. For many years I have not seen at Fallodon the vast flocks of peewits that used to visit us in autumn and winter, and which were probably composed largely of foreign birds.

The lapwing quickly picked up in numbers following protection and adapted well to the shift in emphasis in agriculture from pastoral to arable practices. Spring corn with shorter vegetation and larger fields with unimpeded visibility both suited them. However, changes in arable farming and the decline of the true mixed farm have seriously affected the lapwing in the last thirty years or so. A survey undertaken in 1987 showed a seventy-per-cent decrease since 1961. The emphasis in agriculture today is on winter cereals which produce a growth too tall for breeding lapwings. They prefer to nest on bare land adjacent to grass, which is important for rearing the hatched chicks. With the decline of the mixed farm this pattern is vanishing. Management of grassland has also changed for the worse. Silage-making with fertiliser produces a dense tall growth ready earlier than is the old-fashioned hayfield. These recent changes in farming techniques have driven this pretty wader away from its traditional stronghold in the south east of England to northern regions like Cheshire.

I remember well as a boy the excitement when my grandfather's keepers at Blenheim brought in plovers' eggs. More recently when living at the Lince I used to enjoy watching the parent birds feeding with their fluffy chicks in the parkland sheepwalks up by the Monument.

A charming description of the lapwing and the anxiety caused by the human egg-thief is portrayed by one of our greatest nature writers, W. H. Hudson, in *Hampshire Days*:

> Worst of all birds that can have no peace in their lives so long as you are in sight is the peewit. The harsh wailing sound of his crying voice as he wheels about overhead, the mad downward rushes when his wings creak as he nears you, give the idea that he is almost crazed with anxiety; and one feels ashamed of causing so much misery. Oh poor bird! Is there no way to make you understand without leaving the ground that your black spotted, olive coloured eggs are perfectly safe; that a man can walk about on the heath and be no more harmful to you than the forest ponies and the ragged donkey browsing on a furze bush and the cow with her tinkling bell? I stand motionless, looking the other way; I sit down to think; I lie flat on my back with hands clasped behind my head and gaze at the sky and still the trouble goes on – he will not believe in me nor tolerate me. There is nothing to do but get up and go away out of sight and sound of the peewits.

Friday, 29 March

I arrived home to the unforgettable sight of a peregrine falcon circling the yard – the first I've seen in Derbyshire and it was taking a close look at our bantams. It was quite unmistakable, a large powerful bird with pointed wings and a shortish tail. I suppose it could have been an escaped bird (they are commonly used for falconry) or maybe it was merely moving north to its nesting grounds having spent the winter at some coastal estuary. There are now an estimated eleven hundred pairs in Britain and a tenth of the population nests in quarries. I think there are more quarries in Derbyshire than any other county in Britain. I have only seen a peregrine stoop once and that was on the Blackwater meadows at Needs Ore. Some say they can reach speeds of up to two hundred miles an hour when diving. The peregrine has had a chequered history since the turn of the century but is now back in numbers. I always look forward to seeing them on Jura. Every year a pair nests on a ledge in the narrows that lead into Loch Tarbert. If you are lucky when you take the boat through you are greeted by their shrill chattering call.

George Montagu, the famous ornithologist who died in 1815, tells us just how common the peregrine used to be:

> From its nature it is limited to certain districts, for it inhabits only the mountainous parts, or where it can settle in security upon the shelving rocks of some stupendous cliff. With us, therefore, it is

> chiefly confined to the bold and rocky parts of our coast, where it breeds. From its habits, therefore, it appears to be less common than it really is; for, in fact, it is nearly as plentiful a species as any in England, one or two of the commonest sorts excepted; there is not a part of our coast from north to south where the cliffs rise to the height of three or four hundred feet, but they are found scattered in the breeding season.

Between the wars when there were many more large estates than there are now, peregrines were heavily persecuted by gamekeepers. Large numbers were shot during the Second World War when pigeons were used to carry messages, and then in the 1950s and 1960s they were badly hit by pesticides. The peregrine fed on prey that in turn had fed on contaminated insects and this led to the bird laying thin-shelled eggs which broke. In addition to all this the peregrine was subjected to the theft of its eggs and chicks. Recovery began with the phased withdrawal of organochlorine insecticides. An increase in their food supply has also helped, particularly with the availability of domestic pigeons.

E. W. Hendy firmly places the peregrine among the royalty of the British bird world:

> She was a splendid creature, and in magnificent plumage. The black patches at the sides of her head set off her white breast, delicately pencilled and freaked with umber and pale brown, and her bright yellow claws. And her eyes! What a consuming fury blazed forth from those small pools of pitch! I moved nearer and she took to the wing, circling above me, a blunt-headed, short-winged bird, winnowing the air with strong, swift wingbeats. Soon she returned to the eyrie, stooping almost perpendicularly for the last twenty feet, as though striking at a quarry, and stood there keening and cursing. Her rage was awe inspiring. Impotent though her hate was, I felt humbled before it.

PEREGRINE FALCON

APRIL

Monday, 1 April

There was a huge flock of fieldfares over the park in the morning. This was almost certainly part of the northerly migration back to Scandinavia, although I have seen them at Parwich Lees well into May. The fieldfare is the largest of our winter thrushes, and Grey thought it the prettiest:

> The fieldfare has no bright colour like the redwing; it is not quite so large and fine a bird as the mistle thrush; but in variety of shades of colours it is the most beautiful of all our thrushes. In the last twenty years or so a small number of birds have nested in Scotland.

A warm clear evening. We left for dinner at Melbourne around 7.15 p.m. but only after I had been entertained to a virtuoso performance by a joyful blackbird high up in our copper beech.

Wednesday, 3 April

Spent the day in our Leeds office and arrived back home in the evening to find a female wheatear sitting on the stone wall opposite the lime kiln. The wheatear and the chiffchaff are our earliest arrivals and along with the redstart I think the wheatear is the prettiest of our visiting migrants. I find it hard to believe that just a few weeks ago this elegant little bird was probably a thousand miles south of the Sahara. I don't know whether they stay and nest with us or move up to the higher ground; there are certainly plenty of nest sites in our stone walls. We are on the 650-foot contour at Parwich Lees but to the north of the house one runs quickly up to the limestone plateau which is over 1,000 feet. They are easy to identify, showing their distinctive white rump when they fly away.

WHEATEAR & LIME KILN

Apparently the name is derived from the Anglo-Saxon words meaning 'white arse'. It was practically dark at 8.15 p.m. when I locked up the bantams and a robin was still singing. If artificial light is nearby, a robin will sing even at night. Our daffodils are now in full bloom – we are that much later than the south; they were out in London some weeks ago.

Thursday, 4 April

Arrived home from Sheffield to watch the curlew displaying over our valley for the first time this year. The purpose of the display flight is to mark out territorial boundaries. He climbs with rapid wing beats, hangs in the air and then glides down, often rendering his lovely bubbling song. In our big meadow I found a decapitated female mallard which had been half eaten by a fox – no doubt picked off a nest.

Friday, 5 April

Visited three companies in Nottingham and Derby and then drove home though Cromford. It was here in 1771 that Sir Richard Arkwright built the first water-powered cotton mill in England; it was driven by the outflow from the Bonsall Stream and the Cromford Slough which drained the lead mines at Wirksworth. A pair of mute swans were busy building their gigantic nest on Cromford pond. Happily our mute swan population has recovered dramatically. In the 1970s numbers declined drastically on the Thames, Avon and Trent river systems as a result of lead poisoning. Mortality as well as reduced breeding success was found to be caused by the ingestion of fishing weights cast aside by Britain's four million participants in coarse fishing; swans picked up the lead pellets with grit and seeds and accidental poisoning became for them the main cause of death on lowland rivers. A ban on these weights began in 1987. A 1990 survey estimated that there were twenty-six thousand birds in Britain, a near forty-per-cent increase on the 1983 survey. Everyone will be pleased except a handful of poor farmers who will have their meadows puddled and overgrazed.

Saturday, 6 April

One or two goldfinches are beginning to arrive back and are ironically bringing with them a spell of slightly colder weather. They are one of the most attractive of our birds and their tinkling canary-like song will enliven the garden through to the autumn. Every year I notice their return around the second week in April and they will stay with us as late as November. Our nesting birds move south earlier and the October/ November birds are almost certainly moving down from further north. More than eighty per cent of the British population winter in Belgium, Spain and France. We see the occasional bird in the winter. I always remember a pair feeding on a thistle in deep snow by the side of our lane. The contrast of the crimson, yellow, black and buff against the fresh fall of snow was unforgettable.

It was Edward Grey's Bill that in 1888 finally led to the protection of the goldfinch (Wild Birds Protection Act). Because of its musical song and colourful plumage thousands of goldfinches were trapped and sold as cage birds. This led to a huge decrease in Britain in the nineteenth century. In 1860 it was alleged that over one hundred and thirty thousand were being caught each year near Worthing which lies on the main migration route. Since the goldfinch is a seed eater, with the introduction of set-aside under the Common Agricultural Policy the future of the bird looks as bright as its plumage. There are now an estimated three hundred thousand pairs in Britain.

Sunday, 7 April

Drove south to Needs Ore. Jeremy and Derek came down for dinner, before which I enjoyed a long walk around Blackwater.

It was a lovely sunny evening and so clear you felt you could reach out and touch the Isle of Wight. As I walked through the lush meadows the background music was provided by thousands of screeching black-headed gulls and hundreds of 'growling' dark-bellied brent geese. It can't be long before these small seashore-loving geese make the journey back to Siberia to breed. They were in the process of flighting out to the mouth of the estuary to roost having spent the day feeding on eel grass growing on the salt mudflats. It was only when I saw a solitary bird next to a greylag goose that I realised how small they are; in fact, on the water, from a distance, they look very duck-like. In the 1920s and 1930s the population of brent geese decreased drastically due to a failure of the eel grass. However, the disease affecting the grass disappeared and the number of brent geese in the south east of England has steadily increased from fifteen thousand in the 1950s to around a hundred thousand today. Numbers do tend to fluctuate from year to year depending on breeding success.

Three soloists stood out against this background chorus and perfectly captured the atmosphere and exhilaration of a spring evening at Needs Ore. There was the plaintive mewing call of the lapwing uttered during his joyful tumbling display; there were the wild piping calls emanating from a group of noisy yet colourful oyster catchers; but the sound that I found most evocative of the estuary was the sharp 'teu-hu-hu' call of the redshank, which has given it the nickname 'sentinel of the marshes'. I was lucky enough to watch what I imagine was a cockbird perform his acrobatic territorial switchback display flight. He would rise and hover with quivering wings like a humming bird and then glide down uttering a single 'tu-tu' call which became more and more rapid as the bird floated to the ground. I suspect Grey ranked this outpouring of happiness alongside that of the curlew and lapwing:

> Redshanks in the breeding season have notes that may be compared to yodelling; they utter these in a very conspicuous joy flight.

English Nature has created some highly effective 'flashes' in the Blackwater Meadows and it was from behind a man-made mound that I watched a group of fifty golden plover at the water's edge. These were the first such birds I had seen at Needs Ore and were probably *en route* for their moorland nesting sites. They were developing their summer plumage and their black bellies could be plainly seen. The fact that the black patch does not extend up to the chest denotes they are of the southern race. Around twenty-five thousand pairs breed in Britain but ten times that number spend the winter with us. I have heard their mournful whistle while stalking high above Glenbatrick on Jura. I have seen nesting birds

whilst walking on the hill at Allenheads in May. But my real recollections of the 'goldie' are tied to snipe shooting in the Uists in October. Edward Grey describes the attractive plover in *The Charm of Birds*:

> When served on a dish, [the golden plover] is so like the peewit in body that it can be distinguished only by the absence of a hind claw. When alive it is very different in appearance and flight. It 'yodels' very pleasantly in spring. The call note heard frequently in autumn and winter is a single very plaintive whistle.

The golden plover is declining as a breeding species in Britain and would suffer to a greater degree if grouse shooting was ever banned. Being a moorland nester they react in the same way as the grouse to poor habitat management. They suffer from overgrazing by sheep which causes heather to give way to grassland. Tree planting in the highlands and Flow Country has also resulted in loss of habitat and an increase in predators. They prefer short-rotation burned moors (especially those next door to pastureland) which denotes a well-managed grouse moor.

When I had completed a circuit of Blackwater I took a short walk up the creek in front of the cottages towards Gull Island in the mouth of the estuary. The high-water mark is bordered by a swathe of whin bushes. Three particular birds were perched on top of this mass of yellow. The female linnet was part of the furniture but I certainly did not expect to see a male kestrel with his blue-grey head sitting so low down. The trio was completed by one of nature's most attractive offerings – a cock stonechat perched on top of a sprig of gorse in full bloom. It has a black-and-white neck with distinctive white patches and a lovely chestnut breast. In many ways its movements remind me of a whitethroat. It is an incessant mover, with a bouncy jerky flight. It rises like a helicopter only to dive back into the cover of the gorse. Then it will perch prominently for a few seconds and recover its breath. Now it flicks its tail and gives the loud call note which sounds like two pebbles being struck together and which gives the bird its name.

I found a stonechat's nest a few years ago situated in the grass by the fishing hut on the Oisedale River on Jura. A combination of its agitated call note and the midges nearly drove me mad as I tried in vain to extract that elusive seatrout. The stonechat prefers a heathland habitat and loss of this, due to intensive agriculture and urban and recreational development, is the main reason for the bird's decline. As they remain with us all year round they are also susceptible to cold winters. It is estimated that the number of stonechats in Britain has more than halved in the last twenty years and that we are now down to around fifteen thousand breeding pairs.

In the creek itself were two waders. A solitary black-tailed godwit with its long legs had waded far out into the water and plunged its whole head under while probing the mud. It took off in a frenzied corkscrew across the water and propelled itself upwards, showing off its distinctive white rump and wing bars. It then dive-bombed out of sight. The grey plover was present, of course, but the journey north cannot have been far from its mind. In anticipation of the breeding season it looked a little less dejected. Its posture was more erect, and its plumage less drab, giving a hint of the beautiful spangled black to come.

Monday, 8 April

Walked along the creek before breakfast. A delightful sunny morning with the usual chorus of screaming gulls. The tide was going out, thereby exposing a breakfast table for the waders. A classic sunrise over Cowes and Spithead which allowed me to pick out clearly the church tower and masts of the yachts in Yarmouth harbour some nine miles to the west. The low sun also reflected on the russet breeding plumage of a group of twenty black-tailed godwits that were feeding in the mudflats in front of the cottages. This was as many as I've seen at Needs Ore. A couple of the birds remained with us for most of the day. After gorging themselves they curled their heads under their wings and, standing on one long elegant leg, went to sleep.

This lovely spring morning produced two significant events in our bird calendar; the first sighting of the swallow and the first song of the willow warbler. In fact they must have been coming in for a day or two as no sooner had I arrived back in Derbyshire (around 6.00 p.m.) than two swallows were sitting on the telephone wires in Parwich and our hawthorn bank was full of willow warbler song. If you asked the most disinterested city dweller his opinion of the first sign of spring, he would say the arrival of the swallow. It is a much loved and attractive bird that flies in to spend the summer with us from South Africa. Its numbers have declined noticeably in recent years. Mortality occurs both from the effects of bad weather on the long migration and the effects of droughts in their winter quarters. As a result of the latter birds arrive back in poorer condition and raise smaller clutches. In Britain changes in farming practices that reduced the supply of nest sites and the availability of insects have also been responsible for their decline. Improved farm hygiene, intensive livestock rearing, modern buildings and the use of pesticides make a farm less suitable for swallows.

If you asked that same city dweller to describe a willow warbler he would probably not even know of its existence, let alone that five times as

many willow warblers visit us each year than swallows. This Needs Ore male willow warbler was announcing its arrival from deep within a blossoming blackthorn bush. The females are smaller and arrive a week or so later and are attracted by the singing males in their established territories. The only occasion I have found a willow warbler's nest was on 25 May 1991 – my forty-first birthday – and I was staying at Needs Ore. It was situated on the ground under a gorse bush in front of the cottage. It was a tiny, beautifully constructed domed nest lined with feathers, and the parents were busy feeding their young.

Edward Grey ranks as one of the foremost amateur ornithologists we have produced this century but he only developed his interest as a young man, as evidenced by Seton Gordon in *Edward Grey and his Birds*:

> Edward Grey was not, as a boy, interested in birds. He told me that he remembered at the age of twenty-two hearing a very loud song in a tree. He struck the tree and a wren came out, and that is how he came to know the wren's song. He said he did not know the song of the chaffinch until he was twenty-six.

The fact that he only acquired a knowledge of birds later on in his life and after he came down from Oxford is also evidenced when Grey writes about the willow warbler in *The Charm of Birds*:

> I have never been in any part of England where it is not common; in the woods about Fallodon it is so abundant that the song forced itself upon my notice before I had begun to take any account of small birds: all day and every day in May and early June, when I was in the woods, the song of one willow warbler after another was in my ears: it was impossible to ignore it. Not knowing from what bird it proceeded, I called it 'the everlasting bird', because the song seemed never to cease. In the South of England one expects to hear it in the first week in April. The song is particularly pleasant as well as frequent. It is a succession of slender and delicate notes, forming a completed sentence, which is repeated again and again at short intervals. The bird is a desultory singer, uttering its song as it flits about the bushes, searching the leaves for insect food. The notes have a very endearing quality of their own. They suggest something plaintive – as if the bird were pleading. 'A cadence as soft as summer rain' has occurred to me when listening to the song, which is peculiarly touching. It is entirely without any note of bravado, exultation or challenge, such as is suggested by many other songs. To all who find pleasure in birds, the arrival and first hearing of the willow warbler each spring is a moving incident.

While we ate lunch, bathed in sunshine, we watched the screeching gulls mobbing the carrion crows above their nesting grounds. No sooner do the black-headed gulls think of laying than the crows start patrolling the saltmarsh for eggs and clicks. Ask my ducks how ruthless they are. A gullery, like a rookery, is a good example of safety in numbers. The communal effort more often than not will see off such a predator.

Tuesday, 9 April

A sunny spring morning with a pleasant breeze. While working in the conservatory, I heard a rather unusual song which I initially thought was a rusty performance from a chiffchaff moving north. In addition to the two-part call (which is why I confused it with a chiffchaff), the bird uttered a repetitive single warbler-like note but harsher (a 'tic' rather than a 'howeet'). With a little help from the binoculars it was immediately evident that a cock pied flycatcher had arrived – a surprisingly early visitor as they normally appear from their West African winter quarters from mid-April to late May.

Once you recognise the song you cannot fail to observe them. Not only are they very colourful but they are vigorous singers and incessant movers, usually around a potential nest site. They are much more restless than their cousin, the spotted flycatcher, constantly flicking a tail or rather oddly raising one wing. E. W. Hendy, in this book *Bird Watching* (1928), has a chapter on the pied flycatcher and he describes the cockbird as follows:

> Though not much larger than a marsh or coal tit, and not very dissimilar in general appearance, his spruce black-and-white plumage marked him out as distinct from either of these. Breast, waistcoat, wing-bars and forehead were of a sleek and shining white which contrasted finely with the glossy black of his other feathers. His song, too, was a far more elaborate affair than anything a tit could ever imagine, and his spasmodic flight suggested at once kinship with his cousin, the spotted flycatcher.

Interestingly enough Edward Grey makes no mention of the pied flycatcher in *The Charm of Birds*. This is particularly strange as the bird has an attractive musical song. We must assume that he just wasn't familiar with the pied flycatcher, which didn't frequent Hampshire and Northumberland. Its stronghold has always been oak-dominated deciduous woodland in the west of Britain and it has only started extending its range since the war. This expansion has coincided with the provision of

nest boxes in other parts of the country. There is no better example of this than our home at Parwich Lees in the Derbyshire Dales. Before April 1993 I had only seen pied flycatchers on the River Arrow in Herefordshire. In February the same year the Derbyshire Wildlife Trust put up seventy boxes on my land and that summer four pairs of pieds nested at Parwich Lees. They had been coming down the valley unnoticed for hundreds of years but had not stayed owing to a lack of nesting sites. Any suitable holes in old trees would have been occupied by the tits before the pieds arrived. Last year we had only two nesting pairs. Apparently there was a shortage in other strongholds in the country suggesting mortality in their winter quarters.

Wednesday, 10 April

We left Parwich Lees to catch the flight to Gibralter on a glorious spring morning. We are *en route* to Sotogrande in southern Spain to spend a few days' holiday with friends. The sun had burnt off the light frost well before breakfast. The grass is just beginning to green up but the wind is still in the north.

The chaffinches and dunnocks were singing boisterously in their territories although I have yet to hear a chiffchaff in Derbyshire. A cock pheasant chucked and whirred in the hawthorn bank to be answered by one after another up and down our valley. A woodpigeon cooed restfully across on the Tissington bank. How their peaceful song reminds me of my Hampshire days.

A COCK PHEASANT CHUCKING & WHIRRING ...

As I sat in front of our house contemplating both our Andalucian holiday and the lovely view that I am always loathe to leave behind, a group of starlings quietly whistled and chattered like an expectant congregation awaiting the arrival of the bride. A great spotted woodpecker 'drummed' from the old sycamore and a nuthatch was 'reeling' in the copper beech. A pair of the latter were feeding on the nuts yesterday so with luck they will use one of the nest boxes. A green woodpecker 'yaffled' from the lime-kiln woods and his mate seesawed into the oak trees in the valley bottom. Their laughter no doubt helps them keep in contact as they go about their courting. In much the same way the drumming of their close cousin signifies the staking out of a territory. From the top meadow I caught a few distant notes of a skylark. What a tragedy it is that their numbers are falling so dramatically. We are currently paying a high price for our ruthless drive for greater efficiency in agriculture.

The jackdaws are building in a hollow branch of ash just over the ha-ha wall. They are messy devils – there is a big pile of sticks on the ground below the nest site. At least they are not still building in our chimneys. We used to collect jackdaws' eggs at Blenheim when I was a child. They nested in the old oaks in the park and their eggs have a dark rich yolk similar to the eggs of the plover, gull and moorhen and are considered a delicacy. It will not be long before the young mallard are hatching. The drakes look most handsome in their green livery. I have caught five magpies around the ponds which should save some early broods. Bullfinches were softly piping in the hawthorn bank where yesterday evening I came within ten yards of a vixen. She sat and watched me for several minutes from under the canopy of a hawthorn bush. There is a good deal of fieldfare activity in the locality which almost certainly means they are starting to move north. A pair of teal visited my ponds this week, probably taking the same route. The little drake whistled musically.

Sotogrande is situated at the most southerly point of the Iberian peninsula. Not for everyone does it conjure up images of luxury yachts, polo, golf and an endless round of bridge parties among a fast international set, in short, the world of wealthy expats. For those fortunate enough to appreciate natural history, an Easter visit to this famous Spanish resort is a cast-iron guarantee of an enchanting holiday.

After the abundant winter rains, the woods are carpeted with wild flowers and the lush valleys are grazed by seemingly docile fighting bulls. Nowhere is the romance of birds better evidenced than on these southern shores of Andalucia. One of nature's most enduring mysteries is underway. The great annual migration from Africa to the northern nesting grounds is reaching its peak.

The garden at our house in Sotogrande has been moulded out of the ancient cork-oak forest. The air is scented with jasmine, wistaria, rosemary and orange blossom. The grapefruit trees are heavy with fruit. The dawn chorus in this garden gives more than a taste of what we can expect on an early May morning back in England. The main contributors are the blackcap and blackbird. The wren, chiffchaff, great tit and greenfinch are all present. From somewhere out in the forest the first cuckoo announces his arrival, which is an emotional moment in anybody's calendar. One particular bird stands out through the very power of its song – the star turn, of course – the nightingale, a bird that has sadly become a rare performer in England, so much so that few people today can lay claim to having heard one north of the Thames.

Although Grey only made one official foreign visit during his eleven years as Foreign Secretary, he would have felt quite at home in our garden in Sotogrande. Three out of four of his favourite songsters were performing. Only the bubbling spring notes of the curlew were missing.

♂ BLACKCAP

For sheer quality he found it hard to better the blackcap:

> For perfection or moving quality of voice I should place the blackcap with the blackbird and nightingale in the first class of British songbirds. His song is loud, exceedingly sweet, but also spirited; it is not very long, but is frequently repeated: there is no great variety, but the thing done is absolutely perfect. There is not a note that fails to please or to be a success. The tone does not stir us so inwardly as that of the blackbird, but it is sheer delight to listen to it. Of the blackcap indeed it has been said that, like the gypsy before the castle gate, he sang so very completely.

With its dark red eye and scolding alarm call, the Sardinian warbler brings a native flavour to the garden, although it can easily be confused in appearance with the blackcap and in songflight with the whitethroat. It is probably still too early for a visit from the beautiful golden oriole.

As the nightingale's range retreats southwards so too is there a corresponding shift to the north by certain other species. One such example, which is a regular in our garden at Sotogrande, is the serin, Europe's smallest finch. It produces a soft jingling song that reminds me of our own self-effacing dunnock. This dumpy little yellow bird was first recorded breeding in Dorset in 1967 and has since nested in other counties across southern England.

A mile or so away down on the River Guardiaro two other birds can be found which are now resident in small numbers on Britain's southern shores and which Grey would have been unfamiliar with a century ago. The cettis warbler is a secretive bird with an explosive voice which frequents the reed beds on river margins. It was first recorded breeding in Britain in 1972 and together with the blackcap is one of two migrant warblers that now overwinter, the largest numbers being found in Kent. The little egret, an elegant snow-white heron, common in the Mediterranean, is now found throughout the year on Britain's southern coasts, although it has yet to breed.

The Guardiaro Estuary provides a welcome staging post for numerous waders on their long journey north. A small flock of sanderling ran rapidly up and down the beach with the washing of the waves. A

common sandpiper bobbed nervously on the shore. I wondered whether it would be soon prospecting for a nest site on the banks of one of our great Scottish rivers. Higher up the river, a little ringed plover whistled mournfully from a gravel bank thrown up by the recent storms. They run around the sandbanks like clockwork toys and are distinguishable from the larger ringed plovers by their yellow eye stripe, pale legs and black beak. In flight there is the absence of a wing bar. This tiny wader is yet another example of a bird that has increased its range northwards into Britain. They first bred at the Tring Reservoirs in 1938 and represent one of our most successful conservation stories. They favour man-made nesting sites, which includes gravel pits, coal-mining complexes and sewage farms. I have even seen them running around the tracks in the Crewe marshalling yards.

Aside from the nightingale there is no bird more evocative of Sotogrande that the bee eater. With its colourful harlequin plumage it would surely be in more suitable company with the exotic fauna of a tropical rain forest. With a far-carrying liquid cry, it is a bird that is more often heard than seen. The bee eater has much in common with the martin family. It nests in colonial burrows like the sand martin and as it glides over the river on outstretched wings, it closely resembles a large house martin.

Thursday, 11 April

At Sotogrande you are well placed to make any number of day sorties into the heart of Andalucia. Today we decided to take to the hills. There are few more attractive railway journeys than the two-hour run from San Roque to Ronda. The bulky nests of the much loved stork astride electricity pylons decorate the route. As you snake your way off the floodplains and into the hanging white mountain towns of Jimena, Gauchin and Cortes, from the comfort of your window seat you can enjoy the migrating raptors that have glided northwards over the Straits of Gibralter on the mid-morning thermals. The most conscientious travellers are the black kite and honey buzzard, which mix with the local eagles and vultures in the mountains. Ronda, which boasts the oldest bullring in Spain, built in 1775, sits on an upthrust of rock with impressive cliffs. The town is split by a geological fault and through the resultant deep gorge runs the River Guadalevin. The two parts of the town are linked by a bridge over the gorge. It is here I love to watch the acrobatic choughs. What taste these birds have when it comes to choosing a home! Only last July I used to wake up to their cartwheeling antics along the spectacular raised beaches of Glenbatrick on the Isle of Jura.

Friday, 12 April

If you have the strength to drive further afield, a visit to La Laguna de Fuente Peidra near Antequera will not disappoint. It is the second most important breeding site of the greater flamingo in Europe, after the Camargue. But my favourite pilgrimage remains the two-hour drive to the Bonanza Salinas which lie to the north west of Jerez. Along the route, which the locals call 'the valley of the bulls', corn buntings perform their rather irritating jangling song from the gnarled and rickety barbed wire fences. Bonanza is a little fishing village on the banks of the Rio Guadalquivir, which is navigable up to Seville. On the north side of the river, opposite the Salinas, lies the celebrated Coto Doñana National Park. The Salinas are extensive saltpans that use natural methods of sun and wind for their evaporation process. Their position near the mouth of the river and the Doñana makes an ideal site for drawing in migrant waders. During the spring migration, avocets, black-winged stilts, black-tailed godwits, redshank and little stint feed in the shallow lagoons.

As we approached Jerez we stopped off at the Laguna de Medina. In normal dry conditions – unlike the current year – the lake is a favourite haunt of flamingos and many different species of wildfowl. With the recent rains the inhabitants have dispersed far and wide across the countryside. The white-headed duck, which is currently under threat from our own ruddy duck, is often present.

We rounded off a wonderful day around Jerez with a visit to Antonio's restaurant a few miles to the north west of the city. At this converted *finca*, surrounded by neat vineyards, we enthusiastically attacked the delicious fresh fish landed at the nearby Atlantic port of Sanlucar, and washed it down with ice cold local sherry.

Sunday, 14 April

Arrived at Sandwich Bay to stay with the Seymours after a four-hour train journey. Rest Harrow was built in 1910 by Nancy Astor – the first woman MP and my friend William's grandmother – for seaside and golfing holidays. The family would spend August here before moving up to Jura for September. It is a large Edwardian house with a very sunny atmosphere. Like our own Hardwick Hall, the house enjoys 'more glass than wall'. The rooms are light and spacious and decorated in sky blue and white. Rest Harrow has the spirit of a large east-coast American house. This is hardly surprising as Nancy Astor was an American, as indeed was her architect. Julian Seymour proudly states, 'It reminds me of a small version of one of those grand houses in Newport, Rhode Island – if you can call a house with sixteen bedrooms small.' One of its more interesting eccentricities is that the bathrooms were installed with two sets of taps, one for hot and cold freshwater and one for hot and cold seawater! Another unusual feature is a wind dial set horizontally on the hall ceiling. In the eighteenth century it was by no means unusual to set such a wind dial vertically on the chimney-piece and to connect the hands with a weather-vane on the roof. The house sits astride the shingle beach and enjoys an extensive garden. A few miles offshore, a famous red lightship plays sentry to the treacherous Goodwin Sands. Rest Harrow is surrounded on all sides by interesting habitat for birds. The Deal and Sandwich golf courses lie south and north with large tracts of uncultivated dunes, scrub and grassland. Behind are the water meadows long ago reclaimed from the sea and now pastureland for large numbers of sheep and cattle. A few miles walk north up the beach towards Ramsgate lies the Stour Estuary which is home to thousands of waders, particularly in the autumn and winter months.

In the same way as the black-headed gulls provide the background music at Needs Ore, so the skylarks and corn buntings furnish the 'everlasting choir' at Rest Harrow. The links habitat provides the perfect surroundings for these two drab yet musical birds to thrive. Unfortunately both species, which ironically are for the most part found on open arable land across England, seem to be on the decline. The corn bunting has suffered from more intensive agricultural practices being introduced over the last twenty years or so. As with the lapwing the main problem lies with the propensity to plant winter corn rather than spring corn. Skylarks also like to nest in immature crops and, what is more, winter planting results in a lack of weeds and stubble for the birds to feed off at a vital time of the year. An earlier harvest prevents second broods and use of pesticides reduces the availability of summer insects and weeds.

In Edward Grey's day the jangling song of the corn bunting could be heard right across downland Britain. Nowadays it is totally missing from the west and north of the country and aside from Sandwich I know of no other place where its rather irritating song – like the jingling of a set of keys – is so prevalent. Grey uncharacteristically finds it hard to award much merit to the bird:

> It is not altogether kind to write much or tell the whole truth about the corn bunting – his person or his song. The tendency of buntings is to be robust rather than slender but the corn bunting is the cart horse among them all. He has the habit, too, of sometimes taking a short flight with legs hanging down, as if it were too much trouble to tuck them up neatly in flight like other birds: this adds an impression of slovenly disposition to clumsiness of body. Though the largest of our four common buntings, the bird is the least beautiful in plumage. The males of the other kinds all have some distinction of vividness of colour. The male corn bunting is content to be as dull as his mate, who in turn is duller than other females of this tribe. For a perch the bird prefers telegraph wires or a wire fence. Corn buntings must have been pleased when the abomination of wire took the place of green hedges or honest posts and rails grown and made on the country estate. On wire then, by preference, the corn bunting will perch and grind out the noise that is his song. This suggests to me the sound of two hard

> pebbles one against the other. There is neither melody nor pleasant pattern in his song. On the Hampshire wires and where wire fences are sadly on the increase, it is impossible in midsummer to miss the corn bunting and his 'song'. He thrusts himself upon our notice.

As I walked across the Deal golf course before breakfast the air was full of skylark song. It is easy to understand why they have become one of our best loved birds. They were stacked up in the sky like jets waiting to come into Heathrow. If one was singing a hundred yards or so up another was a speck in the sky above him. Their sustained song can last for five minutes without a pause and is performed as the bird ascends, hovers and descends again to the ground. Grey was a great admirer of Wordsworth and both men had an obvious fascination for the heavenly world of the skylark.

> I came across a small volume of verse written by a young airman in the war. There was no evidence that he knew Wordsworth's poem on the skylark, but one of the experiences that he described as most pleasing or glorious was the sensation of being high up alone in the sunlight. When Wordsworth wrote, 'A privacy of glorious light is thine', his imagination had penetrated to what men would feel in the skylark's place. Without giving the bird human attributes, he had linked its flight and song to human feeling. This is an achievement in poetry that 'fancy', however beautiful, cannot accomplish.

Monday, 15 April

Overcast with a rather cold north-west wind. All the children went off to Howlett's Zoo while Julian and I went for a walk across the water meadows at the back of the links. The heavily grazed fields are dissected by a series of reedy dykes whose banks were decorated in places with cowslips. They provide the perfect home for reed buntings. The cockbird is most handsome with his black head and bib and distinctive white tail feathers. Buntings in general are reasonably tame birds. The corn bunting is probably the most confiding of all and I passed within a yard or so of one sitting on a fence post. Once they are comfortably ensconced on their perch they seem quite oblivious of all that goes on around them. In the end, Grey can't resist finding something positive to say about them!

> Yet at last, in spite of the inferiority of the corn bunting, of which the bird itself is so completely unconscious – for its whole demeanour is that of self-satisfied content – one gets a sort of humorous affection for it.

YELLOW WAGTAIL & YELLOWHAMMER

On our walk we came across two of Britain's most gaily coloured birds. One was another member of the bunting family – the yellow bunting, more commonly known as the yellowhammer. A cockbird with its bright yellow plumage sitting among the blackthorn blossom is a truly lovely site. The bird I was really hoping we would meet was the yellow wagtail. It gives itself away by both its characteristic sharp wagtail call note and its bouncy flight. Maybe he's not as pretty as the grey wagtail but like the cock yellowhammer it is unusual to come across a bird with so much yellow in its plumage. As with the green woodpecker you get the feeling you are gazing at the exotic – a bird from some far-off land. And in a way, of course, you are. The yellow wagtail, unlike its two cousins, migrates to spend the winter in West Africa and returns to nest with us in April. This is the perfect country for yellow wagtails – damp meadows and fields by water where they can feed on insects disturbed by the cattle. Whether these birds have just arrived and will move north to the high ground or whether they will stay and spend the summer, I do not know. They are yet another example of a bird which has contracted its range as a result of the intensification of agriculture. They have particularly suffered from field drainage and the replacement of grassland with cereal crops. *The New Atlas of Breeding Birds* estimates that during 1988–91 there were an estimated fifty thousand pairs in Britain.

Tuesday, 16 April

Arrived home at 6.00 p.m. after getting on a train at Sandwich at noon! The journey was made a good deal less tortuous by my discovery of two volumes of Edward Grey's *Twenty-Five Years* on a Rest Harrow bookshelf. It was raining when I arrived back – the first rain for a couple of weeks. The grass is greening up well, as is the hawthorn. Broken duck eggs outside the enclosure – crows or magpies?

Friday, 19 April

Spent the night at Bywell in Northumberland with the Beaumonts and got up at 4.30 a.m. to drive to Allenheads. I was met by the head keeper, Robert Grainger, at 5.30 a.m. and we drove up on to Kilhope Moor to watch the blackgame at their traditional lek. Black grouse are polygamous and the lekking ground is where the blackcocks display and establish a pecking order. The best time to witness this strange ritual is at first light during the third week in April. A light fall of snow covered the hill and curlew were calling for miles around. Robert said that to be on the hill at this time of year was the greatest place on earth, and I wasn't going to argue with him. The lek was in a grass field just short of the heather and

BLACKGROUSE AT LEK

with a good covering of rushes at one end. Long before you caught sight of the birds with the naked eye you could hear an eerie bubbling chortling sound wafting across the valley. With the help of the telescope we counted around twenty blackcocks and two greyhen. The latter do not normally visit the lek in numbers. The birds in the middle were obviously the dominant males. All the cocks had their beautiful white tails fully spread and with extended necks they jousted like knights of old. Occasionally the odd bird would flutter up into the air, but there was definitely more 'bark than bite'. Even the two hens had accepted the competitive spirit and were chasing each other around. Robert says there are probably over a hundred blackcocks on his moor at Allenheads. They are poor breeders with the greyhens laying small clutches and being less than attentive mothers. A Newcastle University graduate who has been studying the local population for some time says the leks can move from year to year and in a clockwise fashion. The blackgame population at Allenheads is one of the few concentrations in the country where the birds are thriving. This is because the greyhens are not shot, the foxes are well controlled and there is plenty of suitable habitat. Blackcock are traditionally birds of the fringes of moors and woods. They like young conifer plantations; also a diversity of plant and shrub species, particularly dwarf willow, blackberry, birch scrub and hazel bushes. This was once widespread habitat until modern agriculture led to reclamation of almost every acre, encouraged by grants and subsidies. Livestock grazing pressure is now intense in many areas and agrochemical spraying leaves areas devoid of protein-rich insect life – vital for newly hatched chicks.

A few years ago a survey was undertaken at Kilhope which showed it enjoyed one of the highest nesting densities of waders in the north of England. The curlew, lapwing, golden plover and redshank all nest here in good numbers; there are even a few dunlin. Robert says the grouse are in terrific condition and have started laying. Given reasonable weather next month he is hoping to double last year's bag.

Saturday, 20 April

An uncomfortably strong cold north wind that brought rain. I took Marcus out in the Land Rover in the morning to try and shoot a rabbit with the 2.2. I noticed that the redstarts had arrived for I saw two cockbirds hopping around the rabbit burrows on the limestone banks.

These birds, like the pied flycatcher, frequent the oak woods of western and northern Britain. Large numbers arrive with us in Derbyshire to nest and they particularly take to holes in our stone walls. As long as the entrance is large enough they also occupy nest boxes. In 1993 we attracted three pairs to our boxes at Parwich Lees and this increased to four pairs last year. These attractive warblers will contribute to any garden in the summer; they are very active birds, constantly flitting through the branches and flicking their chestnut-red tails. Grey felt that the cockbird was probably the most beautiful of all our summer visitors.

> There is one aspect of the redstart that differs from that of all these April-coming songbirds. None of these are brilliant in plumage; their beauty is quiet rather than gay: the plumage of the male, with the

exception of the blackcap, is the same as that of the female and does not alter much, if at all, after the breeding season is over. But the cock redstart has colours that arrest the eye: he is indeed one of the most beautiful of our birds; and it is a plumage of the breeding season; afterwards comes an eclipse that places him more nearly on a level with the female; but in all redstarts the patch of reddish colour on the tail coverts, from which they get their name, is constant.

Redstarts winter in Africa and are widely thought to have been affected by the Sahel drought. Their numbers, like those of the whitethroat, can fluctuate greatly from year to year depending on circumstances in their winter quarters. Warde Fowler suggests this when writing on an Oxford spring in his *A Year with the Birds*:

> Another bird, too, which is often called a warbler, has of late become very common in and about Oxford – the redstart. Four or five years ago they were getting quite rare; but this year [1885] the flicker of the red tail is to be seen all along the Cherwell, in the Broad Walk, where they build in holes of the elms, in Port Meadow, where I have heard the gentle warbling song from the telegraph wires, and doubtless in most gardens. The redstart is so extremely beautiful in summer, his song so tender and sweet and all his ways so gentle and trustful that if he were as common, and stayed with us all the year, he would certainly put our robin's popularity to the proof. Nesting in our garden, or even on the very wall of our house, and making his presence obvious by his brilliant colouring and his fearless domesticity, he might become, like his plainer cousin of the continent, the favourite of the peasant who looks to his arrival in spring as a sign of a better time approaching.

In my three years or so at the Lince in Blenheim Park (one hundred years after Warde Fowler was writing) and only a few miles from Oxford, I never set eyes on a redstart.

Sunday, 21 April

The wind has gone round to the south and is not quite so unpleasant. Marcus and I went for a walk down the Bletch before church. The north wind took out one of the rooks' nests in the night leaving only two solid structures in our rookery. Our first spring (1987) produced twenty-two nests so this says something about the decline of Britain's rook population. A heron flew down the Bletch and was aggressively mobbed by three rooks until it was a safe distance away from their nests.

We saw the Tissington 'white hare' in his bottom meadow. I thought it was a cat at first as it galloped away and perched on a stone wall at a safe distance. It had a snow-white neck and chest.

The willow warblers are in fine song despite the weather and the first cuckoo flowers are out in the duck enclosure, as are a few bluebells on the drive. The cock pied flycatcher continues to occupy its territory in the old tennis court – waiting patiently for the females to arrive. Its song and harsh 'tic' call note makes it easy to identify. The striking black-and-white livery adds a touch of the exotic to the spring garden – this bird is a class act.

After lunch Marcus and I walked down through the hawthorn bank to feed the ducks. We put a fox out of a bush about thirty yards away. When I see one this close I am always surprised how red they look. The fox is a sleek killing machine but there is no denying its beauty. We found another mallard's nest in the enclosure with seven eggs. I've got another broody so I might lift these eggs as well. They have a much better chance of hatching and surviving this way. There is not enough cover at this time of the year and as a result the crows and magpies more often than not find the eggs. In addition, if they hatch there simply isn't the insect life to sustain the ducklings.

Thursday, 25 April

I took Marcus to school in Ashbourne and then drove north to our Leeds office. I woke up to a blackcap singing in the small wood by the walled garden. It was still singing when I returned in the evening and I watched it through the binoculars fidget among the branches. It is the song one most looks forward to out of all those of the summer visitors.

The song can easily be confused with that of the garden warbler who will arrive next month. Edward Grey describes the blackcap's elegance:

> In appearance blackcaps are very distinct from garden warblers: the size and shape are alike, but the blackcap is an exception to the rule among our warblers that both sexes should have the same plumage. The prevailing colour of each sex is a soft grey, but the male has a black cap and the female has one of rich brown on the top of the head. The general appearance of both is of elegance and good taste.

An increasing number of blackcaps now spend the winter with us (maybe two thousand birds). British breeding birds will migrate to the Mediterranean and North Africa but those that winter with us have probably come from Eastern Europe. I remember so well the first time I identified a blackcap. A pair were playing in a shrub at the edge of the lawn at the Lince in Blenheim Park. What struck me most was the contrast of the brown cap and the black cap. In the same way as Grey wrote when describing the dipper in *The Charm of Birds*:

> It was another moment when the song of a single bird penetrates to the affections and abides thereafter in the memory.

Stan White came round to give me the annual cheque for the summer's grass keep. He lost a pair of lambs to a fox last night. One had been taken away and the other had blood and bite marks around its neck.

Lots of swallows diving low across the ponds when I walked down this evening. I found another mallard's nest in the enclosure. It was covered up and beautifully camouflaged with down.

Friday, 26 April

Left Parwich Lees at 6.30 a.m. for Anglesey and arrived at the farm near Valley three hours later. The farm is just over three hundred acres of varying qualities of grassland around Lake Traffwll and is about a mile as the crow flies from Rhosneigr, the well-known seaside resort. It is a paradise for birds, particularly wildfowl and geese. The RSPB are keen to acquire eighty acres of 'bog' from us and turn it into a reserve. They

TRAFFWLL, ANGLESEY & SNOWDONIA

plan to plant a large reed bed to attract back the bittern and marsh harrier. In addition they intend to buy the lake bed from Welsh Water which will leave our farm buildings in the middle of an exciting new reserve. We are therefore considering ploughing back any funds from the sale of the land into the buildings and developing a farmhouse which can be split into two or three units for holidaymakers who have a special interest in birds and wildlife. Lake Traffwll is a favourite wintering site for numerous wildfowl. In the spring and autumn a variety of waders who use the 'western flyway' call in on their long journey north or on their way home later in the year.

The lake was not as busy as usual but today it played host to a number of tufted duck, gadwall and greylag geese. There were a couple of pairs of great crested grebes and a large colony of black-headed gulls nesting on one of the islands. A solitary crow dive-bombed the gull colony which caused total confusion, and the success of the 'safety in numbers' strategy was soon demonstrated as the predator was driven off. It flew on to a rock by the lakeside, no doubt to compose itself for another attack. A quick glance through the binoculars demonstrated that it was a hybrid between a carrion crow and a hooded crow. It had a grey front and a black back. The hybrid zone for these two birds runs from the Clyde up to Caithness, so it was a good way south. The grey hooded crow and the black carrion crow can interbreed and produce fertile offspring. Hooded crows are mainly distributed across north-western Scotland and Ireland and tend to occupy the higher ground and Western Isles. The zone where interbreeding occurs is narrow which suggests that the hybrid birds are less successful breeders than either of the pure forms.

A large group of white wagtails (between fifty and a hundred) were feeding on insects in a field by the lake. Their plumage is much lighter than that of the pied wagtail. Pied wagtails are a subspecies of the white wagtail and breed regularly only in Britain and Ireland. White wagtails breed from Ireland to the Mediterranean and are seen in Britain on passage in spring and autumn, especially on the west coasts. This was the first time I had seen white wagtails in Britain. In *A Year with the Birds*, Warde Fowler gives as good a description of the bird as any:

> The white wagtail is as comparatively rare in England as our common pied wagtail is abroad. The two forms are very closely allied, our pied wagtail in winter very closely resembling the white bird in its summer dress. The difficulty of distinguishing the two caused me to pay great attention to these white wagtails whenever I saw them. If you see a bird in summer which has a uniform pearl-grey back, set off sharply against a black head, the black coming no further down than the nape of the neck, it is the white wagtail. You must look at his back chiefly; it is by far the most telling character. The male pied wagtail has at this season a black back and the female has hers darker and less uniform in colour than the genuine white bird.

We thought we saw a flock of whimbrel in the distance. I saw a group of these migrating birds behind Traffwll's farmhouse when visiting in the first week of May 1992. That same week I came across a flock of around forty when walking the Arun Valley with Roddy Balfour at Burpham, which is just south of the Amberley Brooks. In August 1988 I managed to get very close to a small group of whimbrel by hiding in one of the bunkers on the Deal golf course. These birds were on their way back to their African wintering grounds and were using the eastern flyway, merely stopping off to refuel. The whimbrel is a smaller version of the curlew with a shorter and less curved bill, stumpier legs and a more rapid wing beat in flight. It is definitely tamer than the curlew and when you move in close you can observe two distinctive black bands of feathers on the crown giving the effect of two white streaks which are absent in the bigger bird.

The whimbrel is much scarcer than the curlew, being predominantly a bird of the Arctic, only touching down in Britain on its long migration flights. Britain is at the southern edge of its breeding range: around two hundred and fifty pairs nest in the very north of Scotland and the Shetlands. The whimbrel is known as the 'seven whistler' and there is no call more evocative of Dr Syn's desolate and inhospitable marshes than the sound of its wild whistle.

WHIMBREL & CURLEW-(behind)

Saturday, 27 April

An overcast day with a light yet cold east wind. Played tennis in the morning on a pretty court on top of a hill in Parwich. We performed to a chorus of willow warblers in the surrounding hawthorn bushes. It is easy to understand why the young Edward Grey referred to the willow warbler as 'the everlasting bird'.

The terriers found a blackbird's nest low down in the same box bush that last year housed the hedge sparrow. They killed the nestlings – it broke my heart to think of all that lost song. It was also the first nest of a garden bird found this season. It's early so maybe it will build again.

In the afternoon I successfully sat eight mallard eggs under a broody. There were nuthatches calling all around the garden and across the valley. They have such a wide variety of calls. The rook that lost its nest in the gale last week has totally rebuilt it – we are now back up to three.

Sunday, 28 April

A lovely day but still with a fresh east wind. We played tennis in the morning at Lower Hurst Farm with Andrew Sebire. A small flock of 'chacking' fieldfares flew north, high overhead; it shows how late they set off back to their nesting grounds in Scandinavia.

In *The Charm of Birds* Grey asks why our winter visitors never sing in Britain:

> I have seen fieldfares at Fallodon at the end of the first week in May: by that time all our resident birds are in song: many of these have been singing for weeks or even months. But if the song of any of these winter birds is heard in Britain, it is but a fragment. Every year we are familiar with these three species (redwing, fieldfare, brambling), but unless we go abroad, we live out our lives in England and never hear their song. Is it because they cannot sing the home song in any but their homeland?

A nuthatch was calling throughout our game; they are very successful birds that are constantly increasing their range northwards. After tennis we drove down to the fishing temple on the banks of the River Dove. A substantial part of *The Compleat Angler* must have been produced at this spot in the 1660s when Isaak Walton was staying with his friend the local squire, Charles Cotton.

In the afternoon I successfully sat another six mallard eggs under a broody. We then picked up the horses from Lower Hurst and put them out on the lush grass at Parwich Lees for their summer holiday.

TUFTED DUCK : GREY'S BRIDGE ON THE ITCHEN.

Tuesday, 30 April

A pair of wild tufted ducks have arrived in the duck enclosure and it is to be hoped will find a nest site as they have in the past.

If you walk on to Grey's bridge below his cottage site at Itchen Abbas, 'where the strong clear current still bends the anchored weeds and water grasses, pointing their heads down towards Winchester' (G. M. Trevelyan – *Grey of Fallodon*), you are invariably confronted by a small group of diving ducks uttering an angry growling call as they make their clumsy takeoff downstream. These are tufted duck which have achieved an astonishing expansion of their range over the last century, making them Britain's most successful breeding waterfowl. Although the first pair bred in Britain in 1875, the real expansion has only come about in the last thirty years or so with approximately two thousand breeding pairs in 1960 increasing to around seven thousand today.

At the turn of the century Edward Grey would undoubtedly have been familiar with tufted duck. He had at least one pair in his Fallodon collection and would probably have seen them wintering on Alresford Pond. However, they would have been a very rare sight on the River Itchen in summertime. Our current breeding population is now augmented by over sixty thousand migrants which come in from Iceland, Scandinavia and Russia to spend the winter on our larger freshwater lakes. From a nineteenth-century breeding rarity, the tufted has become our commonest diving duck.

W. H. Hudson makes no mention of the tufted duck while staying at the Cottage in *Hampshire Days*. Kelsall and Munn in *Birds of Hampshire* (1905) state: 'The tufted duck is a common winter visitor to our inland waters and coasts, now nesting in a few localities.' The same book quotes the Honourable Alick Baring writing to Kelsall from the Grange near Alresford in 1889: 'I am hoping that the tufted duck may breed with us. I have noticed it as late as mid-April but never afterwards.' In 1890, Baring writes: 'Since writing to you I am glad to say one pair have nested on the lake – the nest was built in the thick branches of a dogwood bush, very little above the level of the water, like a coot or moorhen.' Another passage in the book quotes Dr Bowdler Sharpe in 1896 stating that he had seen two pairs at Avington at the end of May and he believed that some remained to breed there. He states: 'For years past this species has been a regular winter visitor to the lake at Laverstoke – generally ten to twenty individuals which arrived in October and remained until April – and in 1899 a pair remained to nest, since when they have bred regularly.'

The primary reason for the success of the tufted duck is that like the mallard it tolerates human contact and has taken advantage of man-made bodies of water. The extraction of gravel along the floodplains of our lowland rivers to satisfy the insatiable appetite of our construction industry has provided the tuftie with hundreds of acres of new habitat and a plentiful supply of food.

The tuftie is a social bird and in winter is often seen in the company of the pochard in large rafts of over a hundred birds. Looking west from the Grand Bridge at Blenheim in February you can nearly always spy a sizeable gathering of our two most common diving ducks. These two birds do not compete with each other for food which is why they enjoy each other's company. The pochard is a vegetarian and the tufted is carnivorous. It would seem that the increased abundance of freshwater molluscs maybe a significant key to the tufted's range expansion. Two mollusc species, the zebra mussel and the Jenkins spire snail, both of which are important food for the tuftie have recently become widespread and abundant in British freshwater. Tufted ducks will dive down to around fifteen feet and stay submerged for over thirty seconds.

It is easy to understand why the tuftie has become more prolific than the pochard, as it readily adapts to concrete-banked enclosures and new gravel pits where vegetation is sparse. The nesting habits of the tufted duck also play an important part in their overall success. They tend to build later than other ducks – in May and June when the vegetation is much denser – and this, coupled with a propensity to nest on islands, means they suffer less from predators like foxes. Tufted ducklings are hardier and more independent than other young ducks. A few years ago I watched a brood on my ponds that looked no bigger than bumble-bees. They were only a day or so old yet they were swimming and diving freely and popping up on the surface like tiny corks.

Wednesday, 1 May

It is perhaps appropriate that on the final day of my diary I should visit the site of Edward Grey's cottage. I was expecting to feel a sense of personal sadness now that the house at Bramdean is sold and my year with Grey is over. Instead I felt a contented gratitude for his contribution to the pleasure I derive from birds and birdsong, for Edward Grey wrote in his Introduction to his book *Fly Fishing*:

> Nor are we all equally attracted by the charm and changes of the season and by natural beauties, nor all equally interested in the life of the country. The gift of being pleased by these things is one of the most precious possessions that a man can have within him, but it is rare to find it at an early age. In boyhood it is generally dormant, and it is not this we think of when we realise that angling is often taking us to the most beautiful places in the country at the very best times of the year, and then we feel a new sense of gratitude and a crowning

· THE LIME AVENUE & REMAINS OF GREY'S COTTAGE ·

> delight. There comes a time when the beauty of the day or of the place seems to possess us, so that the thought of angling ever afterwards becomes full of beautiful associations, delightful meadows and woods, of light upon water, of the sound of streams, till in the recollection of days that are past, the vision of these things perpetually rises up and fills us with joy.

A man who helped mould world events at the beginning of the century spent the happiest days of his life fishing and enjoying his birds on the banks of the Itchen. It was the Cottage that inspired *The Charm of Birds*. Grey and Hudson have both contributed incalculably to my awareness of nature's mysteries and my love of birds. The cottage that played such an important part in their lives has played no small part in my own. It took over in a spiritual way from the Lince.

I felt a great sense of reassurance. Nature's changing seasons come around again and again, bringing with them their own special beauty and charm. There is forever an event to look forward to and the continuity reminds me of the lovely inscription on the Blenheim boathouse, 'May thy craft glide gently on as the years roll down the stream.' It was this very continuity that helped Grey through the stresses of office and the several personal tragedies he suffered throughout his life. When one of his nephews was killed in the Great War he wrote to his sister Mrs Graves:

> It is difficult in these dark days not to become disheartened and discouraged. I find that what helps me most is watching the stability of Nature and the orderly procession of the seasons.

Looking at the ruins of the cottage, I felt an awareness of my own mortality and the insignificance of my own being in the wider context of nature and her ever turning wheel.

My feelings at leaving this part of Hampshire must have been similar to W. H. Hudson's when he wrote the final paragraph to *Hampshire Days*. As another happy visit to Grey's cottage draws to a close, he describes a late September day with the birds in the Itchen Valley:

> The early hours are silent, except for the brown owls that hoot around the cottage from about four o'clock until dawn. Then they grow silent, and the morning is come, cold and misty, and all the land is hidden by a creeping white river mist. The sun rises and is not seen for half an hour, then appears pale and dim, but grows brighter and warmer by degrees; and in a little while, lo! the mist has vanished, except for a white rag clinging like torn lace here and there to the valley reeds and rushes. Again the green earth, wetted with mist and dews, and the sky of that soft pure azure of yesterday and of many previous days. Again the birds are vocal: the rooks rise from the woods, an innumerable cawing multitude, their voices filling the heavens with noise, as they travel slowly away to their feeding grounds on the green open downs; the starlings flock to the bushes and the feasting and chatter and song begin that will last until evening. The sun sets crimson and the robins sing in the night and silence. But it is not silent long; before dark the brown owls begin hooting, first in the woods, then fly across to the trees that grow beside the cottage, so that we may better enjoy their music. At intervals, too, we hear the windy sibilant screech of the white owl across the valley. Then the wild cry of the stone curlew is heard as the lonely bird wings his way past, and after that late voice there is perfect silence, with starlight or moonlight.

EPILOGUE

On 21 August 1996, in a state of no little excitement, I made my first visit to Fallodon. I was warmly received and hospitably entertained to lunch by the current owners, Mr and Mrs Peter Bridgeman, and their daughter Davina.

The final entry in the 'Fallodon Green Book', dated February 1906, shortly after Dorothy Grey's death, states:

> It is my wish presently to make a record of all that she did in the house and in the garden, in the hope that someday when I am gone the place may again belong to someone who will love it and be grateful to her.

Edward Grey's wish has come true. The house and gardens are today lovingly cared for by the Bridgeman family. The treecreepers continue to roost behind the bark of the giant wellingtonias. The spotted flycatchers conduct their aerobatics from the magnificent beech in the middle of the lawn. The red squirrels are fed in Dorothy's sunken garden. Grey's pond, recently dredged, provides a happy home for several families of mallard and moorhen.

A few yards from the duck sanctuary, under the shade of the trees they planted together, lie the ashes of Edward and Dorothy Grey. Emanating from the canopy, the restful song of innumerable woodpigeons gave me the distinct feeling that Fallodon is still very much their home.

BIBLIOGRAPHY

Noel Cusa, *Tunnicliffe's Birds*, Gollancz, 1984
Henry Douglas-Home, *The Birdman*, Collins, 1977
J. Flegg, *Birds of the British Isles*, Orbis, 1984
W. Warde Fowler, *A Year with the Birds*, Macmillan & Co., 1891
Seton Gordon, *Edward Grey and his Birds*, Country Life, 1937
Edward Grey, *The Charm of Birds*, 1927
— *Fly Fishing*, 1899
— *Twenty-Five Years*, 1923
— *The Fallodon Papers*, 1926
E. W. Hendy, *Birdwatching*, Cape, 1928
Edith Holden, *The Country Diary of an Edwardian Lady*, Michael Joseph, 1977
W. H. Hudson, *Hampshire Days*, Longman Green, 1903
— *A Foot in England*, Hutchinson, 1909
— *Birds and Man*, Duckworth, 1915
Revd C. A. Johns, *British Birds in their Haunts*, SPCK, 1885
Jan Karpinski, *Capital of Happiness*, Michael Joseph, 1984
Kelsall & Morris, *Birds of Hampshire and the Isle of Wight*, Witherby, 1905
Robert Massie, *Dreadnought*, Little Brown, 1990
Revd F. O. Morris, *British Birds*, Groombridge, 1880
E. M. Nicholson, *Birds in England*, Chapman & Hall, 1926
Robin Page, *The Fox and the Orchid*, Quiller Press, 1987
The Reform of the Common Agricultural Policy, RSPB, 1988
Alan Richards, *Birds of the Tideline*, Dragon's World, 1988
A Scottish Naturalist: The Sketches and Notes of Charles St John, Anthony Atha, 1982
Eric Simms, *British Warblers*, Collins, 1985
— *Natural History of Birds*, Dent, 1983
Mary Soames, *The Profligate Duke*, Collins, 1987
G. M. Trevelyan, *Grey of Fallodon*, Longmans, 1937

LIFE OF SIR EDWARD GREY

1862 Born in Chester Square, SWI
1875 Winchester College
1880 Balliol College, Oxford
1880 Sir George Grey (grandfather) dies. Grey inherits Fallodon (two thousand acres and baronetcy)
January 1884 Sent down from Balliol
June 1884 Returns to take a third in Jurisprudence
July 1884 Private Secretary to Sir Evelyn Baring
October 1884 Private Secretary to Childers, Chancellor of the Exchequer
1885 Marries Dorothy Widdrington
November 1885 Elected Liberal MP for Berwick-upon-Tweed
1885–6 Builds wildfowl collection at Fallodon
February 1887 Maiden speech on Ireland
1890 Builds the Cottage on the Itchen River
1892–4 Parliamentary Under Secretary at the Foreign Office (under Rosebery)
1895 Vice President of RSPB. Liberals now in opposition
1896 Amateur real-tennis champion at both Lords & Queens
1898 Director of North Eastern Railway
1899 *Fly Fishing* published
1904 Chairman of the North Eastern Railway
December 1905 Foreign Secretary in the new Liberal Administration
February 1906 Death of wife Dorothy in a driving accident
June 1910 Celebrated 'Bird Walk' in Hampshire with Theodore Roosevelt
1913 George Grey (brother) killed by a lion in Africa
3 August 1914 Grey's statement to House of Commons on the outbreak of the First World War
December 1916 Resigns as Foreign Secretary with break-up of Asquith's government
May 1917 Fallodon burns down
1919 Chaired committee to review Wild Birds Protection Act
1922 Married Pamela Glenconner
February 1923 Cottage at Itchen Abbas burns down
1925 *Twenty-Five Years* published
1926 *The Fallodon Papers* published
1927 *The Charm of Birds* published
1928 Chancellor of Oxford University
1928 Charles Grey (brother) killed by buffalo in Africa
1928 Wife Pamela dies
September 1933 Grey dies at Fallodon